# INSIDE THE
# HERMIT KINGDOM

# INSIDE THE
# HERMIT KINGDOM

## A MEMOIR

## YI SUN-KYUNG

KEY PORTER BOOKS

*Although this book is based on actual events, some persons' names have been changed to protect their identities.*

**Canadian Cataloguing in Publication Data**

Yi, Sun-Kyung, 1967–
      Inside the hermit kingdom : a memoir

ISBN 1-55013-904-5

1. Korea – Description and travel.  2. Yi, Sun-Kyung, 1967–
– Journeys – Korea.  I. Title.

DS922.463.Y5    1997     915.1904'43    C97-931313-9

The publisher gratefully acknowledges the support of the Canada Council for the Arts and the Ontario Arts Council for its publishing program.

Key Porter Books Limited
70 The Esplanade
Toronto, Ontario
Canada M5E 1R2

THE CANADA COUNCIL | LE CONSEIL DES ARTS
FOR THE ARTS | DU CANADA
SINCE 1957 | DEPUIS 1957

Design: Jean Lightfoot Peters
Electronic formatting: Frank Zsigo

97 98 99 00 6 5 4 3 2 1

*For my parents,*
*Tae-Sik and Chung-Hae,*
*with love and gratitude*

*The house may be falling into ruins, gates and doors off the hinges, poverty staring in at every chink, and yet, if only sufficient ceremony and commotion is kept up, the owner's position as a man of importance is assured, appearance, not reality, being the aim of life.*

*Rev. James S. Gale*
*A missionary to Wonsan, Korea*
Korean Sketches, *1898*

# Contents

# Prologue

# ITAEWON ELEMENTARY SCHOOL, SEOUL, SOUTH KOREA, 1975

"Pay attention, boys and girls. There are fourteen Communists. Our heroic soldiers kill seven red bastards. How many are left?"

I shoot up my hand, stand tall and proud like a real soldier, and look at the portrait of our president, Park Chung-Hee, hanging above the blackboard as I recite my answer, to the teacher's approval.

Although I am the tallest girl in the class, I sit in the front row because I am the teacher's pet. I am the smartest, the best dressed, and my father works for the U.S. Army. He and the Yankees are defending our country from Communists, and it is my duty to grow up and become a soldier and work alongside him. It is fate, and you can't fight fate.

I am only eight years old, but I am already a fiercely loyal patriot. In art class I draw posters depicting Communists with horns and red faces. They are devils. Everyone knows they don't look like us. In social studies class my friends and I laugh at poor North Koreans who have nothing to eat. Our textbook shows a family sitting on a dirt floor in a house with barred windows. Parents and children have rags for clothes and no shoes. Their miserable faces and sunken eyes stare at Kim Il-Sung's portrait hanging on the wall. Kim Il-Sung is an evil man. He divided our country in half.

The same textbook has a picture of colorful flowers, happy children and parents having a picnic on a bright, sunny day. This is South Korea. Democracy. Thanks to the Americans, we are free. As long as they are here, we are safe.

As I walk home from school, I am on the lookout for spies. They are everywhere. They dig tunnels from North Korea so they can invade us and start another war. But our smart soldiers catch them just in time, sending them scurrying back.

Anyone seen wearing dark sunglasses and a trenchcoat is accused of being a spy. I am tempted many times to call the spy hotline, but I am ashamed to admit I can't remember the number. It flashes across the bottom of the television screen all the time, but I can't call it to mind.

As usual, my classmates and I take the long way home, just to walk by the American army base and salute the Big Noses. Sometimes they give us Hershey chocolate bars and gum, which taste much better than the broiled silkworms I eat for snacks. But I am not there for that. I just want to admire the soldiers.

Yankees are so tall and handsome. Their fine, short hair is the color of the sun, and their big, round eyes are as blue as the sky. I have a crush on every one of them.

They are here to protect our country. Americans are heroes and Gen. Douglas MacArthur is our savior.

# Prairie Princess

My family and I immigrated to Canada in 1976. That year, a billion Chinese mourned the death of Chairman Mao, and Vietnam was still trying to believe that the war was finally over. But I was too young to realize that. I was nine years old, and all I knew was that I was going on an airplane for the first time in my life.

With nowhere to go when we got to Canada, we checked into a hotel in Regina, Saskatchewan, and waited for our lives to begin. My parents' silence told me that this wasn't a holiday, and that we weren't going back home.

That was the year Montreal hosted the Summer Olympics. My eyes fervently searched the TV screen for signs of the Korean flag. With a flood of national pride came a sharp pang of guilt for having abandoned Korea. I was convinced that I had deserted my own country, and therefore deserved any misfortune and humiliation that came my way. To my child's mind, there was something terribly wrong with what our family had done.

When we lived in South Korea, my father always wore a fine, three-piece tailored suit with shiny black shoes, and my mother had a maid to do the housework. I went to a private kindergarten, where the teachers paid undivided attention to me. It was a fine life. Then, it seemed to me, we decided to throw it all away. My parents had come to Canada to seek a better life, yet here we were, saving egg cartons and McDonald's foam containers to use as dishes. My father wore old jeans with a cheap pair of shoes he bought at a bargain center. He fixed cars and cleaned toilets for a living. My mother, who had never worked a day in her life, washed dishes at the same hotel where we were once guests.

My parents were petrified as they tried to negotiate their new environment, and as hard as they tried to put on a brave face, their eyes, shimmering with fear and uncertainty, betrayed them. Silenced as we were by the language barrier and overwhelmed by the alien culture, the simplest task, such as making a doctor's appointment or asking the bus driver for directions, became a traumatic, anxiety-ridden experience my parents preferred to avoid. So they turned to their children. We answered the phone and translated the bills and letters from the bank. Eventually they even counted on me to attend parent–teacher interviews on their behalf.

With injured pride, my parents suppressed their frustration. Only their deep, heavy sighs revealed what they could not express. There was very little I could do but watch, as my own anger and resentment built. Then, one day, the situation exploded.

My father had brought home his latest purchase from Canadian Tire. I don't have the faintest idea what it was now, but I know it came with an instruction book because that was what the fight was about. He had asked the children to help him translate the instructions, but we forgot all about it. A few days went by, and my father became increasingly irritable, which we all pretended not to notice because it was impossible to keep up with his unpredictable moods. Finally he lashed out, accusing the children of undermining him. "You ignore your own father because you think he is a stupid idiot!" The words stung me. We had just forgotten, and a simple reminder would have sufficed. But not for my father. He searched for meaning in the smallest gestures and responded accordingly. And this was one of those times when he had horribly, and unfairly, misconstrued the situation, as if there was a family conspiracy to mock him.

He was the head of the house, and his orders were to be carried out promptly. When he said "Jump," we had to jump as high as possible. (Asking "How high?" would be missing the point.) After all, as my mother liked to remind me, in the ancient days, when filial piety was carried to extremes, children drank poison given to them by their parents, without uttering a word of protest. They not only drank every last drop, but they did it with a firm conviction that their death sentence was a well-deserved punishment, even though they might not always have known what crime they had supposedly committed.

As the eldest child, I bore the brunt of my father's anger and hung my head in shame for setting a bad example for my siblings. It was my duty to guide them through life and make sure that they met my parents' expectations. Their failure was my failure, and in turn, my failure was my parents' failure. In our family, no one made independent decisions and no one took responsibility for his or her own actions. I would later discover that these were national traits that made Koreans suspicious by nature and instinctively distrustful of one another.

## II

I could never meet my parents' expectations, and I knew I'd be a disappointment to them for years to come. The very first sign of this came about a month after we arrived in Canada. When my parents tried to enroll me in school, I was told to come back when I could speak English. My sisters, ages four and seven, were young enough to pick up the language and assimilate, but at nine I was too old to do so. So for my first year in Canada, I went to Regina's only English as a Second Language class for children, at Thompson School. There were only about a dozen students in the class: a few Chinese, a girl from Yugoslavia, and a handful of Koreans. The members of the three nations spent more time plotting and conspiring against one another than learning English. *Equality* was not a word that existed in anyone's vocabulary, and it never occurred to us that we could be friends. From the very first day of the class, we saw one another as potential threats, and we were ready to wage the bloodiest battles to protect the little territories we had already carved out for ourselves. Insecurity and fear had brought out the worst in us.

The primary battle raged between the Chinese and the Koreans, with Esplansa, the prima donna from Yugoslavia, caught in the middle. None of us could figure out why she was in our class, since she was white and looked like a bona fide Canadian to us. She had high cheekbones, stylishly shaped eyebrows, and long brown hair tied neatly in a ponytail. Next to her, I looked like a peasant who had just come in from the rice field.

Our desks were set in a semicircle, but we soon arranged them so that the Koreans were on one side and the Chinese on the other. Esplansa, not quite sure where to go, left her desk in the middle, staying neutral. The Koreans helped each other cheat on spelling tests; the

Chinese held secret meetings to pick whom to beat up after school. The two sides glared at each other, threw erasers and pieces of chalk across the room, fired spitballs, and stuck out their tongues. We screamed and shouted in our own languages, and when that didn't seem to get us anywhere, we armed ourselves with an English dictionary and searched for words to insult and offend. Our class would have made a fine case study about tribalism that inevitably leads to civil war. The fighting persisted for a whole year without a ceasefire.

This was more than our poor teacher could handle. In many ways, Mrs. Anthony, big and generous, epitomized Canada. But to us, little immigrants from oppressed Third World countries who were used to a daily dose of corporal punishment in school, the first Canadian authority figure we were exposed to was a pushover. When Mrs. Anthony welcomed us and embraced us with her liberal Canadian spirit, we all thought we had died and gone to heaven. We were strangers to the overwhelming kindness and incredible patience that Mrs. Anthony demonstrated day in and day out, behavior that made us uncomfortable at first.

But once we figured out that it would be easy to win her affection, and therefore a few extra grades, we showered her with gifts, which she accepted reluctantly. She drew the line when envelopes full of money mysteriously started to appear on her desk. Angrily, she proved that Canadians, too, were capable of raising their voices. Dumbfounded, we tried to defend ourselves. For a change, the Chinese and the Koreans got together and shared what few English words we knew to explain to the teacher that it was common practice in our countries to pay money to the police, teachers, bosses, and even friends. Hearing about our long-standing tradition, she wrote the word BRIBERY on the blackboard and spent the next day explaining to us what it meant. Such a thing did not exist in Canada, she said. "No money." She shook her head so violently that I thought she was going to hurt herself. "Police, judge, teachers—no money. No, no money," she repeated vehemently.

Things changed after the bribery scandal. The fighting subsided, the desks were rearranged, and the border was erased. But the peace was short-lived. Now the Koreans had turned against one another and the

Chinese were fighting among themselves. It seemed more important for us to have enemies than friends because we needed something to channel our anger and frustration. We stubbornly refused to get along because none of us wanted to admit that we could be happy in our new school, in our new country. I hoped that if I complained enough, my parents would eventually surrender and go back to Korea.

Until my parents relented, I preoccupied myself with daydreams and memories so I wouldn't forget what it was exactly that I wanted to go back to. At night, I lay on the bottom of my bunk bed and proceeded with my nocturnal ritual. Safely snuggled under the blankets, I stared at the soft glow of the night-light and gently coaxed my mind to go back in time, to the streets of Seoul, and escaped into my memory until I drifted off to sleep. It was like watching a favorite old movie for the hundredth time, except in this case I was the heroine. This was a movie about my life. Sometimes I fell asleep before the end, and my dreams picked up the story line, rearranging and distorting the scenes, enticing the truth to flirt with fiction. When that happened, it was sheer panic that woke me up, sending me into despair for having forgotten yet another piece of my childhood. It was important for me to remember things exactly as they were because, as far as I was concerned, when we left Korea my childhood had ended.

But as hard as I tried to preserve the memories, they were quickly fading. With each repeated scene, a detail or two disappeared until— poof!—nothing. In less than a year, my movie became a silent flick because I had forgotten the lines for my characters; in two years, the names and faces of friends, teachers, and relatives were also lost. But once in a while, something would trigger a recollection and I'd be running down memory lane again. This happened once at a classmate's birthday party, where they served Neapolitan ice cream with cake.

The first time I'd tasted the tricolor dessert was back in Seoul, when my father brought it home one night after many hours of drinking. The ice cream, which was almost unheard of in Korea at that time, was either given to my dad as a gift by one of his American army buddies or, more likely, purchased on the black market. With his face flushed from whiskey and eyes droopy from fatigue, my father stumbled into the house singing loud enough to disturb the entire neighborhood. Ignoring my mother's protests, he woke up my sister and me. "I brought you a delicious treat, my princess," my father slurred into my ear. "Wake up and say hello to your father." I wiped the sleep from my eyes and dutifully sat on my dad's knee. He carefully unfolded the ice-cream carton, exposing the soft, satiny block of strawberry, vanilla, and chocolate delight. My sister and I devoured it greedily, but two little girls can only eat so much. When we finally put down our spoons in surrender, my father became visibly upset. "Why, Daddy brought it just for you girls, and this is all you can do?" he cried. "Now, eat before it melts." A whole carton of ice cream! I looked down and saw that it was already melting, forming a little pool by my feet. Not to disappoint my father, I did as I was told.

My father used to bring all kinds of stuff from the army base. I was the only kid in school, for example, who had the privilege of eating rice smeared with ketchup, peanut butter, or cheese. And people dropped by our house just to have coffee, a rare and exotic drink that didn't come cheap. Instant coffee with powdered cream and cubes of sugar was the real delicacy, served with apples and pears, peeled and thinly sliced.

Years later, in Canada, I used to get embarrassed showing old family pictures to my friends because they would always want to know why the brand-new toaster oven was displayed on top of the piano, why the refrigerator sat so prominently in the living room, and why empty liquor bottles lined the bookcase like trophies. It was because these were all American products, the ultimate sign of wealth, success, and superiority. I don't think our toaster oven was ever removed from the glass case we worshiped it in, and I doubt we even knew how to use it, but that wasn't the point. It was for show, and in Korea, appearance was everything.

## III

After completing my ESL course, I enrolled in Wascana Public School, where I found myself among farm children with freckles on their faces and teachers who had never seen an Asian kid before. I was something of a novelty, and as a result had the honor of joining some of my classmates for lunch at their homes. Their mothers, excited to meet a girl from the Orient, felt obliged to share their culture by opening the refrigerator door to show what Canadians liked to eat—perogies, pickles, and a lot of cheese.

I kept many secrets from my Canadian friends and teachers, who curiously asked about my life back home. Although my family had been better off than many others, and we'd been the only household in the neighborhood with a telephone and a television set, we had still lived in a Third World country. Out of pride, I could not bring myself to admit that we'd had no indoor plumbing and no hot running water. Blocks of coal were used for cooking and heating the house. And there was no way I was going to confess that I'd bathed only once a week, at a public bathhouse with a hundred other women, or that I'd been routinely checked for lice.

The truth was a menace. I couldn't kill it, so I changed it—just a bit at a time. I really didn't see any harm indulging in creative storytelling—not until it was too late.

*I lived in a house. I lived in a big, fancy house. I lived in a mansion with iron gates.*

That's how it started. Just a small lie. Then, before I knew it, my childhood had turned into a complete fantasy. A fairy tale. I told my stories with such relish and vigor, I even convinced myself, for a while.

I told people that I was really a princess who was next in line to rule the country called Korea. Most had never heard of this country before. Even my teachers asked where it was.

I patiently explained to my round-eyed friends that I lived in a grand house that was safely protected behind majestic iron gates. "To keep the common people out, you understand," I said nonchalantly. My audience could only nod their agreement.

Picture steep steps that lead into a gorgeous courtyard with a beautiful garden, I started the story, sparing no adjectives to describe my dream home. *Cherry trees blossomed and water lilies bloomed. The house didn't look anything like the matchboxes Canadians call home. It had many rooms with hardwood floors and silk screen doors. Every weekend, my parents hosted a party for important people in the U.S. Army, where my father worked. Dressed in a dazzling ball gown, my mother would greet them while the servants offered glasses of champagne and Korean delicacies to the guests. I was allowed to stay up as late as I wanted and watch my father speak English to the Yankees, who brought me presents and candies. They did this not just because I was a princess, but also because they wanted to flatter my father, their boss.*

"You had servants?" came a question from the audience.

*Many. I even had my own personal servant, but I had her fired when I caught her destroying the doll my father had brought for me all the way from New York. The doll had mechanical eyes that opened and closed. I used to sit for hours admiring her blue eyes and long eyelashes, the longest I had ever seen in my life. She was my treasured possession. So imagine my devastation when the maid cut off all the eyelashes. I cried for days, long after the maid was let go.*

I babbled on and on. It was the only time I wasn't conscious of my accent, and my voice didn't drop into a mumbling whisper in embarrassment. My elaborate stories were the only thing that kept the kids from their cruel teasing and name-calling. As far as they were concerned, I was a princess from some exotic land far away, not just another dirty chink with buttonhole eyes. I had to keep up the myth. For the first time, I was grateful that I was the only Korean—the only Asian—in the whole school. The chance of being caught out was remote.

*My chauffeur drove me to a private kindergarten, and I had a personal seamstress who sewed all my dresses. For my first birthday, I received gold and precious gems for presents. Nothing but the best for a princess of the Yi Dynasty, the clan who had ruled Korea for five hundred years.*

"Then why did you come to Canada?" they asked.

"We were escaping from the Communists. North Korea is always trying to invade our country, you know," I answered confidently. "My father had a chance to go to the United States or Australia, but he picked Canada."

Truth and fiction, facts and lies. They were all one and the same in my mind, as long as I had an audience to fool. The first few times I told the story, my heart beat so fast that I thought it was going to burst. Then, gradually, I told it as if I had truly lived the life of a princess.

When the children dispersed without a trace of suspicion on their trusting faces, I held my breath for a moment and thought, Got away with it again. But I wondered how much longer I would be able to keep up the false identity I had given myself. All Canadians couldn't be this gullible and naive.

Still, I couldn't stop myself. My mother became a fine lady who hosted tea parties in the afternoons for her friends who also had too much money and time on their hands. They idly sat around on a plush white sofa drinking tea from the finest china, I boasted to my friends. A beautiful painting hung above the fireplace, and a crystal vase full of red roses sat on the coffee table. Of course, Koreans don't have tea parties, never mind drink tea. And we sit on the floor. I had never laid eyes on a sofa until I came to Regina. And the fireplace! Even I had to admit I went a bit too far with that one. No house in Korea, not even the presidential palace, would have a fireplace.

With just a minimal grasp of the language, I had somehow managed to fool all those around me. So far, I hadn't said a word of truth since the day I arrived in Canada. But I wasn't losing any sleep over it, because I didn't feel any ties to Canadians. They weren't my friends. My father cleaned their trash and my mother washed their dishes. That was enough. I owed them nothing more.

# IV

I soon began to realize I was never going to fit in at my school. Most of the children stampeding to their lockers ignored the teachers in the hallway, but I automatically stopped in midstep, not quite sure what to do. I was told I didn't have to bow. "Just say hello and smile," the principal had suggested—but I couldn't bring myself to act so casual and relaxed, not in front of authorities.

Canadian students chewed gum during lessons and talked back to the teacher. Some even fell asleep in class. Teachers said "please" and "thank you" and kids said "yeah." Those who didn't finish their homework went unpunished, not even earning a slap on the head. Students didn't have to remain after school to polish the windows and sweep the floors; janitors were hired to do that. I was the only one who went home with a bundle of books under my arm after school; the other kids didn't know the concept of studying. To my surprise, teachers actually gave students class time to do homework so it wouldn't ruin their evenings and weekends. And when they occasionally assigned homework, it was usually followed by a sympathetic look and an apology. Imagine a teacher apologizing to students.

Everything was backward in Canadian schools. It was cool to sit in the back of the class, not the front. Talking and passing notes during lessons were a must; otherwise, you were a "brown-noser." Sitting up straight and paying undivided attention pegged you as a "green snot." Even with my limited English vocabulary, I knew these weren't compliments. Anything that involved color to describe you was bad. I managed to figure out this much after I was referred to as a "yellow chink." Native Indians were called "red bums."

I usually finished my sandwich on the school bus coming home. Although I noticed other kids throwing away their food if they didn't like what they found in their lunch boxes, I felt too guilty to follow their example. It was too much like throwing away money, which I knew my parents didn't have very much of, and besides, I couldn't throw out something my mom had made for me. But I had to admit that peanut-butter-and-jelly sandwiches were overrated and never tasted as good as they looked on *Sesame Street*. Still, my mom insisted on making them because that's what Canadians supposedly ate for lunch. It was very important to my parents that I learn to become Canadian as soon as possible. "It's the only way to survive," my mother said, as if our very lives depended on it.

## V

In 1979, I was sworn in as a Canadian citizen. The citizenship judge proclaimed that it was a day of celebration and pride, but I remember feeling a sense of loss instead. My dream of going back to Korea seemed to drift further and further away, and I no longer fantasized about coming home from school one day and finding my grandparents sitting in the living room. Feeling confused and angry, I joined the other Canadians-to-be and sang "O Canada" and pledged my loyalty to the Queen without knowing the significance of the gesture. I didn't even know she was a real person. When it came time to swear on the Bible, however, that's where I drew the line. I put the wrong hand out and only pretended to give my loyalty to Canada. For months afterward, I was afraid that the RCMP were going to come and arrest me.

Shortly after my family officially became Canadians, Korean president Park Chung-Hee was assassinated. On October 26, 1979, the director of the Angibu, the Korean Central Intelligence Agency, shot the president dead. Martial law was declared and the whole nation went into a frenzy. Extra troops were mobilized in and around the Demilitarized Zone (DMZ) between North and South Korea, and Gen. Chun Doo-Hwan moved into the Blue House and became the next military dictator. I watched mass student demonstrations on TV in horror, and learned about the death of hundreds of civilians. It was then I first began to realize the truth about South Korea. It seems it was not as free a country as I was told all along.

Things got awfully confused in my mind, and I tried to figure them out using a childish logic. If North Korea was a Communist country where people weren't free to do and say what they pleased and South Korea was a democratic country but people still weren't free to do and say what they pleased, what was the difference between the two? If South Korea was neither Communist nor democratic, then what was it?

All my life, I had taken it for granted that South Korea was a democratic country no different from Canada and the United States, and I was distressed to discover otherwise. Feeling cheated and deceived, I started paying closer attention to the evening news to find out the truth about my country. I also eavesdropped on conversations among Korean men when they discussed politics. At first they seemed to support the anti-government protests led by university students and labor groups, but they soon grew annoyed by the endless civil unrest in Korea. The students were only a handful of radicals, they charged, who weren't excelling in classes so they went out looking for trouble. To many Koreans, intellectuals and civil-rights activists seemed like Communists. In their minds, anti-government equaled pro-Communist.

The news images of soldiers and the riot police beating up students in Seoul made me think of my childhood hero, the Army Lady. She was one of my mother's closest friends, and she chose a very daring career for herself. When all her friends got married and started families, the Army Lady joined the military and became an officer, an incredible achievement for a woman in Korea. She joined the army at a time when women were discouraged from even wearing pants, although this was the late sixties and the early seventies. I could only imagine what kind of battles she had to fight both at home and at work to overcome all the obstacles and barriers that stood in her way. And I could only imagine how she must have felt when she became an officer and watched the men salute her. I remember visiting her in the army barracks and thinking, I want to be just like her when I grow up.

Years later, when she was about forty, the Army Lady married a fellow officer. My mom glowed as she studied the wedding pictures that arrived in the mail. The blushing bride, wearing her white satin gown, stood by her man with her head lowered. Her new husband was dressed in his army uniform marked with shiny medals. I was shattered. I had secretly believed that the Army Lady and I were fellow travelers who had rebelled against our male-dominated culture and declared our independence, but she had given up the fight to have a baby. When she gave birth to a son, she knew she was blessed.

In Korea, of course, a woman's worst crime in life was failing to produce a son for her husband and his family. It wasn't that long ago when mothers named their daughters to reflect their resentment: Soun (disappointment), Sosop (pity), Put'ong (anger), or Yukan (regret). I grew up watching Korean movies and soap operas where women fell on their hands and knees to beg forgiveness, and mothers took their own lives because they couldn't have a son.

As the first-born child, I instinctively knew I wasn't supposed to be a girl. Neighbors and relatives didn't hide their disappointment and practically told me to my face that I was a mistake and that I'd be responsible for my mother's misery. It was enough to give me a complex, and soon I refused to wear dresses and asked my parents if I could join the Boy Scouts. I thought the next best thing to having a son was to have a daughter who acted like one.

Though my parents showed me nothing but adoration and spoiled me with the best of everything, it was impossible to ignore the cultural message that said a woman was a worthless piece of property. I can still recall the women at the market who taunted my mother because she had enrolled me in a private kindergarten. When my father took me to restaurants, the waitresses came and teased him for showing so much affection to his daughter, saying, "Imagine how much more he would adore her if she was a boy." Adults talked as if I wasn't even there, and offered condolences to my parents for their bad luck.

After three daughters, my mother finally gave birth to a baby boy. But she was too busy packing boxes and preparing for the move to sit back and enjoy the long-awaited child. A month after my brother was born, we came to Canada.

# VI

Thanks to the old Hollywood movies I had watched in Seoul, I was under the grand illusion that all North American men looked like Clark Gable and all women dressed like Audrey Hepburn. So I didn't know what to think when I saw half-naked Indian chiefs dancing around their teepees, Inuit fishing outside their igloos, and men in red uniforms riding their horses into the sunset, all in a film, courtesy of the Canadian embassy in Seoul, introducing my new country.

In the end, neither Hollywood nor the National Film Board prepared me for the stark reality of Regina, Saskatchewan, where Canada geese, wheat fields, and grain elevators were the capital's main attractions. The land was as flat as the eye could see, the winters were unfit for human survival, and the city was one big, naked suburb.

Our family felt completely isolated and lost, and I am not sure how we would have survived the loneliness if it hadn't been for the other Korean families who also seemed to have made a mistake in the choice of their final destination. For the first couple of years after our arrival, the twenty-some Korean families were inseparable. Evenings and week-ends were spent visiting, reminiscing about Korea, and crying on one another's shoulder. We all tried our best to shut out all that was Canada and re-create a little Korea in our own living rooms.

The biggest event of the year was the Korean community's annual summer barbecue, a full-blown production with days of preparation and anticipation. Mothers spent hours on the phone planning an elaborate menu that consisted of at least three or four different kinds of kimchee, pounds of *bulgoki*, half a dozen pots of rice and side dishes, as well as potato salad, doughnuts, Kentucky Fried Chicken, and pizza for the children and non-Korean significant others. Corner-store families, too busy to prepare Korean food, usually brought the Western food, along with cases of soft drinks and bags of chips. Every year, the night before the picnic, my parents stayed up past midnight cooking and packing the ice chest. It was a rare time when my parents acted like friends, joshing each other and laughing jovially. My father meticulously carved paper-thin slices of roast beef and marinated them in a bowl of soy sauce and garlic, while Mom busily attended to three things at once: frying dumplings, boiling noodles, freely tossing chili powder and sesame seeds into a big container of kimchee that sat in the middle of the kitchen floor. Mom selected bits of food with her fingers and fed them to my dad for a taste test. That was the extent of spontaneous affection they were capable of showing, especially when the children were pre-sent. She would chat amiably the whole time about how the Canadian way was so much simpler. Hot dogs and hamburgers. No fuss, no muss. Koreans made everything difficult and cumbersome, even eating. She stopped talking only long enough to taste the food before continuing with her monologues. She talked about the days of the Korean War, my grandparents' health, the fate of senior citizens at the nursing home where she worked, who was bickering with whom in the community, and the future plans for her children, as if all these topics were some-how intricately linked.

This evening of bliss soon turned into a morning of frenzy, however, with the wake-up call coming at the ridiculous hour of eight o'clock on Saturday morning. My father, extremely impatient and excitable, rushed the whole family and chastised my mother for taking half the kitchen with her. Every year, it was the same pre-picnic conversation.

"We're not feeding the whole community," Dad would snap.

"We stay up half the night cooking. Why shouldn't I take it?" Mom would reply sheepishly.

"Too much! They won't all fit in the ice chest." Sigh, groan.

"I don't hear you complain when you eat it." Mom always had the last word.

We were almost always the first to arrive at the picnic area at Fort Qu'Appelle, a provincial park just outside Regina. Station wagons and minivans pulled into the parking lot, and people piled out with boxes of food, cases of soft drinks, rolled-up blankets and mats, raincoats and umbrellas, baseball bats and soccer balls. From a distance, we looked like refugees on the run.

After the feasting, the afternoon was spent playing baseball and soccer and running three-legged races. For the sake of the women and the children, silly games were also a part of the day's activities: running through an obstacle course balancing a Ping-Pong ball on a spoon, and playing find the candy by burying your face in a mound of flour. Then there were games that were fraught with sexual overtones, though this was lost on the children. Two players, of opposite sex and similar height, faced each other with a ball placed between them at chest level. They had to carry this to the finish line without using their hands. Naturally, the best way to secure the ball in place without dropping it was to squeeze it by standing close together. In a culture where public displays of physical affection raised eyebrows, this game stirred up a lot of commotion, inviting jokes and teasing from the participants' spouses, who watched uncomfortably on the sidelines.

One year, my mother, being the creative sort, invented a game that topped even the carry-the-ball game. An orange was dropped in a stocking and tied around a contestant's waist so the fruit hung between her legs. The objective was to hit a soccer ball with the orange to push the ball forward. The harder the thrust, the farther the ball rolled. Most women, shy and embarrassed, never made it to the finish line, while the men yelled and shouted encouragement. Even passersby stopped to observe what they must have thought was a most peculiar ritual of the assembled Orientals.

As the years went by, fewer and fewer families showed up for the picnic. Many had moved to Vancouver or Toronto, and soon only a handful of us remained. The women showed their age, and the men didn't move as quickly on the soccer field. The children, all grown up, sat around idly and awkwardly bowed their heads to greet the adults who inquired about their plans for university and summer jobs. My mother, who still brought too much food, busily chatted away with the other women. It was then that I began to understand my mother's efforts to keep peace in the community. This was her world. It was all she had.

Although the Korean community in Regina was pitifully small, we had more than our fair share of fights, gossip, scandal, rivalry, competition, and even fistfights. We were like a dysfunctional family all trying to live under one roof, constantly whispering, exchanging sidelong glances, taking sides, transferring our loyalty, and holding grudges. As in every family, however, there was also a lot of love, caring, and generosity. Unfortunately these qualities were too often buried beneath the immediate desperation to survive and cope in a country that was foreign and intimidating to all of us.

Most of us had arrived in Regina in the mid- to late seventies, and the future had never looked so uncertain. Parents came with children and babies in their arms, eager to start a new life. Like my own parents, they believed Canada was where miracles happened, where money and opportunity came knocking at your door.

Though everybody clung to one another and sought comfort in numbers in the beginning, the honeymoon was short-lived. I soon started to see the true nature of Koreans. Competition and one-upmanship were impossible to ignore; jealousy and envy were embarrassingly transparent; and superficial gestures and false modesty were grossly exaggerated.

When one family bought a piano and signed up their children for lessons, every single family in the community did the same. Now that the children were well assimilated into Canadian society and their English wasn't a problem, the parents urged them to concentrate on their music lessons. Practice, practice, practice.

At the spring piano festivals, Korean kids dominated the prize winning. Of course, this meant more to the parents than to the children, who would gladly have given their right arms to quit. It was even worse when some kid picked up a second instrument. From then on, at least one child in each family was pressured to play both the piano and the violin. Luckily for me, my second sister was that one child in our family.

The funny thing was that none of the parents in the community had any background or interest in classical music, and most of them didn't even like it. And no one wanted a professional musician in the family because that wasn't a real career. Playing the piano was strictly a hobby, an extracurricular activity, but no one treated it that way, least of all the mothers. The piano transformed them into dictators with fire in their eyes. When they weren't browbeating the children to practice, they were on the phone with their friends, comparing notes. In their saccharine voices, mothers praised their rivals' children and denied that their own had any talent to boast of.

"If only my daughter practiced even half as hard as your child," they'd say, and add, "I have all the confidence in your daughter. I mean, look how smart her parents are ..."

After these friendly chats, they then turned on their children and demanded to know why they couldn't practice as long and hard as so-and-so's children. "You go to the same conservatory and you have ten capable fingers. What's wrong with you?" Mother would lament, standing in her work uniform, as if I needed reminding that she had to work to pay for my lessons. "Is it so much to ask after all the sacrifices I've made? When I was young in Korea, I was so poor, I couldn't even dream of such a luxury ..."

These small, inter-family rivalries were our parents' way of measuring their success in Canada. After all, the children were the reason they had immigrated in the first place—we were their investment in the future. Still, their obsessive preoccupation was driving the children mad. I, for one, could hardly wait to get away.

# VII

By the time I started high school, my parents had transferred their anxieties from music to books. I halfheartedly committed myself to a career as a doctor because that was the goal of every immigrant child, most of whom only wanted to make their parents happy and compensate for their years of sacrifice. But in my case, it wasn't meant to be. Owing to either a genetic failure or a severe lack of attention, I could not wrap my mind around the wonders of physics and chemistry, not to mention calculus. In biology, the mere sight of earthworms and frogs laid out for dissection made me queasy. Confounding my teachers, who had bet on this Asian kid to earn perfect grades, I barely passed science and math and amused myself reading Dostoevsky instead.

When my parents realized that they weren't going to have a doctor in the family, they were neither disappointed nor surprised. They had high hopes for their children, naturally, but even they couldn't expect that much. "Our family doesn't have that kind of brain," my mother, who believed everything was hereditary, observed with nonchalance. "Just finish university and find yourself a good husband," she pleaded. That was all she asked of her daughters. My dad, who couldn't bear to look so far into the future, asked for even less. "Don't bring white boys home!"

Once my mother saw that women in Canada, married or single, had to have a career and work until age sixty-five, she suggested that I become either a schoolteacher or a piano instructor—a respectable day job so I could play the dutiful wife in the evenings. It was my fate as a woman, she stubbornly insisted, and argued that there was no other way. Look at Margaret Thatcher! The Queen of England! Two of the smartest women in the world, with all the power and glory, yet they still married. "That goes to prove that a woman needs her man and children." She nodded her head emphatically. "And another thing, married women with children age with more grace and dignity. I see this at work every day," she explained. "They are not as selfish and impatient as the women who have been single all their lives. Those ones are impossible."

"Who cares? They're old, Mother. I'm not going to sacrifice my life just so I can wrinkle gracefully," I protested. "Besides, I hope to die before I get wheeled into a nursing home."

"Don't talk about death in front of your mother. And as always, you miss my point. Nothing is more physically demanding and painful than giving birth to a baby, and nothing tests your patience more than a husband. They will teach you more about life than a thousand books."

"Mother, I don't want to live your life," I complained. "You and Dad bicker constantly, and all you do is worry about us. I don't want that."

"It's called life," she said matter-of-factly, showing no sign of being hurt by my words. "Believe me, all the success in the world will still leave you feeling lonely and empty if you don't have a family to come home to at the end of the day."

On and on. Our conversations continued like this for several years. Every day after school I'd come home and sit in the kitchen and talk to my mother for an hour while she frantically prepared dinner. The poor woman didn't even have time to change out of her work uniform and catch her breath. It was very important for my father to see his dinner ready on the table the minute he walked in the door at five o'clock. He had no patience when it came to his empty stomach. And as if to make my mother's task that much more difficult, my brother had never learned to acquire a taste for Korean food, so Mom had to cook a separate dish for him. "So much easier to cook for the old folks," she used to mutter under her breath. "You just grind everything up."

Despite numerous heated discussions about sharing housework in what was supposedly the Canadian way, our family never assimilated to that degree. It was unthinkable for my mother, and even her daughters, to imagine the man of the house standing over the stove with a pair of chopsticks stirring noodles. And it broke my father's heart to see his only son and heir making a peanut-butter sandwich when he had three sisters to serve him. To my father's credit, though, he did the vacuuming and loads of laundry and even dared to set foot in the kitchen when we had big dinner parties.

My mother's wisdom began to make sense to me as I got older and discovered men. But at the time, her words sent me climbing the wall in frustration. I was not only outraged at her absolute refusal to even entertain the idea that there might be more to life than serving men and popping out babies, but it also disheartened me to think that all that lay ahead was for me to repeat my mother's life. Marriage was one thing, but marrying a Korean man was something else altogether. It was hard enough to find Mr. Right without restricting myself to Koreans. In my eyes, Korean men were all the same: domineering, controlling, and stubborn. In other words, they were all like my father.

I grew up in absolute terror of him. His quick, explosive temper followed by days of brooding ruled our home. He never raised a hand to us, but one look at his dark, moody face almost made us wish for a quick death. Everybody tiptoed around in his presence and automatically checked the tension barometer on entering the house. His moods, which varied from minute to minute, determined the atmosphere. Sometimes he went weeks without uttering a single word to my mother after a fight.

Inevitably, with his fierce temper and my rebellious nature, there was chaos. Like all teenagers, I ignored the house rules on drinking, dating, and staying out late. At first I did my best to avoid confrontations with my parents, who armed themselves with their immigration-and-sacrifices speeches, guaranteed to reduce me to guilty tears. But I couldn't live like a hermit. When I couldn't bring myself to defy them outright, I came up with a brilliant idea and decided to call on Angela to fight my battles.

Angela was my alter ego. Angela was me.

When I first enrolled in school in Canada, the principal, Mr. Barlow, informed my parents that I'd never make any friends with a name like Sun-Kyung. No Canadian would be able to pronounce it, he observed, insisting that I adopt an English name. My parents agreed that it would be one way to assimilate more quickly. It never occurred to them to object, especially when the suggestion came directly from an authority figure, and a white man at that.

Although my name, Angela, was randomly picked, my second sister's name, Sue, had an uglier origin. When Yu-Kyung was introduced to her Grade 2 classmates, they teased her and called her "chop suey," which she didn't understand. Hearing the name-calling, the teacher added insult to injury by announcing to the class that since Yu rhymed with Sue, as in "chop suey," this would be my sister's new name. She was stuck with it.

This was during the seventies in the Prairies, where Yu-Kyung and I were the only Asian kids in a school of several hundred white students. We didn't know that it was our right to say no to the name changes. Out of ignorance, I remained Angela for about a decade.

I must admit, however, that at first it was fun to be somebody else for a change, and I took the opportunity to alter my identity altogether. My parents were eager for me to become Canadian, so I decided to go to extremes and change my personality as well. Like Superman and Clark Kent, I became Angela to the outside world and changed back to Sun-Kyung at home.

I ate bologna sandwiches at lunchtime, and rice and kimchee for dinner. I sneaked smokes in the girls' washroom and skipped classes at school; at home, I practiced the piano and studied in the evenings, planning to become a doctor to make my parents proud. I could argue openly with my teachers without fearing the consequences, but found myself staring at my feet with my mouth shut when Koreans talked to me. Being out in the world meant I was able to escape the constraints of my cultural conditioning; being at home meant a return to being an obedient and submissive daughter.

Angela went out and got drunk with her friends; Sun-Kyung came home and knelt in front of her parents and apologized until the small hours of the night. Angela dated white boys against her father's wishes and lied about it shamelessly; Sun-Kyung compensated for the lies by hustling several summer jobs to help her parents with the mortgage.

Angela used her piano practices at the music hall as an excuse to stay away from her family as much as possible; Sun-Kyung received a piano performer's degree, with honors, to make up for the guilt of not being home. Angela foamed at the mouth with contempt for gossip-mongering Koreans; Sun-Kyung was a role model for all the other Korean children in the community. Angela had Sun-Kyung's permission to be the bad girl who was filled with curiosity and mischief because Sun-Kyung was too responsible and inhibited to do it herself. Angela had the courage to be spontaneous and adventurous, constantly testing and challenging her limits, while her alter ego was a self-controlled conformist whose raison d'être was to make her parents happy and proud at all cost.

It was a severe case of cultural schizophrenia, and though I became deceptively good at changing identities at the drop of a hat, the emotional strain was making me dizzy.

# VIII

Like the creation of my alter ego, the words "No speak English" were essential to my survival for a long time. These three magic words made people feel sympathetic toward yet another newcomer and, to my relief, also tended to make them shy away and leave me alone. The phrase even proved to be a good excuse if I didn't want to be bothered by door-to-door salesmen or telemarketers. Of course, there were always those who insisted on talking anyway, pronouncing each word very slowly and very loudly, as if I was deaf and mute. One time, an Avon lady stood outside my door and babbled for twenty minutes about a tube of lipstick. She shouted the whole time with a silly grin on her face. "VERY-SEXY-RED! BOYS-GO-CRAZY! JUST-THE-RIGHT-COLOR-FOR-YOU!"

Even though my English has improved greatly over the years, I am still far from comfortable with it. Luckily my friends and colleagues are used to my accent. Still, when I'm feeling lazy and sloppy, I quickly resort to pidgin English and speak abruptly, with exclamation marks, as if I am giving orders: "Don't!" "Problem! Need to talk!" "Eat lunch!"

And if I am really comfortable and under the influence of alcohol, a Korean word will slip out here and there. When I am especially tired, it is not unusual for me to decide, in mid-sentence, that I no longer want to complete my thought, my voice trailing off into mumbled nonsense until I stop moving my lips.

For years, I tried to improve my speech with everything from private voice lessons to singing lessons from an opera singer to poetry reading sessions with a sweet old retired teacher who always served tea and biscuits. But they were all in vain.

Eventually, I became obsessed with my language abilities, or the lack thereof, and refused to speak unless absolutely necessary. At university, I never asked questions during classes, especially when they were held in big lecture halls where a few hundred students could witness my handicap. I'd walk down the hallway after class hearing a voice in my head. That voice spoke perfect English, the way the words are supposed to sound, but damned if I was able to manipulate my mouth to duplicate it.

From years of practice, I developed a habit of carefully constructing a sentence first in my head, then double-checking it to make sure the nouns and verbs were in the right places. If there were any words that were tricky to pronounce, I carefully mouthed them silently before speaking. I learned that lesson the hard way when my Grade 6 teacher told me to go to the next classroom, Grade 7, and ask to borrow a pair of scissors. I knocked on the door and tried to fight off the intimidation of those "senior" kids who were staring at me, enjoying the distraction from their lesson. Since I went to school surrounded by kids and teachers who all sounded the same—white—I was under the illusion that I sounded like them, too. So imagine my shock and humiliation when I finally mustered the courage and asked to borrow a pair of "sae-jjors." The whole class burst out laughing. I stood there dumbfounded while the teacher mimicked my mispronunciation. "You want a pair of sae-jjors?" he mocked. "Here you go. Here's a pair of sae-jjors." I had to walk to the front of the class and get the scissors from the teacher and walk back out. Since then, I have never been able to say "scissors" without thinking of that incident.

Then there were the articles *the* and *a*. Useless words as far as I was concerned, with no meaning, no context. A teacher explained that the article *the* was applied when referring to a specific thing. So the next day I decided to put it into practice and asked my classmates, "Where's the Karen?" No sooner had the students started giggling than I realized I had made a mistake. The teacher never told me about the exception to the rule.

In university, I took a French class that was compulsory for my degree. Needless to say, it was Mission Impossible. The language demanded too much twisting and twirling of my tongue and called for unnatural gurgling sounds to spill out from the back of my throat, distorting my features and leaving my jaw tired at the end of each class. It just wasn't natural for someone like me to even attempt to learn French. The French words just got buried beneath my Korean and Canadian accents, a cruel and unusual punishment for both the professor and me. So with a wink and a nudge, he agreed to pass me based only on my written exams.

My inability to speak French was distressing because I feared it would interfere with my plan to become a journalist in a country where French was the other official language. I tried my best to take some comfort from my ability to speak Korean, but I knew that it would be of very little use for a foreign correspondent in Europe or Central America.

The romanticized images of globe-trotting trench-coated reporters and war correspondents in movies were the extent of my knowledge about journalism. Then, one day, quite by accident, I discovered a book in the local library that would change my life. Still only semi-literate, I read for the sole purpose of expanding my English vocabulary, paying little or no attention to authors and literally judging each book by its cover. I'd lug home indiscriminate piles of novels—John Steinbeck, Judy Blume, James Michener, and even Harlequin romances—and toss them on my bed. Then one day, a very special book fell out of the pile. The book was *A Man*, the author Oriana Fallaci.

I was completely awed by Fallaci's portrait of Alekos Panagoulis, founder and head of the Greek Resistance, and her obsession with tracking down this rebel's past, falling in love with him in the process. Mesmerized by the protagonist's passion for life, and the intrigue and intensity between the two lovers, I could only daydream about finding such a man, knowing very well that none existed in Regina.

To my sixteen-year-old imagination, Oriana Fallaci was a literary femme fatale who feared nothing in life. She was everything I imagined a journalist to be: strong, intelligent, tough, and sexy. And single. I had found myself a new hero and a new career.

I was sorry to part with the book after I finished reading it, but consoled myself by copying down Oriana's words on cards. I had finally realized the value and significance of a good book, and how personal a possession it became once you caressed the pages with your eyes and your fingers. I hesitated for days before returning it to the library and decided that I'd buy all my books from then on. Hoping to purchase the library a brand-new copy of the book so I could have "my book" back, I searched all over the city, but without success.

My discovery of books and the joy of reading was a triumphant moment in my life. A revelation. Annoyed I had waited so long, I started devouring books. A small collection began to pile up on the shelf that my father built above my bed. I spent many nights wishing that all the magical words and perfectly composed sentences would somehow mysteriously lift off the pages and float into my head to leave their imprint on my brain.

# Hide and Seek in
# Little Korea

# I

There are three stages of exile: triumphant assimilation, nostalgia, and serene despair. I read this in a magazine profile of Nancy Huston, a Canadian novelist living in Paris. Though I had never considered myself an exile, Huston's words rang so true that I copied them down and stuck them ceremoniously on my bulletin board. I was amazed at first how accurately she had described my life; then I became mildly annoyed. What I'd stumbled for twenty years to piece together, Huston had summed up in that eloquent sentence.

I was on the brink of waking up on the other side of despair when I moved to Toronto, foolishly thinking I was leaving my Korean psyche behind, along with my parents and their friends, in the Canadian prairies. Little did I know that something much bigger and more trying awaited.

# II

There were a number of factors that inspired me to pursue a career in journalism, but in the end it was my parents who influenced my decision the most, though quite unintentionally.

One night, during a halt in the domestic hostilities, my mother said, with a sigh, "You can't fool fate ... you're a horse after all."

According to the Chinese Lunar calendar, used by many Asians for marking celebratory dates like birthdays and the Chinese New Year, I was born in the Year of the Horse, December 12, 1966. This is apparently a bad astrological sign for women, so my mother took fate in her own hands and registered my birthdate using the Western calendar, which pushed the date ahead to January 22, 1967—the Year of the Sheep. This symbol—quiet, gentle, and submissive—was considered more appropriate for women. Of course, my mother hadn't counted on having a black sheep.

That night, watching the news on TV, she muttered under her breath, "You're never home ... you should be a journalist and gallivant around like a horse."

That was when the idea was planted in my head. After a few days of contemplation, I bravely announced my decision and, as I expected, my parents tried to dissuade me. Their objections were many. It was no job for a woman, the hours were long and the assignments dangerous, and the pay wasn't all that great either. They also plucked examples from their home country and tried to inject fears about censorship, threats, and arrests. I knelt before my parents, unmoved, until my mother blurted out, "Besides, English is not your first language and you have an accent. No Canadian will hire a yellow face."

The words hung in the air with nowhere to go. My mother had just opened a Pandora's box of my worst insecurities. I had always regarded my accent as my biggest handicap, a wretched reminder of my short-comings every time I opened my mouth. I knew that I'd never sound intelligent or Canadian, and that people would always assume I was a "Chinaman." In humiliation, I told my parents that I'd work for news-papers, where people didn't have to hear me, just read me.

The decision was reinforced by a family friend who counseled me at my parents' request. When he failed to persuade me to become an accountant instead, he suggested I at least drop my Korean name. I'd never make it as a reporter if people couldn't pronounce my name, he'd warned. To prove him wrong, I permanently removed the name Angela from all official documents and reclaimed my birth name.

Years later, in those moments of despair when it takes me hours to construct a simple paragraph and sleeping on a bed of nails seems more appealing than writing, my parents' voices creep into my head and I shudder with fright. "You think anybody can write? English isn't even your first language ... Try something easier, perhaps accounting ..."


## III


After I received my journalism degree from the University of Regina, at the mature age of twenty-four, I took the bus to Toronto, a three-day trip. I was going to the big city to write for the *Globe and Mail*, the first student from the university to be hired by the national newspaper. I was on top of the world. During the initial interview, I had been cocky and aloof, and told Mr. Globe and Mail that I planned to have his job when he asked what I envisioned myself doing five years down the road. With five hundred candidates competing for the ten summer positions at the paper, I figured I didn't have a chance in hell. Things are very simple in life when there's neither hope nor expectation.

Now, with two suitcases crammed with books and clothes, my parents and I anxiously waited for the departure time, dreading the moment when we had to say goodbye. My dad insisted on leaving the house an hour early for the ten-minute ride to the bus depot. If he'd driven any slower, we would've gone backward. My parents fought back tears, and I knew it would be weeks before they stopped crying. They knew and I knew that I was never going to come back.

My parents were so proud that they announced the news to everybody they knew, including their bank tellers and the ticket agent at the bus station. For my part, I'd been so deliriously happy about finally ditching Regina that I hardly gave a second thought to leaving my family behind. Sitting in the waiting area, I stole a glance at my mother, who sat there with a cold cup of coffee in her hand. She looked pale and vulnerable under the fluorescent light. Suddenly, I was almost afraid to leave her. Never before had I wanted so badly to hug her and tell her that I loved her, but I couldn't. It would've been too melodramatic and out of character for us. Instead, we all pretended that this was just a short trip, as the immigration to Canada had been just a temporary stay. Whatever excitement I felt was suppressed by the guilt of leaving home, deserting my parents. I cried until the bus crossed the border into Manitoba.

My new job was to be short-lived. In fact, disillusioned with journalism, I quit five jobs in five years. Not surprisingly, the daily exercise of delivering the news was nothing like the ideal, romantic fantasy I had conjured up over the years. I had envisaged the country's great opinion makers and news gatherers sweating over their typewriters until late hours, sacrificing everything to uphold freedom of speech. I was under the impression that journalists were married to their jobs and that words were the greatest love of their life. Obviously, I was extremely naive. It was disheartening to learn that journalists, by and large, were not a very bright bunch of people, and most of them regarded their job as just a paycheck. The newshounds were no different from my parents in that they, too, looked forward to weekends and holidays, worried about their children, and bought lottery tickets. Instead of holding animated discussions about Arafat, the plight of women in Third World countries, and the collapse of the Soviet Union, the editorial staff assembled at the water cooler to gossip, compare recipes, and reenact their favorite scenes from *Seinfeld*.

After my summer contract ended at the *Globe and Mail*, I went to the *Kitchener-Waterloo Record*, a daily in a medium-size community just outside Toronto. As grateful as I was to have found a job during a recession, I was depressed to be in a city where the annual beer festival was taken much too seriously and dominated the paper's front page for a week. After hearing one too many reporters reminisce about broken dreams and how a six-month contract had turned into a decade-long commitment, along with a mortgage and a family, I fled without a moment's hesitation. I wrote my resignation letter, dropped it off on my editor's desk at three in the morning, and drove back to Toronto the next day. That job lasted less than three months.

As anticipated, my parents were irate over my lack of responsibility and worried themselves sick thinking that I was homeless and destitute. A Technicolor picture of an innocent small-town girl lost in the mean, cruel streets of Toronto and prostituting herself to survive leaped into their heads. In between sobs and frantic pleas for me to come back home, as if I were a teenage runaway, my parents took turns reasoning with me and uttering threats. Nevertheless, they were practical folks who worried first and foremost about their children's health and well-being. Right now, their concern was the dental plan and the pension that had been terminated along with my employment. Then came the good old guilt trip.

"You quit because you didn't like your job?" Dad asked, as if he had never heard anything so crazy in his life.

"Now you know what your parents go through day in and day out."

Mom jumped in without missing a beat. "You think we like our jobs? When we feel like quitting, we think of the children. Nobody likes their job all the time, but you stick with it. That's why it's called 'work.' How dare you quit on a whim?"

My mother, who had a theory on everything, speculated that I'd been spoiled by the *Globe* experience. I had skipped too many steps too soon to reach the top. Now there was nowhere to go but down.

"But I didn't expect it would be this low. Imagine, unemployed. And so young," she said, clicking her tongue in disapproval. "What am I going to tell the Koreans? My daughter, a *Globe and Mail* reporter, and now a bum. That's not making it in the big city. You should just come home and get a job here."

Taking a deep breath, I tried to explain the concept of freelancing, but I knew it would go in one ear and out the other. They didn't want to hear about an imaginary job that had no dental plan or pension.

"You work when you freelance, right?" Mom asked. "See, why not work at a place that gives you a dental plan if you're going to have to work all the same?" It was hard to argue with her reasoning sometimes.

"Mom, please understand," I said. "This is not about a dental plan, okay? My teeth are fine."

"Of course they are fine," she snapped. "You're young. But wait until you get older. My teeth were fine, too, until I started having children. You have to prepare for your future. You have no husband, no children, and no job, and believe me, you are going to be thirty before you know it."

Logic and reasoning rarely found their place in our family discussions, and no one stayed calm for very long. If by chance a family member restrained him- or herself from expressing five emotions at once, it immediately aroused suspicion. Clearly, either the speaker was terminally ill or a matter more dire was lurking in the background. Emotion and panic controlled our mouths, and the point of discussion, if anyone could remember what it was, stood no chance of being recovered.

With my mother on the kitchen phone spitting out Korean words faster than bullets from a machine gun, and my father clutching the extension in the basement firing questions in English, I couldn't get a word in edgewise. After they were thoroughly exhausted, I dutifully explained myself, alternating between English and Korean, and promised I would look both ways before crossing the street and walk away when a stranger offered me a ride.

Get a job, find a husband—preferably Korean—buy a house, and start a family. An easy-to-follow set of instructions. So why couldn't I do it?

My poor parents. My life seemed so simple and straightforward from where they stood. They had done their job well, and years of sacrifice and hard work were finally starting to pay off for them. So to hear their pride and joy complain about her chosen field so early on in her career and confess that conventional nine-to-five hours didn't quite suit her temperament made them feel like crying. Hurt and disappointed, they reacted as if I had deliberately sabotaged my job to bring misery to their lives. I understood their frustration, but still, for once in my life, I would have liked to hear them say, Well, it's your decision, dear, and just let it be.

The weekly ritual of calling my parents left me drained. Not only did I have to concentrate on my Korean, but I had to gauge the mood they were in and conduct the conversation accordingly. Sometimes I'd call in the middle of a fight, and they'd simply carry on with their bickering as if they appreciated the audience. Often they were arguing about me and my bleak future. Though I always made a conscious effort to sound cheerful and optimistic, a nervous edge to their voices made it difficult for me to play my part.

What I couldn't tell them was that I really needed some time to reevaluate this whole journalism business. I needed to find a niche for myself because I had learned the hard way that spot news and civic politics bored me to tears, and that feature articles and investigative pieces were basically reserved for senior writers. To be a foreign correspondent meant years of laboring away with no guarantee of the desired position, and I knew my impatience would never permit me to diligently work my way up. I thought about television and radio, but my accent discouraged me immediately. I knew I was looking for shortcuts, ways to cheat, but I also knew that there would be a big price to pay for it in the end. Or so went my mother's theory, anyway. She believed that a person was like a tree. Good, strong roots produced healthy branches, but the tree with rotten roots would eventually fall to the ground. Needless to say, I didn't have healthy roots.

## IV

It didn't take too much soul-searching to see why I rejected conformity, convention, and authority figures. After years of being smothered by an oppressive environment dictated by an archaic culture, I had surfaced at last. No one knew me in Toronto. I was anonymous and it felt great. And best of all, I was free of Koreans. I didn't have to look over my shoulder to make sure my behavior wasn't going to be reported back to my parents.

I had come to Toronto to shed my past and create a new identity for myself. Finally, I had time and space for Angela and Sun-Kyung to merge and give birth to a new person, Sunny. To achieve such a task, I believed it was essential to stay away from Koreans until I was strong and confident enough to stand alone, as an individual. I wanted to feel comfortably detached. So it seems strange to me now that I voluntarily joined an ultraconservative newspaper that was nothing more than a propaganda rag for the South Korean government.

Watch my mouth, mind my manners, improve my Korean, don't smoke, dress respectably, go to Korean church, and find a suitable young man. Advice and warnings rolled off my mother's tongue when I told her about my new job with a Korean community newspaper. It was my worst nightmare come true, but unpaid bills and the sheer desperation born of my father's threats to send Mom to baby-sit me in Toronto drove me to give Koreans a try.

Delighted and shocked, my parents hoped that the new job would encourage me to change my negative attitude toward Koreans and help me appreciate the special bond that supposedly existed only among our own kind. "See, Koreans stick together. We take care of our own," Mom announced triumphantly. She was in for yet another disappointment, however, and this time it wasn't for lack of trying on my part. I think my chances of survival would have been better if I had walked through a minefield instead.

I had proposed that the paper publish a national weekly English supplement for young Korean Canadians to help bridge the gap between parents and children; the old world and the new; traditional values and Western ideas. Interracial dating and marriage, women's rights, unequal treatment of daughters and sons, violence against women and children, divorce laws, the community's isolation and ghettoization, xenophobia and homosexuality were all urgent issues that needed to be addressed. Ultimately though, the publisher had little tolerance for "radical" ideas, and the community even less.

Toronto's Korean ghetto was a closed enclave, and it wanted to stay that way. Its fifty thousand members were ruled by absolute conformity; a refusal to play by the rules meant instant ostracism. They lived in fear of gossip and rumors but also thrived on them. As one Korean warned me, "If I start a rumor that you farted, in an hour the whole town will be saying that you had diarrhea, and in a day people in Seoul will have heard about it also."

Toronto Koreans were no different from Regina Koreans, with one significant exception: their attachment to the church, Toronto's social mecca, where worship was incidental. Ironically, the church was the most unforgiving place, a place where members were quickest to judge. Divorced women were asked to leave the choir and were shunned by the congregation. Men were pressured to change their political allegiance and conduct their business according to the dictates of the Korean Businessmen's Association. Parents forced their children to go to church in hopes that they would meet other Korean kids and, with luck, a future spouse.

People came to church to catch up on the latest news in the community—who was new in town, who had gone bankrupt and had to return to Korea, whose child was getting married, whose son was going to be a doctor, the latest hot spot for golfing, and scandals involving congregation members. Most scandals were mundane, like somebody's daughter seen smoking and hanging around with Canadian kids who dressed strangely, or somebody's son getting rejected by a medical school. But for a group of people for whom saving face was everything, any unpleasant news about their children was a disgrace. The real heart stopper was the extramarital affair, and there was more of that going on than anyone cared to admit. Stories of wives sneaking out for a couple hours while their kids looked after the store, and husbands backing out of a golf game for an afternoon roll in the hay could be heard as people whispered in restaurants and subways. Once in a while, you heard intimate details about men who had lovers, and even children, back in Seoul. That usually came out in the open only when a husband was forced to confess to his wife about the other woman, who was blackmailing him until she got her end of the bargain: money and a visa to come to Canada.

Again, the incredible pressure to save face discouraged people from talking about their problems with their friends. Frustrated with immigrant life, husbands vented their anger by beating up their wives and verbally humiliating them in public. Tied to their corner stores as much as eighteen hours a day, parents lived their lives through their children, browbeating them to become doctors and lawyers. When teenagers got pregnant, they were sent off to Korea for abortions for fear that their family doctor in Toronto, who happened to be Korean, might spread the news. A child with a mental illness or physical disability was discouraged by the parents from making public appearances at church, social gatherings, and other Korean functions. Senior citizens were often lonely and neglected, and divorced women were openly criticized and harassed by members of the community. Sensational talk shows like *Oprah* and *Geraldo* would never survive in Korea. No one was into confession, and everybody was into hiding.

The number of churches in Toronto was disproportionately high compared with the size of the Korean population. Congregations ranged from several hundred people to only half a dozen families with the worship taking place in somebody's living room. Internal politics and constant bickering were the main reasons for one more church appearing on the scene. Instead of working out their differences and agreeing on a compromise, impatient and quick-tempered Koreans would head off to start a church of their own and recruit new members. It was the same with local newspapers, businesses, political organizations, and social groups. Everybody was a minister, an elder, or a president of some group or another. Stripped of their status in Canada, where university degrees and work experience from the old country were no longer valid, they had to be recognized and appreciated as somebody, no matter how small or inconsequential the role.

Koreans are a proud people. They are proud of their culture, heritage, and traditions, but sometimes I found it difficult to see why. For a country where foreign invasions were practically an annual event and whose greatest contribution to the world was the Moonies, the prevailing arrogance and feeling of cultural superiority were inexplicable. The Chinese were "dirty yellow bastards." The Japanese were hated but envied even more. Native people were dismissed as an uneducated and uncivilized group, with no one seeming to notice that we share similar Mongolian origins. And of course, the white men were superior beings, a separate entity altogether.

This deep-rooted racism was brought home to me one day in a Korean grocery store where I often purchased spices and other delicacies to send home to Regina. It was still early in the morning when I entered the shop to satisfy my craving for rice cakes. The store was empty except for a West Indian woman who curiously studied the labels and ingredient lists of anchovy soup paste, pickled fish, and instant noodles. She wrinkled her nose at the pungent smell of kimchee and ran her hand over the rough texture of a strip of dried seaweed that was the size of half a sheet of plywood. Amused and always flattered when a culture other than my own shows interest in Korean food or customs, I was tempted to go and offer my limited expertise in barley tea and fish cakes. It wasn't unusual for restaurant and store owners to ask me for help with the translation when non-Korean customers came into their establishment. I once explained how to make Korean-style sushi to a Canadian, arranged an overseas delivery over the phone for the store owner's wife, and saved a nice-looking Caucasian man from ordering a bowl of beef intestines. Naturally I thought this customer might need similar assistance when I saw her wandering in the aisles. But that wasn't the case.

With arms folded across her chest, the store-owner's wife tiptoed two steps behind the customer throughout the store. It was hard to tell if this was her idea of being inconspicuous or if she was just plain rude. She exchanged sidelong glances with her husband, who protectively draped his arm over the cash register. Their body language and facial expressions were openly hostile. They were so preoccupied with the foreigner that I'm sure I could've easily walked out with an armful of groceries without getting caught. I looked at the black customer, but she pretended nothing out of the ordinary was taking place, as if this kind of blatant racism was not new to her. When she left the store empty-handed, the store owner loudly cursed his bad luck and scowled. His first customer of the day not only happened to be black, but hadn't spent one bloody penny in the store. Superstition dictated that this was a bad omen for the next twelve hours. Just to confirm his suspicions, I dropped my rice cake on the counter and walked out of the store without buying a thing.

Such experiences might well have soured me on Koreans forever, but I saw my job at the paper as a second chance to learn about and understand these people. So, with a mixture of repulsion and fascination, I analyzed and dissected Little Korea from within, like an anthropologist studying a fossilized culture.

Gays and lesbians were subhuman, black people were primitive and lazy, and violence against women was a "real" man's expression of anger. Korean law gave automatic custody of children to the father in divorce cases, and rape was rarely reported to the police and almost never made it to court. When it did, the whole family was covered in shame and the victim was blamed for ruining the life of somebody's precious son. In one perhaps apocryphal case, a rape victim in Seoul was chastised by the judge and convicted of assault for biting off her attacker's ear.

"We have a saying in Korea," said a voice from the editorial desk. "Women, children, and dogs need to be beaten occasionally to keep them in line." Then another remarked, "Until a few years ago, wives couldn't even eat at the same table as the men. They ate leftovers. Now, there's no end to what women want."

What was more frightening than their words was their conviction that women were a lower form of life. As far as they were concerned, women had no rights, only sacred duties: to obey, respect, and serve their fathers, husbands, and sons.

The paper was run like a sweatshop. Canadian labor laws and workers' rights did not seem to apply to this Korean outfit, and the staff members laughed incredulously at the mere mention of the words *union* and *overtime pay*. Everybody, including the senior editor, punched time cards, and when five o'clock came, people looked around apprehensively, not wanting to be the first one to leave the office.

The newsroom was all male, and it was the quietest I had ever encountered. There were no story meetings, no assignment editors, and no reporters who left the office to cover events. The phones didn't ring and the fax machine was idle. All the copy was written in longhand and given to a typist.

The paper was divided into two sections: news from Korea in the front, and Canadian news in the back. The news staff basically spent their days ripping off stories from the Korean wire service and other local Korean papers. A couple of reporters who had an adequate knowledge of English scanned the English dailies for Canadian news. They weren't looking for story ideas but articles to translate. Without credit or any acknowledgment of the original source, articles about the Quebec separatist movement, the Ontario government, and the Blue Jays were translated word for word and run in the paper, complete with pirated photos, which were meticulously cut out of the source paper with an X-Acto knife and transferred onto ours. This practice explained the absence of bylines. These people were committing the worst crime in journalism and publishing the evidence. Thinking that they didn't know any better, I approached the chief editor and gently reminded him of copyright violations and the unlawful act of plagiarism. "This is the way we've always done it," he said and walked away.

All the staff addressed the owner and publisher of the paper as "Mr. President," while his personal assistant and wife was "Madame." The boss flirted shamelessly with the female staff, ignoring reproachful looks from his wife, and urged me to enter the Miss Canada-Korea contest. There was no coffee break, and lunch was half an hour, or however long it took you to eat. Under the watchful eyes of Mr. President and Madame, no one wanted to appear idle.

Lunch was prepared by one elderly woman who cooked all morning to feed about thirty people in a small kitchenette where five or six employees at a time took turns eating at the table. No one brought sandwiches and hardly anyone went out to eat. While people hungrily shoveled rice into their mouths with chopsticks, the cook plopped herself down in a chair and lamented her fate. When her son asked her to come to Canada, she complained, she didn't think it was to slave away as a cook. She had never worked a day in her life in Korea, so why was it that she had to break her back in Canada? What good was a son when he couldn't even take care of his old mother? She adored her grandchildren but didn't want to raise them, especially when her cunning daughter-in-law took full advantage of her services. In her most melodramatic voice, the old cook would recount the bad breaks in her life. She'd never known peace or happiness. First, it was the Japanese bastards, then came the Communist sons of bitches. And when Korea was just about to become a rich country, her son had lured her away and trapped her into more years of hardship. "Oh, look at me now," she cried as she slapped her knee in frustration.

I ate silently as I listened to the afternoon performance and was taken aback when people interrupted her to complain about the food. The fish was too salty, the kimchee wasn't spicy enough, the soup was bland, the rice was overcooked, and the meat was too tough. The men, especially, treated the cook no differently than they would a wife in their own kitchen. Get me more rice. Get me water. I felt embarrassed for them and humiliated for her, but that was only me. I was the outsider.

The minute I joined the paper, I lost about a dozen points with my new colleagues: I was a single woman living alone who didn't go to church. In the eyes of Koreans, as long as you were without a significant other, you were considered a lesser being. It was difficult for them to accept, never mind understand, the fact that I lived alone. This was seen not as a sign of independence but as a failure to live within the bounds of tradition, and therefore a disappointment for my parents. It was also a sign of promiscuity.

Of course, I had prepared myself for uninvited comments and criticisms. However, the degree of harassment and discrimination I was expected to endure came as a sick surprise.

It began as harmless teasing from the older staffers. "Miss Yi, you should get married." "Miss Yi, I know a nice, young man ..." "Miss Yi, I have a son ..." "Miss Yi, do it for the sake of your poor parents ..." I smiled shyly and politely and walked away. Soon the younger ones joined in. The women were catty and wondered aloud if I was still a virgin and if I dated white men. Then the men at the office decided to take my marital status as a personal insult. A male staff member asked sarcastically what kind of Prince Charming I thought I was going to get by holding out. This invited giggles and laughter throughout the office, and encouraged another man to speak up: "Your value is going down." Apparently women are evaluated like precious metals: they start out as platinum, around the ripe age of sixteen, and diminish inexorably to gold, silver, copper, lead, and rusty metal. According to this scale, I was slowly drifting down in value from copper to lead.

"What kind of man do you want to marry?" a male voice in the office inquired.

"Someone who is taller than me," I said curtly.

The room fell silent. I was the tallest person working at the paper, with all the men at least an inch shorter than me. After that, they picked on my incorrect use of Korean grammar and the shabby way I dressed. During editorial meetings, when I dared to raise my voice or argue a point, I was met with snide remarks. "Just because you worked at the *Globe and Mail*, you think you are better than us," one of the writers said when I corrected his spelling mistakes.

In less than a month, I was demoted from editor of the English supplement to assistant editor. The way they announced the change was so remarkable that I almost forgot to feel insulted and had to remind myself I was the injured party. One day, on the front page of the Korean-language section, the paper ran a picture and a brief interview with the supplement's new editor. It was none other than the Einstein whose spelling mistakes I had just finished correcting. My name was nowhere to be found. It was as if I'd never existed, never mind the fact that I was the one who got the whole thing started in the first place. This was how I found out that I had just lost my job. Not a word from Mr. President or anybody else. Just like that, I was out of the loop.

When I confronted the publisher, he said it was nothing personal. "We didn't think you were right for the job after all," Mr. President said. There were some complaints from both the editorial staff and senior members in the community that a woman my age shouldn't have the privilege of such an important position at the paper. It just didn't look good. A woman doesn't have the same weight or influence as a man. "The readers have more confidence this way," the publisher informed me. He nodded when I asked if I was being demoted because of my gender and age and marital status. He also pointed out that my editorial decisions were highly questionable. The first generation had strong objections to my articles challenging Korean values and highlighting the problems of the community.

After my demotion, South Korean government propaganda and anti-Communist rhetoric took the place of articles on wife abuse and profiles of young artists. Stories on pro-democratic rallies and student protests in Seoul were banned. Any articles that questioned traditional values that conflicted with Canadian ways, or even hinted that young people should stand up to their parents about their own beliefs, were censored. None of my story ideas even saw the light of day.

I spent my last month at the paper provoking the staff members and threatening to report them to Canadian authorities. I made noises about starting a union, reminded the other employees of their rights, and intimidated the publisher's son, who worked as an errand boy at the paper. I got on the phone with my friends, spoke passionately and loudly about how Koreans were exploiting their own people, and challenged the editorial staff to a healthy debate on xenophobia.

Finally, the day of judgment arrived. The showdown was in the publisher's grand office, which was lavishly furnished with leather couches and a big oak desk and had doilies everywhere: round doilies on the armrests, a square doily on the coffee table, another doily under the telephone, and yet another one for his family portrait on the desk. A Korean flag stood majestically in the corner and a beautiful work of calligraphy hung above the doorway. The office looked as if it truly did belong to a president.

Seated behind his oak desk, Mr. President remained silent for a moment, trying to regain his composure. I had rattled him by choosing to sit only two feet away and loudly cracking my gum. I knew I was getting fired, but I wasn't prepared to let him off the hook easily. All the anger I had suppressed over the three months at the paper surfaced, and for the first time in my life I wasn't going to hold back just because he was a Korean.

"I don't think you should work here anymore," Mr. President began.

"Oh, why?" I asked, acting surprised. "Did something happen?"

"You don't fit in."

"I am not here to fit in. I'm here to work."

"People don't like you," he said, shaking his head slowly. "They feel very uncomfortable and tense around you."

Launching into the speech I'd been working out in my mind for weeks, I took pleasure in watching his face turn pale. I threatened to sue him personally for sexual harassment, discrimination, and wrongful dismissal. I accused him of not knowing the first thing about running a paper and of being guilty of plagiarism. "If the Canadian newspapers knew what you were up to—stealing from them—they would take you to court so fast you wouldn't even know what hit you," I said. "And they would make you pay for every little article and photograph you stole over the last couple decades and more. Trust me. I know." Of course I didn't know, but the important thing was that Mr. President believed every threat I uttered.

A few days later, I got a call at midnight from a family friend who was also a friend of Mr. President's. They had gone to university together in Seoul, and in our culture that means you are practically blood brothers. The facts that you were never friends in school, didn't graduate in the same year, and didn't even know each other then are all inconsequential. This was yet another way of establishing one's position on the social ladder.

Distraught, the publisher had called his buddy and recounted the day's events, confident that his "senior brother" would sort out the mess. Though Mr. President hadn't understood half my speech, which I gave in English, he recognized enough key words to get my message. He was concerned that I'd tarnish his reputation in the community. The friend, acting as mediator, tried to reason with me over the phone. Speaking as an old family friend who had watched me grow up, he asked me not to pursue legal action against the paper. Of course I had no intention of actively carrying out any of the threats I had made, but I didn't let him know that. The fact that Mr. President took me seriously was a great achievement in itself.

When I didn't respond, the mediator tried a more reliable tactic. I was too young to be involved in scandals, and it would embarrass my family and jeopardize my future, he said. The whole thing was an unfortunate misunderstanding that arose from cultural differences. Mr. President gave me an opportunity because he was proud to meet such an impressive young Korean girl who had achieved so much. He meant well. And please understand the delicate situation here. The publisher is my friend. We went to school together. You are also the daughter of my very dear friend. Let's just forgive and forget.

As much as I resented the patronizing tone of the mediator, who spoke to me as if I were twelve years old, the Korean side of me understood the code. If I didn't let go, my actions in Toronto would generate gossip that would inevitably reach the community in Regina, humiliating my parents and tormenting them for months to come. It just wasn't worth the trouble.

V

Regrettably, my experience in Little Korea didn't teach me anything I didn't already know. It did nothing to refute my suspicions and everything to confirm them, driving me further away.

Usually I had no problem slipping off one mask to wear the other. On automatic pilot, I could switch from a subservient, painfully modest, and shy maiden into a loud, boisterous, and opinionated bitch. I was living a lifestyle, not a life, so acting came easily to me. It was a win-win situation. If I behaved in an "immature" and "unseemly" fashion, Koreans blamed it on my Canadian upbringing, while Canadians assumed my pessimism and sarcastic streak were inherently Korean. But one day I woke up tired of it all. Caught between half-lies and half-truths, I wasn't sure where I was anymore. Playing Korean proved to be a full-time job and it left me emotionally exhausted.

Out of work again, I freelanced in between jobs and unemployment checks. The *Globe and Mail* experience and my ethnic background seemed to guarantee my entry into the country's most desirable news organizations. As both a woman and a visible minority, I could do no wrong in a place and time ruled by political correctness. With affirmative action, appropriation of voice, and the famous Anita Hill case in the air, I felt untouchable. As my journalism professor used to joke, all I needed was a wheelchair to win the "disadvantaged and oppressed" title.

Regardless of my qualifications, I was always conscious of my minority status, which inevitably played a part in the hiring process and generated suspicion and resentment among my co-workers. I did quit on principle on a couple of occasions, but there were other more basic reasons I ran in disgust. Wherever I worked, inflated egos, professional jealousy, mediocrity, and petty office politics seemed to take precedence over everything else, stripping grown men of their dignity and integrity. When television, a medium I worked in briefly as a researcher, was demystified for me, my disillusionment was complete. I hadn't realized that a whole army of researchers, producers, editors, and technicians worked behind the scenes to make one anchorperson look and sound intelligent and worldly.

I was quickly running out of places to go for future employment. With each change of season came a new job—print, TV, and radio. Bored and unsatisfied with what I had seen and accomplished in a whirlwind tour of the media world, and barely two years out of university, I was seriously contemplating going back to school to get a few more degrees and live on student loans for the next twenty years. I was sinking deeper and deeper into depression when I was granted the chance of a lifetime.

# The Invitation

My most recent job was at a morning radio show for the Canadian Broadcasting Corporation. My title was production assistant, but I was nothing more than a glorified secretary. As had been the case with most of my jobs, I was unsatisfied and eager to quit. But I had promised myself that I would stay for at least one full year, even if it meant waking up at four in the morning every day to get to work on time, to prove to myself that I wasn't a quitter. It was February of 1994, and I had about six months to go.

After my shift, I spent most of my time upstairs, hanging around at *Ideas*, a critically acclaimed radio documentary unit. The team consisted of about a dozen producers who worked with freelance journalists, critics, writers, and academics on sixty-minute documentaries that explored a wide range of social, cultural, and economic issues of both national and international import. For me, *Ideas* was an oasis of creative sanity in a corporation constipated by bureaucracy.

I had met Max Allen, one of the producers, at a media function when I was employed as a researcher for *The National* on CBC-TV. Max was a draft dodger who was considered an eccentric by many of his colleagues and friends, and he did very little to demystify that image. He would wear one of his half-dozen identical black suits for seven days straight, changing only his tie each day, and he kept his white, cotton-fluffy, curly hair neatly trimmed. Max was rather proud of his anti-social reputation, and enjoyed immensely the controversy his latest Valentine's Day program had sparked among *Ideas* listeners and CBC upper management. Exploring the mysteries of the female orgasm, Max had included a segment with a woman giving a live, on-air demonstration of the height of her sexual ecstasy. But this was no ordinary orgasm. When the woman climaxed (she was masturbating crouched over a mirror), it sounded like a waterfall crashing against the rocks. She completed this demonstration by advising her listeners to have beach towels ready if they tried this at home.

Max's views on pornography, homosexuality, and prostitution didn't exactly correspond to those of the national broadcasting corporation, and it was precisely his rebellious ways that I admired. He preferred to be called a storyteller rather than a journalist, and unlike most producers at the CBC downplayed his talents and achievements. Max was a workaholic in love with radio.

Max became my producer and mentor when I began offering unsolicited opinions on immigration and multiculturalism in Canada—thoughts heavily tainted by my experiences in Regina and Little Korea. Taking great delight in my anecdotes, Max urged me to make a documentary and joked that it would be better than therapy.

Entitled "Neighbours," the resulting documentary was a critical look at Canada's newcomers, especially those who voluntarily segregated themselves and harbored prejudices from the Old World. Of course I was especially hard on Koreans. As expected, this caused all kinds of grief and controversy in the community, and my parents were almost ashamed to admit that it was their daughter who was responsible. The resentment and anger finally subsided when the documentary was nominated for an award. To my parents and their Korean friends, this was a sign of the acceptance and approval of mainstream society. They therefore conceded that the program wasn't as bad as they had initially thought.

During the production of the documentary, I had to resist censoring myself and second-guessing every observation I had made over the years about Canada's blindness to the ugly side of its so-called cultural mosaic, especially when it came to my own community. As I wrote my script and opened my family's own immigrant experience to public scrutiny, I kept hearing the nagging voice of my mother and was discouraged from being true to my beliefs.

In the end, however, my biggest problem proved to be my lack of self-confidence when it came to broadcast journalism—I had to speak into the microphone. Even Lorne Tulke, one of the CBC's greatest technicians and a man who had worked with Glenn Gould, could not make me sound Canadian. I tried to convince Max to hire someone else to read the script instead, but he wouldn't hear of it. He pointed out that my defeatist attitude was more of a problem than my accent, which he swore was hardly noticeable.

During the recording, he sat with me in the studio and painstakingly went through each word, each phrase, and each sentence until I had it right. Max was a perfectionist. Night after night, we were locked in the studio, and I helplessly watched as he circled vowels and consonants to indicate emphasis, underlined the words *women* and *woman*, *this* and *these* to highlight the differences in pronunciation, and changed the words I couldn't pronounce properly. He then leaned back in his chair and closed his eyes and cued both the technician and me to continue recording.

In the end, Max literally cut my words with a razor blade and patched them together into sentences, which sounded miraculously coherent and natural. When the documentary was nominated for an award, Max told everyone with enthusiasm and pride about my talent as a storyteller, as if he had had nothing to do with the program.

When Max announced the day before the awards ceremony that he had a surprise assignment for me, I thought he was joking, so I played along. Sure, I'd go to North Korea. This will give me an excuse to quit my job, I said. But Max was serious. He had already talked about it with Bernie Lucht, the executive producer of *Ideas*, and they had both agreed that with my language and cultural knowledge, I would do a wonderful job of telling stories about North Korea.

"I've already alienated most South Koreans," I cried. "And now you want me to go after the North Koreans, too? You're out of your mind! Anyway, no one can get into North Korea. That much I know about the country," I stated with authority. "And they don't like South Koreans. That's me."

"You're Canadian," Max reminded me. "And I can't think of a better person than you to go there and find out what they are all about. You speak the language and you know the culture."

"Max, I don't know anything about North Korea," I confessed.

"Then now is a good time to find out."

My heart was racing. Max was serious, and I could hardly hide my excitement. It would be a real coup if I did somehow manage to sneak in there and do a report on the land that was once known as the Hermit Kingdom. But I quickly dismissed the idea. It was simply impossible to go to a country like North Korea. If it wasn't, other journalists—famous veteran journalists—would have been there already. I didn't even have a real job as a reporter.

And I had another problem. After "Neighbours" aired, my parents were beside themselves with embarrassment. "We should never have told our friends about the program," my mother wailed. "Is this what you do as a journalist? Betray your own people?"

Now I had to tell them I might be going to North Korea. I didn't know how I was going to explain this one.

## II

"Mom, I'm going to North Korea," I said, anticipating an emotional outburst.

"Don't talk nonsense," Mom said curtly. "They don't let people like you in the country."

"I'm just researching. Nothing's for sure, but I thought I'd tell you anyway because you read Korean newspapers and just in case you knew …"

"Do you know what kind of place North Korea is? I don't have to remind you that you're South Korean. They lock up people like you and throw away the key. They can kill you and there's nothing we can do about it because they're going to say you were in there spying," Mom said, reciting the fears of every Korean of her generation.

"Mom, just think," I insisted. "This is going to be fabulous for my career."

"You're turning my hair gray," she snapped. "What good are you dead? I was hoping you'd find a nice Korean man in Toronto. Every week, I think you'll tell me you found somebody, but you only call to tell me you quit another job …"

"I didn't quit my job yet," I said defensively. "I'm going to quit only if I get to go to North Korea."

# III

The world had forgotten about North Korea, and so had I. It was a tiny, insignificant country that North Americans couldn't have cared less about. But after forty-odd years of hibernation, North Korea had suddenly decided to wake up and take the world by storm. In 1993 the country had threatened to withdraw from the Nuclear Non-proliferation Treaty. Then, in the spring of 1994, Kim Il-Sung made international headlines with his renegade weapons program. Everyone wanted to know whether North Korea was building nuclear weapons. Did it have the capabilities to do it? Did it perhaps already have nuclear weapons?

Why was all this happening now, when I was trying to quietly sneak into the country? The timing couldn't have been worse. In the midst of the nuclear guessing game, the last thing the country was going to do was open its doors to a Western journalist.

# IV

What little I knew about Korean history and the Korean War, I had gleaned as a child from reruns of *M\*A\*S\*H\**, the one television program that drove my father into a fit of rage. He not only cursed the Americans for turning a tragic situation into comedy, but seeing Chinese actors playing the parts of wounded Korean soldiers and orphaned children was like having salt rubbed into an open wound. Blood rushed to his face and spread down his neck as my father vented his anger about the Chinese Red Army. It was almost heartbreaking to watch him recall the past. Though he was one of the fortunate few who hadn't lost family members or fought in the war, my father had witnessed its destructiveness and lived through the years of poverty that followed. His eyes brimmed with tears as he tried to explain the Korean War to his teenage daughter, who was more interested in catching punch lines on the sitcom than listening to a history lesson.

I'd barely hide my annoyance when my father drew a map of

Korea and urged me to pay attention during a commercial break. Striking a quick line across the Korean peninsula with a black Magic Marker, he indicated the 38th parallel, Panmunjom, the DMZ, and the Military Demarcation Line with tiny Xs and Os, explaining that they were dangerous and forbidden places only soldiers were allowed to enter. Never in my father's wildest dreams did he imagine that ten years later I'd be standing on those Xs and Os. Never did he imagine that I'd visit the DMZ, one of the world's most perilous spots, from both sides of the border.

In the West, the Korean War is often referred to as the Forgotten War because the Americans "didn't win." Sometimes it's not even called a war but a conflict. A "conflict" between the Americans and the Soviets, who fought their Cold War on foreign soil. The Korean War produced neither winner nor loser, victory nor glory. The longest armistice negotiations in history simply brought the fighting to an anticlimactic ceasefire, robbing the soldiers of the opportunity to at least rejoice in the end of the war.

Compared with the infamous and well-documented Vietnam War, the Korean War—a three-year battle between Chinese-backed North Korea and United Nations–backed South Korea—has had little coverage. According to government documents and war historians, the death toll was between two and four million. At least a million Koreans were killed; 35,000 Americans died; and the United Nations suffered about 140,000 casualties. Hundreds of thousands of Chinese also lost their lives, and ten million Korean families were separated by the border.

When Kim Il-Sung's troops invaded South Korea in the early morning hours of June 25, 1950, the South Korean and American troops were poorly prepared and ill equipped for war. The Communists seized Seoul within days and slaughtered more than twenty thousand Korean civilians during the next four months. Survivors, including many soldiers, took refuge in Pusan until the sixteen-nation force under the United Nations flag came to their rescue. In command was Gen. Douglas MacArthur. In what is considered a brilliant strategic move, General MacArthur planned a surprise attack on the port city of Inchon and pushed the enemy back north. An air raid at Pyongyang turned their capital to ashes and left six thousand civilians dead. Just when it was thought that the war was over, the Chinese entered the picture—in November 1950. The fighting continued for three more years.

On July 27, 1953, the Korean Armistice Agreement was signed in the small village of Panmunjom. Its signatories were the U.S. Army, the United Nations Command Delegations, the Korean People's Army of the Democratic People's Republic of Korea (DPRK), and the Chinese People's Volunteers. No nation became a signatory to the agreement.

Many people think it was this armistice that established the border at the 38th parallel, which runs across the waist of the Korean peninsula and cuts the country in half. In fact, the border was created before the war, not after. When the Japanese were defeated at the end of the Second World War, the Allied Forces, many of whom didn't know or care about Korea, drew an arbitrary line across the peninsula and decided to make each half of the former Japanese colony into a protectorate of the two superpowers. The American forces moved into the southern half and the Soviets occupied the northern.

The division was supposed to be temporary, but with increasing hostility between the Americans and the Soviets, and disagreements between the U.S.S.R. and the United Nations over elections and unification issues, the two separate regimes were eventually permanently established. On August 15, 1948, the Republic of Korea (ROK) was declared, with Harvard-educated Rhee Syngman as its president. About a month later, a Soviet-trained officer named Kim Il-Sung became the head of the DPRK.

Since 1953, both sides have been heavily engaged in espionage, disinformation campaigns, and terrorist activities, exacerbating the hostilities of the Cold War. North Korea has been responsible for numerous terrorist acts, including random shootings across the DMZ and an assassination attempt on former South Korean president Park Chung-Hee, which resulted in the murder of his wife instead. In 1968 alone, there were close to two hundred tragic incidents in and around the DMZ that caused the deaths of 17 American soldiers and 145 ROK troops.

In the eighties, this internecine terrorism captured world headlines when North Korean agents planted a bomb in Burma that killed a visiting South Korean delegation which included four cabinet ministers. Then, in 1987, in an attempt to sabotage the 1988 Summer Olympics in Seoul, two North Korean terrorists planted a bomb in a South Korean airliner that killed all on board. North Koreans of course deny all these allegations and accuse the South Korean government of conducting a disinformation campaign. They further charge the Angibu (the South Korean intelligence agency) with sacrificing the lives of its own people in order to boost the sagging national morale.

V

Researching North Korea was like searching for a needle in a haystack. The country was nowhere to be found, not in books, pamphlets, travel brochures, or magazines. The only information available was a small section in the encyclopedia—and even that was outdated. I didn't know anything about the other half of my country. I was taught to hate and fear it but very little else.

Did North Korea have telephones, fax machines, electricity? Did it have currency, food, clean water? What countries did it have diplomatic relations with? How did one get inside the country? Whom did I have to contact to find out?

I called the United Nations and spoke to a North Korean diplomat. He didn't want to talk to me and hung up the phone with neither explanation nor apology. I thought of asking around the Korean community but immediately dismissed the idea. If word got out that I was asking questions about North Korea and the Korean consulate got wind of it, the damage would have been irreparable. The South Korean government would have done everything in its power to stop me from going if it knew about my plan. It seems the only Korean I could trust in this matter was the man who would become my ticket to the forbidden North.

Hidden behind high stacks of newspapers and file folders, Mr. Chun smiled knowingly after I explained the reason for my visit. He kept shaking his head, as if he couldn't believe my nerve. Still, his gentle smile encouraged me to continue begging for help. He finally held up his hand for me to be quiet. Three academics from Pyongyang would be visiting the University of Toronto in June, he said. They would be conducting a seminar on the Juche Idea, a philosophy of self-reliance that apparently ruled every aspect of a North Korean's life, from politics to education to family. Mr. Chun stressed that nothing had been confirmed, but if and when they arrived, he would make the proper introductions and set up a meeting for us.

Chun Choong-Lim was unofficially known as Canada's North Korean ambassador. The country was like a second home to Mr. Chun and his wife. They had visited it more than thirty times since the late seventies, and they had met both the Great Leader, Kim Il-Sung, and the Dear Leader, his son. They knew more about North Korea than all the journalists, academics, and Angibu agents put together, but they kept the knowledge to themselves. The couple was as secretive as North Korea itself and their business just as mysterious.

Mr. Chun was the founder and editor of the *New Korea Times*, a weekly newspaper read by Korean expatriates throughout North America, Asia, and Europe—and banned in South Korea, of course. Operating out of a small office on Spadina Avenue, only a few blocks from the University of Toronto, the newspaper had a staff that consisted of his wife and a colleague. Mr. Chun was also the president and founder of the Organization for the Reunification of Separated Korean Families, making dreams come true for expatriates who had loved ones trapped in North Korea.

Mr. Chun had immigrated to Canada with his family in the early sixties, after working as a reporter in Seoul. In 1975 he started the *New Korea Times* in his basement to voice his opposition to the military regime of President Park Chung-Hee. The paper was immediately condemned by the government, and targeted as a Communist rag. It was now the official mouthpiece for the Communist North, with rumors that it was financially supported by North Korea.

A few days before the North Korean scholars were scheduled to arrive, I got a call from Mr. Chun asking for my help. They were stuck in Beijing, he explained, and the Canadian government had refused to issue them visas. He thought a phone call or a letter from the CBC would pressure External Affairs to speed up the process. I had not told him that I was only a freelance journalist, because it was crucial for me to appear to be legitimately affiliated with the state broadcasting station. Koreans would not have given me the time of the day had they known that I was working independently.

Without these three North Koreans, my research was going to be stalled. I needed them here, in Canada, and Mr. Chun knew how valuable their presence was to me. Stymied, I called the External Affairs department in Ottawa and the Canadian embassy in Beijing. As expected, they told me information on the three men was confidential. I faxed an obscure but encouraging memo to Mr. Chun and informed him that there were "people looking into the situation." When the delegation finally landed at Pearson International Airport a week later, Mr. Chun gave me undeserved credit for their arrival. My futile attempt had scored big points with my comrades.

At the dinner reception for the visitors, Mr. Chun introduced me as if I was the honored guest. He led me to the head table and announced to the three North Korean delegates: "This is Yi Sun-Kyung. She's a journalist and she's single."

I bowed and welcomed the guests to Canada.

"You're very young," one of them observed curtly, and that was that. The trio sat back down with cold, stony faces and I returned to the ladies' table. As at all Korean social functions, men and women sat separately.

At the ladies' table, Mrs. Chun was collecting $20 from each person and asking her to sign the guest register. I obeyed and signed, but not without some reluctance. A record of my name at such an event wouldn't go over very well with South Korean authorities. The sixty-some names in the book were all North Korean sympathizers. Some of them had already visited Pyongyang, and many more were there that evening hoping to get their chance.

I studied the three honored guests. They were true Communist North Koreans, yet they looked so much like South Koreans. They even had the same unhappy expression on their faces. Pak Sung-Dok was the oldest in the group. He was a professor and the director of the Juche Idea Institute in Pyongyang. The professor had a perfectly round face and silver-framed glasses. He looked like Chun Doo-Hwan, the former South Korean president and dictator. Kim Kwan-Gi was a researcher from the same institution. He was in his late thirties but looked like a teenager. His suit was too big for his slightly built body, and he seemed to have an unusually brown, weather-beaten face. He looked exhausted. Lee Myong-Su was a government agent whose job was to keep the two intellectuals in line. He was responsible for keeping records of every word uttered and every movement made by his comrades during their travels.

After a brief speech of welcome by Mr. Chun, someone from the men's table approached the women and requested that a few of us welcome the comrades by pouring them a drink. Mrs. Chun was looking around for volunteers, when a voice rose from the table: "We are not *gisang*. We are not bar girls and this isn't Korea." The voice belonged to a tiny woman sitting across from me. Mrs. Park sat unmoved by the cold, warning glances from her friends at the table.

I had first met Mrs. Park and her husband a few years earlier during one of my freelance stints. At the time, Mr. Park was one of the few Korean Canadians who had visited North Korea and was willing to admit it to a reporter. He went in the early eighties to be reunited with his parents, from whom he had been separated since the Korean War. When the trip was discovered by members of the Korean consulate, they tried to stop him, and even followed him to the airport in an effort to change his mind. When he returned, the family was ostracized by the community and their church, and even their closest friends kept their distance.

Their relatives in Seoul, who had no idea about the trip, called the Parks in a panic in the middle of the night. "The Angibu has been hanging around our house, questioning your behavior," they whispered into the phone. "Smarten up and don't bring us any trouble," the voices pleaded from continents away.

I didn't recognize Mrs. Park until she reminded me of our previous meeting. She looked very chic in a short bob haircut that bounced just below her ears as she moved. A successful diet plan was attested to by her low-cut dress. She proudly admitted that her new image was credited to her grown-up daughter, who had also taught her how to become a feminist after all these years. She was showing off her new power as a woman when she refused to serve the men drinks as requested.

As she sat there, ignoring Mrs. Chun who pinched her arm to shut her up, two women at the end of the table got up resignedly and walked over to the head table to pour the North Koreans a drink. Then another man marched over to the table and practically ordered the women to serve food to the guests. Mrs. Park could no longer contain her anger. The man was her husband.

"You crazy?" she shrieked. "This is Canada. It's a buffet." She spoke each word in a sharp staccato. "Let them get their own food. I'm not moving."

The woman beside her said, "Huhh-ha. Keep your voice down, big sister."

But it was too late—the damage was done. The guests had heard every word.

Mr. Park, with the aid of Mr. Chun, tried to salvage the mood. "This is what happens to us poor men in Canada." He let out a meek laugh. "Our wives lose their manners." With his back arched and his head slightly lowered in embarrassment, he gestured weakly to the buffet table. He looked like an Oriental version of the Hunchback of Notre Dame. I watched in amazement. It was the highlight of the evening so far.

The three Communists got up reluctantly and followed the Hunchback. They declined the plates offered to them with a sharp wave of their hands, and circled the table, returning to their seats empty-handed. The two women who had poured them drinks earlier proceeded to serve them food as well. "It isn't much, but please eat." They bowed and joined the buffet line for their own helpings.

After dinner, the guests entertained themselves by singing. Koreans love to sing. What they are forbidden to say in words, they sing instead, freely expressing love, happiness, and sorrow through songs.

Everyone was jovial. Even the comrades had loosened up with the help of Johnny Walker. As they cajoled one another to sing, I sank lower in my chair, afraid someone would volunteer me. If I refused, it would be considered rude and anti-social, and I certainly didn't want to give that impression. These people were my ticket to North Korea.

Luckily, I was ignored, and the other guests started singing the songs I had heard my parents and their friends sing when I was a child. They were folksongs from the Japanese colonial years, and the lyrics reflected that bitter era. I was startled when the North Korean professor started singing one of my dad's favorites. I used to cringe when Dad sang it, but now it was sending chills down my spine.

A young man, caving in under the pressure from his elders to sing, silenced the room when he broke down crying. "This is such an honor. I have fought alongside my fellow students for reunification," the student sobbed. "This is the first time I have met North Koreans and I now see you're no different from us." The professor put his arm around the student and the two men fell into an embrace. Everyone stood up, clapped their hands, and started singing "Our Wish Is Reunification." The evening had come to an end.

# VI

The next day, I met with the agent, Lee Myong-Su, and the young academic. Mr. Chun had informed me that it was Mr. Lee whom I had to impress.

"He has the power and influence to make things happen," Mr. Chun said. "Make sure you mention reunification. That is very important to them."

Until then, I had no idea that North Korea wanted reunification. Given the intense hatred between the two countries, I thought that was the last thing the North would have wanted.

"Reunification, that's the key word," Mr. Chun reiterated.

I was nervous. They didn't speak a word of English, and I wasn't sure if I could manage with my semi-fluent Korean. But it turned out that Mr. Lee did most of the talking.

"Why do women here all dress like whores?" he demanded to know. "These women, they don't know their bodies and what looks good on them. Many are fat and they insist on wearing tight clothes. That's very unattractive."

Luckily, I was wearing a suit jacket with a buttoned-up shirt, but I knew he wouldn't be pleased with my jeans. More reason to behave like an ideal Korean woman, I thought. I nodded politely without voicing my opinion and spoke quietly and humbly, but only when spoken to. And as tradition dictated, I didn't smoke in front of my male elders.

Mr. Lee listed all that was wrong with Toronto. The streets were dirty, people were badly dressed, the air was filthy, and the food wasn't edible. Niagara Falls was nowhere as beautiful as the waterfalls of his country, he added. His associate sat without saying a word, puffing away.

"There are too many foreigners here," Mr. Lee said.

"Foreigners?" I asked innocently, pretending not to know what he was talking about.

"Too many immigrants," he said.

"North Korea doesn't have any immigrants?" I asked, as a means of double-checking my facts.

"No," he answered, practically jumping out of his seat. "Our country is pure. One nation. One blood." He made a fist with his right hand and punched the air.

Mr. Lee was wearing a dark beige Mao suit and had his hair greased back. He had a thin face, with a sharp chin and narrow eyes that seemed to squeeze his dark-brown pupils. And as the Korean expression goes, he was as skinny as a dry fish stick. He looked cold and intimidating, as though he wouldn't bleed if he were pricked with a needle. I could easily picture him as an interrogator in one of those rooms that had only a wooden chair and a naked lightbulb dangling threateningly from the ceiling.

After he finished venting about Toronto, he asked me the routine questions all Korean adults asked. Are you married? (I guess he wasn't listening when Mr. Chun introduced me at the dinner party.) What does your father do? He meant, what did my dad do back in Korea. I lied and told him that my father used to be a businessman in Seoul. I didn't think he would have been too pleased to hear that he had worked with the American imperialists.

Mr. Lee then said something that made me choke on my coffee: "You should come to North Korea and marry one of our comrades. You can be a true, heroic example of how North and South can be reunified." He then boasted that women all around the world, and named Sweden as an example, requested husbands from North Korea.

"Swedish blondes?" I asked, dumbfounded. I knew from what little press there was about North Korea that Swedish prostitutes were imported to the country for Dear Leader Kim Jong-Il's pleasure, but I didn't think it was meant to be a lifetime commitment.

I changed the topic. I told them that it was important for me to visit their country, that the West had horrible misunderstandings about North Korea, and that I, a Korean with five thousand years of pure Korean blood, would take on the challenge to tell the "truth."

Mr. Lee seemed skeptical, but he admitted that foreign reporters had spread nothing but American and South Korean propaganda about his country.

"Yes." I nodded sympathetically. "But I am Korean and I would be much more understanding. The round eyes—what do they know?"

He agreed, but something told me we were still on different wavelengths. I needed more ammunition. Out of desperation, I threw the following confession on the table. "When the students were demonstrating in South Korea, I wanted to go and join them and fight against the corrupted government."

This got Mr. Lee all fired up. "The students are right. Americans have to leave our country. Only then is reunification possible," he said vehemently. "So you wish for reunification, too. I am very happy to hear you say that."

I didn't say it, but I guess he was reading between the lines.

"You are a flower growing in the midst of foreign weeds," he said.

I was encouraged now. He wanted to hear bad things about the Yankees and their puppet government in South Korea. Coming directly from the mouth of a South Korean, this was music to his ears, I guess.

He didn't care about educating Canadians about North Korea. He just wanted to know I was on North Korea's side.

When Mr. Lee asked me why I had never visited my homeland since immigrating to Canada, I decided to play my trump card. "It was my personal way of protesting against the dictatorial government," I lied.

Mr. Lee was ecstatically happy with my answer. "Someday South Korea shall be free like North Korea," he said. "That's why we want reunification, so our brothers in the South can also live under the loving care of our Great Leader Kim Il-Sung."

Mr. Lee promised me that he would talk to his superiors and try his best to introduce me to the Socialist Paradise.

# VII

July 8, 1994. Great Leader Kim Il-Sung died.

The world was in shock, and once again North Korea was in the spotlight. On CNN, the whole world watched in fascination as thousands of people gathered at the foot of the giant statue of Kim Il-Sung in Pyongyang. Soldiers, women, and children were in a frenzied state of mourning, crying, wailing, and beating their chests. Day after day, the crying continued, and people outside could only wonder if the tears were real.

No one had been expecting it. At eighty-two, Kim Il-Sung had appeared healthy and robust, and had met with former U.S. president Jimmy Carter in Pyongyang just a few weeks earlier. He was engaged in intense negotiations with the United States and South Korea over nuclear weapons, and was scheduled for a historic summit meeting with South Korean president Kim Young-Sam. His death couldn't have come at a worse time.

In Toronto's Korea Town, there were posters that asked, "Is he dead for real this time?" A few years ago, the death of Kim Il-Sung had been falsely reported by a South Korean journalist stationed in Japan, sending the whole country into a panic. South Koreans weren't sure whether to believe the news the second time around.

Ironically, I was almost the last person on earth to find out about Kim Il-Sung's death. I had been out of town with friends at a cottage, trying my best to relax and forget about North Korea for one weekend. When I came back, my answering machine was full of "condolence" messages, but no one told me who had died. One of the messages was from my sister, so I called her up. When I asked her what was going on, she burst out laughing. "Boy, you are slow. What kind of journalist are you?" she asked. "Kim Il-Sung is dead. There are lots of happy Koreans."

My dad was happy and my mom was relieved. To their minds, Kim Il-Sung's death was a guarantee that my trip would never happen. At a loss, I threw up my hands and went in search of the weekend paper.

The next day, I was most anxious to call Mr. Chun to find out whether I should just forget the whole thing, but that seemed too callous even for my taste, so I sent him a bouquet of flowers instead with a card saying, "Thinking of you in your sorrow …" A few hours later, he called to thank me for the carnations and to tell me that he had just received a fax from Pyongyang. It was my invitation to North Korea.

# VIII

Max and I found it extremely odd that the North Koreans would ask me to come at a time when the whole country was in utter chaos. We tried to guess their ulterior motive but came up empty. North Korea was predictably unpredictable.

The invitation injected fear into my friends and colleagues, many of whom thought it was a trap and tried to change my mind. They feared the worst: kidnapping, rape, imprisonment, torture, and even murder.

"Didn't you see *El Salvador*? James Woods almost got killed," a friend shrieked into the phone.

"Different country. Different continent," I said bravely, but she insisted that I was missing the point.

With everybody else sick with worry, somebody had to stay calm and collected. I tried to fight off my paranoia and reminded myself that there was no reasonable proof of the rumors that North Korea was a scary country.

Three days before the trip, I got a call at six in the morning. It was an elderly Korean man who had traveled to Pyongyang a few years earlier with his wife to visit relatives. His voice quavered as he told me that he had stayed up all night worrying about me. He pleaded with me to change my mind, or at least to go accompanied. "It's no place for a young woman," he said nervously. "Think of your poor parents." I tried to calm him down, but to no avail. He finally gave up and asked me for a favor. Could I take some money to one of his wife's relatives in Pyongyang? I didn't have the heart to say no, but after some discussion with Max, I returned the money and apologized. It was too risky, I admitted. North Korean officials could misconstrue the money as bribery, I explained.

Even after I received the invitation—which was simply a two-line statement that said, "Yi Sun-Kyung can come. Pick date for visit"—I approached only those who had already been to North Korea, like the elderly man and his wife, and could share with me their experiences and tell me what to expect. But I found I got more argumentation than information. Like the elderly man, the others tried to dissuade me from taking the trip, and having failed that, they then refused to tell me a single thing about the country. When I became insistent, they would only shake their heads and say, "You have to see it for yourself to believe it. I don't know the words to describe what I saw."


# IX


Toronto to Chicago to Tokyo to Beijing to Pyongyang. Pick up your visa at the North Korean embassy in Beijing, Mr. Chun instructed. What if they change their minds and all this was for nothing? I asked. He smiled and assured me that the visa would be granted. Mr. Chun told me to look for a Korean man at the Beijing airport holding a sign with my name on it. I was to go with him to pick up my visa.

Before I left the office, Mr. Chun leaned over his desk and asked,

"Aren't you scared?" His eyes twinkled with mischief. He was trying to test my will and see if I'd cave in at the last minute. I shook my head, but my mind was uneasy. If Mr. Chun was asking me such a question, even as a joke, maybe there was reason for me to be scared.

The night before I left, I called my parents. They were so emotional that they could hardly speak.

"Mom, don't worry, please," I begged. "I'll call as soon as I get out."

"Please, please be careful," Mom said. "And please watch your mouth. They may be Communists, but they are still Koreans. Treat adults with respect, speak formally to them, and watch your manners."

"Yes, Mother," I said, rolling my eyes.

My father picked up the extension, said, "I love you, honey," and hung up. That was the first time I had heard him say those words to me.

Mom interrupted my tender thoughts. "Eat lots before you go. There's nothing to eat in North Korea. People are starving over there."

# X

My living room looked like a hardware store as I got ready to pack. Equipment: video camera, tape recorder, backup mini-recorder, 35 mm camera, cassette tapes, films, and batteries. Presents for North Koreans: cigarettes for soldiers, pens and pencils for children, makeup for women, disposable lighters for men, and pins and keychains with the CBC logo. Documents: the plane tickets, my passport, traveler's checks, and a copy of the invitation from North Korea. And, of course, my clothes. The trick was to fit all of them into one suitcase, one overnight bag, and one briefcase.

Everything was ready to go except for me.

# Korean Lessons

North Korea is a nation caught in a time warp. Before you enter it, you must leave behind any expectation of normalcy. A visit to the capital city, Pyongyang, is like a dream in which *Alice's Adventures in Wonderland* meets Orwell's *Nineteen Eighty-Four*. Picturesque scenery and smiling children are mere props on a stage set for a psychological nightmare. You desperately wish to wake up and forget the bizarre sequence of events that is unfolding around you, but in a perverse kind of way you are compelled to keep your eyes closed and await the surprises to come.

Before I describe my Pyongyang experience, however, there are a few things that need to be explained.


## The Name Game

North and South Koreans can't agree on anything, not even the name of their own country. They are like spiteful parents who have each decided to call their child by a different name after a bitter divorce. In this case, the troubled child is Korea. She is this skinny, malnourished peninsula, sandwiched in between gigantic China and powerful Japan. For many years, she has been neglected and forgotten; she has been picked on and beaten up by bullies, from the Mongolians to the Chinese and the Japanese. On the map, she even looks physically weak, all shriveled up and ready to crack under the pressure.

In Korean, the name for North Korea is Choson Minjujuui In'min Konghwakuk, or Choson for short. The name dates back to about 2,000 B.C., when it was the name of one of the earliest Korean states, Old Choson.

To Koreans, South Korea is Taehanminkuk, or Hankuk for short. Before the Korean War, Choson and Hankuk were used interchangeably. But after the Korean War (1950–1953), these names were forbidden to people on opposing sides of the border.

Using the name Choson in South Korea is reason enough to be labeled a suspected North Korean spy and get arrested. Similarly, in the eyes of North Koreans, Hankuk does not exist. Both sides simply say *north* and *south* to refer to each other. By playing this absurd name game, the two nations have managed to deny each other's existence.

My first dilemma came when I was confronted with all these choices in names. To please my hosts in North Korea (who had the power to kick me out of the country on a whim), I was expected to call their nation Choson. This was a source of great distress for me because, as a South Korean, it meant betraying my mother country. On the more practical side, I found it extremely difficult to break a lifetime habit of calling South Korea Hankuk and call it something else. After all, the word *Choson* did not even exist in my vocabulary until I made my trip. I am embarrassed to admit it, but I didn't appreciate the significance of this convoluted game until two hours before I entered North Korea. At the Beijing airport, I met a British businessman, also on his way to Pyongyang, who casually warned, "You'll be fine as long as you remember to say 'Choson,' not 'Hankuk.'"

## On Language

I didn't fully appreciate or realize the intimacy of one's language and how deeply it was entrenched in its culture until I tried communicating with my father in Korean. As a child in Seoul, I was a spoiled brat who was spared addressing him formally. I talked baby talk. Then I came to Canada and was encouraged to speak English at home in order to practice my second language. As my English improved, I quickly lost my native tongue. By then I was old enough to understand that I could no longer speak to my father as casually as I did with my mother. When I tried speaking Korean with him, I was conscious of not only the mistakes I was making, but also the emotional distance the language imposed between father and daughter.

The Korean language is rigidly structured to reflect one's position in society. Inferior and superior positions are clearly defined by one's age, profession, and sex. As the Confucian tradition dictates, children are inferior to their parents, students to their teachers, and of course, women to men. Even today, in modern Korea, many women, like my mother, address their husbands as their superiors rather than their equals.

Names are not automatically revealed during introductions, and it is not uncommon for Korean children to grow up without knowing the first names of their teachers or parents. With the exception of close school friends, no one is on a first-name basis. Instead, it's *big brother, big mother* (your parent's older sister), *teacher, yabo* (spouse), or *a-ga-si* (Miss). Married women are usually called by the name of their first-born child. For example, my mother is *Sun-Kyung's mom*.

In daily conversation, the subject of a sentence is omitted. For example, "I'm going now" becomes "Going now," and "Did you eat?" becomes "Eat?" Pronouns are generally avoided. To address somebody as *you* is considered extremely rude, so many immigrant parents take offense when their children, not knowing any better, say *you* when speaking to them. The possessive pronoun *my* is used with extreme discretion. For instance, it is not *my wife* but *our wife*; and it is *our house* rather than *my house*.

Our language reflects a society that urges its people to think collectively, not as individuals; and it is rigidly hierarchical. It rewards community spirit and quashes individuality, encourages anonymity and shuns intimacy.

## Social Conventions

Koreans are reluctant to strike up conversations with strangers, but when they do, they have a great compulsion to get nosy very quickly because that is what our custom dictates. Here's a typical scenario:

Two men are sitting on a train. It's a long journey, so they decide to engage in a conversation. But it's not as simple as breaking the ice by casually commenting on the weather. The two travelers look at each other and immediately conclude that they are of similar age. What follows is a mutual exchange of each other's biographical data, in detail.

The interrogation starts with each other's year of birth. If one man is even a year older than the other, the rules of the relationship are immediately established. But if the two men are of the same age, they must inquire about each other's last name. If they are both named Kim (in a country where there are a several million Kims, Parks, and Lees, this would not be considered a coincidence), they compare family trees, and this can take quite some time. This is followed by a discussion of their place of birth (village, town) and then their educational background and present occupation.

The object of the whole exercise is to find common ground from which the two strangers can build their relationship; more important, it's also an attempt to determine their status in respect to each other.

In my case, North or South, information about my father is always requested even before my name is asked. What's your father's last name? Where was he born? What does he do?

## The Two Kims

One of the problems I had during my visit to North Korea was that I didn't know how to refer to Kim Il-Sung and Kim Jong-Il without offending the people there but still keeping my own integrity. There was no way I was going to be able to say "Great Leader" or "Dear Leader" and still keep a straight face. I suppose I could have attempted to say it in Korean, but I could never get the order of the words right (and Koreans aren't very forgiving when it comes to one's mistakes, intentional or not): *Oui-dae-ha-nun-suryong-nim-Kim-Il-Sung-dongji* (Great Leader Comrade Kim Il-Sung), and *Chi-nae-hanun-jido-ja-Kim-Jong-Il-dongji* (Dear Leader Comrade Kim Jong-Il). It was a real conundrum because any failure to identify them with precisely correct formality could result in a bullet to the head. After all, this father-and-son team is holier than God and Jesus to North Koreans.

I could have referred to Kim Il-Sung as Mr. President, but he was dead, so technically his son was the president. The son, however, had no official title yet. According to the international media, senior members of the government and high-ranking military personnel in North Korea had deep reservations about officially transferring the leadership from father to son. Therefore, Kim Jong-Il was without a title, except for Dear Leader. I could have said Your leader, but sorry, no pronouns are allowed when speaking in Korean. After some thought, I decided not to say their names unless it was absolutely necessary, and even then, to always refer to them in English—Your leader Kim Il-Sung—via the translator. Unlike the language dilemma with my father, I wanted to purposely create an emotional distance from North Koreans by choosing to speak in a foreign tongue.

## *Nunchi*

*Nunchi* is the ability to gauge the mood and attitudes of people in one's immediate surroundings. It's like having a hypersensitive antenna built into one's brain, a survival tool that has enabled individuals to cope in a society that is as oppressive and unbending as ours. Literally, it means "watching one's eyes." It's an important part of the Korean psyche. Culturally, Korea is a country ruled by Confucianism, a system of subordination that dictates filial piety and unconditional duty and loyalty to one's elders. Socially, Korea embraces a caste system that breeds competition, discrimination, and contempt. *Nunchi* is like a sensory detector that helps you to distinguish friend from foe, and truth from lies.

*Nunchi* grew out of five thousand years of living under the constant threat of foreign invasion, internal strife, tribal conflicts, palace coups, and military coup d'états. Conspiracy and betrayal are deeply entrenched in our history; suspicion and cynicism run through our blood. Under these conditions, Koreans could not help developing an unusually keen *nunchi*, which taught them to instinctively distrust neighbors and strangers alike.

Children with "fast *nunchi*" are considered bright and precocious, while those with "slow *nunchi*" are referred to as "dense and slow as a bear." For women, "fast *nunchi*" is a necessity that helps them stay one step ahead in family feuds, which inevitably occur in all extended families. Basically, Koreans communicate through *nunchi* because they are so often forbidden to say what's really on their minds.

## The Irish of the Orient

Koreans have been referred to as the Irish of the Orient for their moodiness and fractiousness. They are dark, brooding, and melodramatic. They are also temperamental and fiery. Everything is personal and nothing is just business. Always pessimistic, Koreans inevitably view the glass as half empty, not half full.

Many Koreans' favorite pastime is to indulge in self-pity and blame all their woes on their tragic past. It's a national malaise. They can't feel sorry enough for themselves. Koreans readily admit that they are a people of tears, and that the Korean War and the Japanese invasion have made them into helpless, pathetic creatures. The way they dwell on their past is enough to give the impression that Koreans are the only people in history who ever fell victim to war, poverty, and imperial takeover. Failing to put things in perspective, they don't seem to appreciate or acknowledge that worse tragedies and horrors have taken place in most corners of the world and continue to do so.

They suffer from convenient amnesia when it comes to the long and tumultuous history of the united Korea before the Japanese invasion in 1910. Koreans were busy fighting among themselves when they weren't driving out the foreigners, and even then they didn't always join forces and fight together. Perhaps if they had managed their internal affairs on behalf of the nation rather than for personal gain, Koreans could have changed the course of their own history and learned to take responsibility for their own actions rather than holding outsiders (Chinese, Japanese, North Koreans, Russians, Americans) responsible for where they are today.

# Socialist Paradise

# I

## August 9, 1994, Beijing: On board a Chosonminhang Korean Airline

The chartered plane had a broken air conditioner and possibly a faulty engine. By the nose of the plane stood a group of men in overalls who took turns poking their heads under the hood. The captain rushed out of the cockpit and down the portable steps to confer with the mechanics and nipped back to the driver's seat. After a few more repeat performances, a tiny, nervous voice came crackling through the speaker apologizing for the delay in takeoff. They were experiencing a "minor" problem. I could only wonder what a "minor" problem was to North Koreans.

Instead of individual storage compartments with doors that snapped shut, this plane featured an aluminum shelf where luggage was precariously stacked, secured only by a yellow string. The slightest turbulence meant an attack of flying suitcases. Expecting luxury items such as individual headphones, miniscreens for movies, and pillows would have been asking for too much. The plane also seemed to be missing a few safety devices, like oxygen masks, life jackets, and an emergency exit. Needless to say, there were no safety demonstrations by the stewardesses, who solemnly huddled in a corner of the plane like shy schoolgirls at a dance.

The three stewardesses on duty were tall and striking. Their shoulder-length hair was neatly tied at the nape of their necks with black bows, and a heavy layer of green eye shadow and quick streaks of rose blush framed their pretty, broad faces. Just as in South Korea, qualifying for an air stewardess job was like entering a beauty contest. Only the young, attractive, and single need apply. But these were no dainty, delicate creatures. They had big shoulders and walked like wrestlers, not too different from the stereotypical Russian women featured in Hollywood movies. Their wrists and ankles were exceptionally thick and bloated, making me wonder if they had the same menstrual cycle, bloating together twenty thousand feet above the ground. And, staying true to the morose nature of Koreans, these stewardesses never smiled. Neither polite nor friendly, the women seemed rather annoyed to find the plane packed with passengers for them to serve.

The $200 (U.S.) for the plane ticket (from Beijing to Pyongyang) suddenly seemed like an exorbitant amount to have paid for a bumpy ride on a Third World bus with wings. A queasy feeling in my gut told me that this was a bad omen, and that I should get off the plane while I still had the chance. But I had come too far to surrender so easily. Besides, there were only two flights a week leaving Beijing for Pyongyang. The alternative was a two-day train ride, but after having witnessed the condition of their aircraft, I shuddered to think what would pass as a train in North Korea. I just hoped the pilot knew how to fly the plane, if he ever got it off the ground.

With no ventilation inside the airplane, the smell of sweat saturated the stale air. After we'd spent almost an hour waiting and drowning in our own perspiration, there was still no sign of it going anywhere. Passengers started to grow restless and irritable, fanning themselves in vain with their hands, newspapers, and boarding passes. My eyes scanned the narrow aisle, and I couldn't help wondering if the seats were assigned according to skin color. Two English businessmen sat in the front row, with several North Koreans in the middle, and some children and adults from Africa crammed in the back.

One of the British men had offered me a piece of his chocolate bar back in the waiting lounge, jokingly calling it the Last Supper. Pleasantly surprised to learn that I was Canadian, he gave me his business card and advised me to call if I needed help. I knew he might very well turn out to be the only ally I had in North Korea. He and his partner had a business consulting firm set up in the Embassy Village in Pyongyang. Reluctant to talk about his business in any detail, the Brit quickly changed the subject by extending an invitation to the foreigners' disco night in Pyongyang on Sundays.

Beside me sat two North Korean men in their late forties who seemed determined to ignore my presence. When I smiled at them in hope of making an acquaintance, they looked back with deadpan expressions. At first I thought I had offended them by wearing a skirt that revealed a hint of my thighs, but then I noticed the Kim Il-Sung buttons on their lapels. All the North Korean passengers, and the plane's crew, were wearing them. I was the only Korean without the sacred pin.

My seatmates wore suits three sizes too big, which made them look as if they had shrunken heads; the Korean women wore polyester skirts with elastic waistbands, and were free of makeup and jewelry. Their skin looked sallow and their eyes were murky brown with an almost yellowish tinge around the pupils. Next to them, I looked embarrassingly decadent, with my gold earrings and black stockings. My fair skin was a sign of a healthy diet full of dairy products. For the first time in my life, I could be accused of smelling like a white man.

People smell like what they eat, and no amount of deodorant and perfume can completely hide the body's natural odor. With Koreans, it's the pungent smell of garlic and fermented soybean that exudes from every pore, while North Americans wear a coat of milk, cheese, and butter on their bodies like a thin layer of paint. When I first came to Canada, the so-called *yangnom* smell was nauseating and inescapable. But after so many years of living among Canadians and consuming their food, I was no longer aware of the smell. I was sure, however, that my fellow travelers could sniff out the foreigner in me.

Finally, the plane miraculously lifted itself to the sky. No explanation was provided for the delay in the departure. Evidently, the engine was fixed but not the air conditioner. To find relief from the stifling heat, the Korean men began to roll up their trousers, revealing an extra layer of pants underneath. They were cotton pajamas, worn like long johns. Candy-cane stripes of red and blue pajama bottoms lined the middle aisle of the plane. I later discovered that the pajamas soaked up the sweat, saving an extra load of laundry.

Flying over China, I was finally confronted with the fear I had managed to avoid until now. I didn't know what was waiting for me at the other end of the plane ride, and that was the worst. There is nothing greater than the fear of the unknown. Of course my South Korean prejudices didn't help either. The stories I had heard about the

Communist North were no more real than childhood tales of ghosts and goblins, but I got goose bumps anyway. Although there was no evidence that North Koreans were actual monsters, my mind kept flashing back to my Grade 2 paintings, where I'd drawn them as devils with horns sprouting from their heads. My mind was playing games with me, and I was flooded with images of jack-booted soldiers hauling me away screaming to a reeducation camp. I was quickly losing my confidence. I sat there shivering, out of fear, suddenly covered in cold sweat.

I was my father's daughter, I thought to myself. So impatient. He was in a rush to come to Canada to find riches; I was in a hurry to go to North Korea to find professional success. I was the first North American journalist to visit the last Stalinist nation on earth for the unprecedented period of three whole weeks. This was a coup. Not even CNN was permitted to stay *that* long. But I couldn't ignore some hard facts: my research on North Korea was skeletal, my experience as a foreign correspondent was nonexistent, and for heaven's sake, *I was a South Korean!* I had a feeling I was in for more than I had bargained for.

The CBC department heads had approved the travel budget and signed the checks; the North Koreans had faxed the invitation and stamped the visa application; and Max had gone out of his way to show me that he had all the confidence in the world in me. For Max alone, I felt obligated to make this trip a success. After all, it had been his idea and he had done an incredible selling job to the powers that be at the cash-strapped public radio network. It was his reputation on the line, and I didn't want to let him down.

When the stewardesses began to serve aluminum trays of unrecognizable edibles for lunch, I finally broke down crying and indulged shamelessly in a bout of self-pity. I wanted to hear some words of reassurance from my North Korean fellow travelers, but nothing was forthcoming. Ignoring my tearful outburst, the two North Korean men heartily ate their dinner of Spam and dry buns and asked the stewardess for another bottle of beer.

Setting aside my dinner untouched, I proceeded to practice my penmanship instead. I had permission from Max to forge his signature, just in case I had to write something official and sign his name to it. From our limited experience with them, Max and I had discovered that Koreans wanted everything in writing. So we obliged. In my briefcase was a stack of letters of request prominently featuring Max's signature, and a pile of blank letterhead as a backup.

I was idly doodling away when a soft chorus of oohs and aahs filled the plane. We had entered North Korea. With my heart in my throat, I slowly peered out the window and saw the mountains. Their majesty restored calm to my heart, and suddenly I felt at peace. But I could hardly ignore the irony. After years of longing to go back home, I had ended up on the wrong side of the border.

## II

The Pyongyang Airport was empty: no airplanes, no air traffic controllers, and no luggage trains. A flat, square building, it sat intrusively in the middle of rolling hills and lush green fields like a concrete matchbox. No city skyline emerged. The only thing clearly visible to the naked eye from high up in the sky was a portrait of Kim Il-Sung, majestically propped up on the top of the lone terminal building. He smiled a gigantic smile at the incoming plane, blinding its passengers with his pearly white teeth, which shone and glinted in the sunlight.

But a closer look at the painted portrait revealed that Kim Il-Sung didn't have any teeth—just a glob of white paint filling the gaping hole that was his mouth. His jet black hair covered his head as convincingly as a bad toupee. Unlike photographs showing the Mona Lisa smile of Chairman Mao or the grim look of Lenin, Kim Il-Sung's image seemed neither intimidating nor authoritative. The incongruity between the benign portrait, which looked as genuine as an Elvis bust in a corner-store window, and Kim Il-Sung's evil reputation was unsettling.

When the plane skidded to an abrupt stop, the passengers were more than anxious to disembark, if only to get some fresh air. Everybody got up, reached for their bags, and stood by their seats, ready to stampede toward the door. But with one stern glance from the head stewardess, we fell back into our damp and warm seats, grumbling like unhappy children who were told to remain after school. Impatiently, the stewardess explained that the plane could tip over if too many people tried to exit at once. For effect, she mimed "I'm a Little Teapot," finishing the performance with a big explosive sound.

Eventually, a portable staircase was rolled up to the plane and, one by one, we were allowed to leave. At the foot of the staircase waited an airport bus to escort the passengers to the terminal building, which was only steps away. It would've been a lot easier and faster to walk, but instead we packed the bus like a can of sardines—only for it to reach its destination with a quick U-turn. As soon as the driver opened the automatic door, a small group of people waiting on the tarmac began waving at the passengers, as if they had been taken by complete surprise. The members of the welcoming committee remarked with excitement that they had been waiting for an hour and were ready to give up when the bus pulled up unexpectedly. For reasons I could not comprehend, they pretended that they had never seen the plane land on the runway, only a few yards away.

The whole charade illustrated the Korean obsession with appearances, where practicality and common sense were readily sacrificed for inconvenience and ceremony, pomp and circumstance. As I'd soon discover, most Pyongyangites made a career out of this.

I was greeted by an entourage of people, including Mr. Lee Myong-Su. Wearing the same beige-colored Mao suit he had worn during our memorable meeting back in Toronto, my host stood with his hands behind his back, acknowledging my arrival with only a quick, indifferent nod. He barely managed to crack a thin-lipped smile and stubbornly remained in his spot, watching as I fought my way through the crowd.

Mr. Lee, my senior minder, introduced me to my interpreter, Park Young-Hee, a university student who was eager to practice her English on a foreigner. When I spoke a few words, she just smiled shyly and bowed. Standing beside Young-Hee was a petite woman in her mid-forties who seemed to be weighted down by her white vinyl purse and big square-framed glasses. This was Lee Hae-il, my junior minder. Not sure of what to say to a total stranger almost half her age and twice her height, she could only size me up with her hard eyes.

A moment of awkward silence was broken by the sudden appearance of a short, stout man who cheerfully shook my hand and welcomed me with a big smile. He was the big boss, Mr. Lee's superior. The round-shaped Big Boss and the chopstick-thin Mr. Lee, wearing identical suits, looked like a comedy duo. As Big Boss disappeared back into the crowd, he and Mr. Lee exchanged a brief look loaded with meaning.

Inside the terminal, another portrait of Kim Il-Sung watched over a handful of soldiers working at the inspection desk and the immigration booth. There were no public telephone booths, no car rental desks, no coffee shops, no magazine and souvenir stands, and no announcements of arrivals and departures.

The soldier at the inspection desk jumped back in surprise when he opened my suitcase. An avalanche of cassette tapes, microphones, wires, and batteries spilled out of my bag, and several little black containers of film rolled off the table. Other soldiers were alarmed enough to rush over and see what was happening. My clothes, which had been used to cushion the equipment, were strewn all over the counter, and I could only stand there embarrassed as the officer tried to untangle my bra from a microphone wire. He searched my purse and found a minirecorder; opened my video camera bag and found more blank tapes and wires.

I felt like an amateur spy who had clumsily tried to smuggle in high-tech toys. The inspector refused to believe that I was a journalist. Ignoring my pleas, he stacked the tapes into a neat pile, lined the wires next to it, and took apart the camera. "Canadian journalist," I said. He stared at me as if I was trying to pull a fast one on him. "Canadian-Korean journalist," I corrected myself humbly. When I showed him my press card, he thought I was challenging his authority. He waved a fistful of tapes in my face, accused me of breaking the rules, and announced that he had no choice but to confiscate all my equipment.

That's when Mr. Lee finally stepped in and pulled rank. He forcefully grabbed the inspector by his arm and yanked him aside to whisper something angrily at him. The soldier returned to the table, hap-hazardly tossed the electronic goods back in the suitcase, and waved me through. Mr. Lee could have saved me the hassle by stepping forward earlier, but I suspected the whole drama was planned to show me who was in charge from there on in.

When I squeezed through to the other side of the immigration booth, Mrs. Lee nabbed my passport and plane ticket and dropped them in her purse. I looked at her apprehensively, but she assured me that they would be returned at the end of my visit, and claimed she needed them to confirm the date and time of my departure. "But I just got here," I protested. It was routine procedure, she said curtly. After less than ten minutes in the country, my minders had managed to strip me of my most valuable possessions. I was at their mercy.

Outside, two cars were waiting: a blue Mercedes-Benz and a burgundy one. I was ushered into the burgundy with Young-Hee and Mr. Lee. I nervously watched Mrs. Lee slip into the blue car with all my luggage and my passport, and worried about the fate of my equipment.

Once we got on the highway, Mr. Lee began a grand speech of wel-come. He addressed me as "reporter teacher" as a sign of respect, and I called him "teacher" in return. Beaming with pride, he told me that Dear Leader Kim Jong-Il had been informed of my visit. I tried not to smirk: If only I was that worthy of attention, I thought.

Though no foreign journalist had ever met or interviewed the man who would eventually be the next president of North Korea, there was no shortage of rumors about Kim Jong-Il in the press. According to the international media, he was an obnoxious man who had as much charisma and charm as a cockroach. He had a notorious reputation as a spoiled playboy who had an insatiable appetite for movies and pros-titutes. He had a private collection of tens of thousands of foreign films; his favorite was *Friday the Thirteenth*. Describing himself as "short and thick as a turd," Kim Jong-Il permed his hair and wore platform shoes to add a few extra inches to his midget-like size. The latest rumors cir-culating the globe involved his lavish purchases of a cognac called Paradis from France to bribe his top-ranking military officers.

"Dear Leader Kim Jong-Il was very happy and proud to learn that a Choson flower had grown up so beautifully and strongly in the midst of foreign weeds and had come back home to her Motherland," Mr. Lee announced tenderly.

I was a "heroic daughter of Choson" who was to be treated with special care and the utmost respect during my visit, he said. My determination to visit Choson apparently "warmed the heart of our Dear Leader Comrade Kim Jong-Il and brought tears of joy" to his eyes. I didn't know whether to blush or laugh. Never before had Korean words sounded so foreign to my ears.

As we continued our drive, I surveyed the passing countryside. I wasn't sure what I had expected to see, but the picture postcard of blue skies and green fields was not it. Barbed wire and soldiers torturing civilians and executing prisoners in broad daylight were probably closer to my preconception of North Korea. Images of terror and bloodshed lurked in my mind, for the South Korean propaganda I had consumed as a child never disappeared completely from my consciousness.

Established on September 9, 1948, North Korea, at 120,529 square kilometers, is slightly smaller than the state of Mississippi. A country of twenty-two million people (half the population of South Korea), North Korea is a tired society on the brink of collapse, where citizens are deprived of the most basic human rights, including food, shelter, and freedom. The people are indoctrinated in the Juche Idea, a philosophy developed by Kim Il-Sung. Self-reliance is its cornerstone, and the Great Leader exploited it to keep the country as closed and secretive as it is today.

Profoundly influenced by Confucianism, Japanese imperialism, and Stalinist-Maoist Communism, Kim Il-Sung embraced the best and the worst of their ideologies and created the Juche Idea, his "own style of Socialism." Though North Korea has diplomatic relations with more than a hundred countries, and became a member of the United Nations in 1991, Kim Il-Sung preached national purity and monolithic unity to justify the nation's virtual isolation from the rest of the world.

When I asked my translator to define the Juche Idea, she recited this mumbo jumbo: "Juche Idea is the idea that the masters of the revolution and construction are the popular masses, and that the masses are the motive force of the revolution and construction. Man is the master of everything and decides everything. The master of one's destiny is oneself. Man is the master of the world." As I'd soon discover, many North Koreans talked in circles like this.

As the country's sole ruler, Kim Il-Sung had been both the president and the secretary general of the ruling Workers' Communist Party until his death. He was a cult figure who had transformed his country into a shrine to himself. There are thirty-five thousand Kim Il-Sung statues and portraits throughout the land.

North Korea is a cashless society, Mr. Lee boasted. Citizens don't pay taxes, and everything is free. Education, health care, housing, and food. As my senior minder reeled off a seemingly endless list of the many desirable features of his country, I pressed my face against the window and blankly studied the empty landscape.

There was not a single car on the highway except for the two Mercedeses, cruising as if they were on the Autobahn. There were no gas stations, highway signs, or truck stops. It was impossible to tell if we were approaching the city limits or driving to China. After about forty minutes, I finally asked where we were going. I had assumed that I'd be checking in to the Kyoro Hotel, where foreign guests stayed, but Mr. Lee laughed and shook his head. I was a VIP, he exclaimed. A very special place had been reserved for me. I smiled meekly and tried to hide my panic. This was it, I thought. I was being kidnapped. When I looked back, I saw the blue Mercedes was no longer behind us.

All my fears dissipated, however, when we drove up to where I'd be staying. A surprised gasp escaped my mouth. What I saw before my eyes was like a spread in *Architectural Digest*. Nestled among the lush green trees were about a dozen pastel-colored mansions perched on a hill, overlooking a lake. Tiny ripples of water shimmered under the sun. Each house was uniquely designed, all urban and contemporary, with balconies and wall-to-wall windows. It was like a scene out of *Miami Vice,* and I half expected to see drug lords and their bikini-clad mistresses sipping champagne under the sun.

The Mercedes stopped in front of a cream-colored four-story house, the smallest one in the group. The four kitchen staff who had been assembled out front smiled and bowed enthusiastically and practically carried me into the house as if I was their best friend.

A large foyer with marble floors led to the library and the open-concept kitchen and dining room. My bedroom was on the third floor, and had a French door that opened to a balcony the size of my apartment back in Toronto. As I stretched and massaged my neck, I spotted a gatehouse on the bridge over the lake. There was a soldier inside, carrying a rifle.

An hour after our arrival, Mrs. Lee walked through the door, making a big fuss about getting a flat tire on the way. It was an acceptable excuse, and I wouldn't have given it a second thought if she hadn't elaborated her story. Nobody on the highway stopped to help, she cried. The cars just whizzed by. I wanted to point out that there were no cars on the highway, but I thought better of it. After all, she was holding my passport hostage.

## III

Dinner was a five-course banquet, complete with wine, beer, sweet liquor, and whiskey. The staff served both Western and Korean dishes: delicate spoonfuls of caviar, boiled quail eggs, jumbo shrimp, rice cakes, and pickled vegetables, including kimchee. The marinated beef, *bulgoki*, was grilled on a flat stone the size of a brick that had been heated for hours in the fire. I marveled at this strange, new way of cooking Korea's traditional dish; the meat sizzled as soon as it touched the surface.

A waiter stood behind my seat and refilled my wineglass after each sip, ignoring my request to stop. The alcohol went right to my head, but I took tiny sips anyway, to avoid offending my hosts. Mr. Lee and Big Boss took turns raising their glasses to toast the "Choson flower who had come back to the bosom of her Motherland." Young-Hee and Mrs. Lee silently picked at their food, and the house staff dutifully watched us eat, drink, and be merry.

After dinner, I stood up to help clear the dishes. I knew there were "servants," but I felt awkward just walking away from the mess. I wasn't used to this kind of royal treatment. The staff, of course, vehemently protested and sent me upstairs to unpack.

I noticed that my bedroom door didn't close fully, but a key was provided for it anyway. As I was organizing my recording devices, I suddenly noticed Mr. Lee standing by the door as still as a ghost. I took a step to greet him when he nodded at the ring on my fourth finger and asked, "Did Reporter Teacher get married since the last time we met?" Then, without waiting for an answer, he instructed me to take it off. There was an authoritative edge to his voice. "Who knows? Maybe we can introduce Reporter Teacher to our handsome comrades," he said, forcing a laugh. "We wouldn't want to discourage any suitors by making them think Reporter Teacher was already married."

It was natural for Koreans to tease young people about marriage, especially women, but Mr. Lee seemed to take it more personally. Maybe he wasn't joking when he said I should become a symbol of Korea's reunification by tying the knot with a North Korean.

The last surprise of the evening was the most terrifying one. Inside the bathtub was a monster that was about two and a half inches long with a hundred tiny little legs. It looked like a scorpion and a caterpillar rolled into one. I froze with fear. After all I'd gone through trying to combat my fears about the Stalinist North, I was paralyzed by a bug. I desperately wanted to go downstairs and get help, but I couldn't avoid thinking again of Orwell's *Nineteen Eighty-Four*, when Big Brother discovered poor Winston's fear of rats. I stood there shaking but finally surrendered. Cursing my cowardice, I ran for help.

That was my first day in North Korea, and it was just the beginning.

# IV

I awoke the next morning and surveyed my surroundings. My bedroom was like a model suite: big, spacious, bright, and air conditioned. It was lavishly furnished with a king-size bed with a red oak frame and matching night tables. The powder room, the en suite bathroom, and the full-length wall-to-wall mirrored closets were the highlights of the show-room. Neither the television set nor the rotary-dial telephone seemed to work, but they blended in nicely with the decor. As I would later discover, the two television stations didn't start broadcasting until three in the afternoon, and the telephone was good for only incoming calls—from my minders. There was also a full-size refrigerator stocked with refreshments and fruits, and an ashtray on the corner table with a fresh package of cigarettes and matches. A Russian calendar dangled on the bare wall.

Outside, the sun was shining and the loud hum of cicadas pierced the silence. It was a beautiful morning without a cloud in the sky. I waved to the man inside the gatehouse on the bridge and went back inside to take a shower.

For breakfast, rice, beef soup, vegetables, fried eggs, yogurt, and toast were served. A starched white napkin was folded in the shape of a fan and delicately balanced on a fine piece of china; a pair of silver chopsticks and matching cutlery were carefully laid out. I didn't have the heart to tell the cook that I never ate first thing in the morning.

I was the pauper who had turned into a prince. I was Cinderella. I was a parasite. Guilt washed over me at the thought of all the starving people, in this case probably just outside the door, who would never even see a meal like this. There was enough food on the table to feed a family of six, and it was being wasted on a foreigner because no expense was too great to impress the "Choson flower."

After breakfast—I tasted a spoonful of this and a chopstick full of that to please my hosts—I asked for a cup of strong coffee, the only thing I had been craving all morning, and went back to my bedroom. The maid—a woman barely out of her teens, who walked around with a permanent smile on her face—had already made the bed, folded my pajamas, and emptied the ashtray. There was nothing for me to do except to wait for my minders. I was anxious to see the city and meet the people and start recording. However, Mrs. Lee had a different agenda—a three-hour mandatory lecture on Kim Il-Sungism 101.

My eyes were drooping with boredom and I squirmed in my seat like a child who had to pee while my junior minder and Young-Hee took turns reciting the state propaganda as though they were on auto-pilot, starting every sentence with "Thanks to our Great Leader Comrade Kim Il-Sung …" It had begun to sound like a Buddhist chant.

"Thanks to our Great Leader Comrade Kim Il-Sung, our people live in a paradise. Our country is free of crime, pollution, poverty, and money," Mrs. Lee said. "It's the unanimous will of the people of North Korea to live as one mind, and nothing in the world could corrupt or weaken that mind."

Amen!

"Thanks to our Great Leader Comrade Kim Il-Sung, our people have built a self-sufficient economy, so we don't have to rely on outsiders for anything," she continued. "Thanks to our Great Leader Comrade Kim Il-Sung and our Juche Idea, our people grow our own food, build our own factories, and take care of our citizens and our nation. The whole world can collapse tomorrow and we will still survive."

The three generations of Kims were ardent patriots whose revolutionary spirit inspired young Kim Il-Sung to become a fearless defender of his country. His great-grandfather worked as a grave keeper for a rich landlord in Pyongyang, and later as a farmer. His uncles, father, and grandfather were all arrested and tortured by the Japanese imperialists, and Kim Il-Sung's younger brother, Chol-Ju, was killed in a battle with the Japanese. Kim Il-Sung's father died at the age of thirty-one, also "fighting for the independence of Korea."

During the Japanese occupation, Kim Il-Sung and his family joined thousands of other Koreans who took refuge in China, then known as Manchuria. In Linjiang, a town in Lianoning province, Kim Il-Sung attended elementary school and learned to speak fluent Chinese. According to the official story, in 1923 Kim Il-Sung walked 400 kilometers from Linjiang to Pyongyang, wearing shoes made of straw. He was an eleven-year-old boy determined to seek his education in his homeland.

"When he was thirteen years old, he walked the same route back to China all by himself with nothing to eat. He had to walk in his bare feet because his shoes had worn out. When people offered him food, he refused. He said, 'How can I eat when my whole country is starving?' and he walked on. Even at that tender age, he was determined to lib- erate the Motherland from the Japanese bastards."

Feeling sentimental about the life of the Great Leader, Mrs. Lee and Young-Hee began to shed tears the size of pearls. My eyes wandered and came to rest on their Kim Il-Sung buttons. Mrs. Lee's was a dime-size pin, whereas Young-Hee's was larger and in the shape of the North Korean flag. I asked Young-Hee about the significance of the different shapes and sizes.

"Everyone has several different kinds at home. We have the freedom to choose which one we want to wear," she explained.

When I looked skeptical and asked if they were emblems that iden- tified the person's social and political status, she denied it and declared, "Everyone is equal in our country."

## V

The heat was unbearable. The sun was scorching hot, and the air sagged from the heavy humidity. Armed with my tape recorder, I escaped into the air-conditioned comfort of the Mercedes. I was sandwiched between Mrs. Lee and Young-Hee in the backseat, while Mr. Lee sat up front. At the gate, two soldiers manually raised the barrier and saluted the passing vehicle.

"The popular masses are always studying and reading the revolu- tionary words of our Great Leader Comrade Kim Il-Sung," Mr. Lee vol- unteered. He was referring to a group of people who sat reading on the edge of the driveway, completely oblivious to the car that missed their toes by only a few inches. It was 36°C outside. Why would they choose to sit on the concrete, in direct sunlight, rather than in the shade?

Mr. Lee explained: "The words of our Great Leader Comrade Kim Il-Sung are so powerful and engaging that readers can't help falling to their knees to continue reading as soon as the pages are opened. Sometimes the reading interferes with their work, but we cannot stop the people from wanting to learn."

When we came back hours later, the bookworms were still there. By the time the driver had parked the car, however, and I had walked down the driveway to ask them what they were reading, there was no trace of them.

I had been warned about the bizarre and inexplicable events that unfold before the eyes of a foreigner, and was told that things were not always what they appeared to be, but I never understood it until my first day out on the streets of the city.

In place of beer advertisements and Calvin Klein billboards, North Korea is flooded with bright red propaganda signs that scream: Determination! Determination!, We Have No Envy in the World!, Reunification Is Our Wish!, Korea Is One!, Victory to Juche Idea!, Victory to Our Great Leader Comrade Kim Il-Sung! Colorful paintings (in bold primary colors) showing Kim Il-Sung with revolutionary workers, Kim Il-Sung with heroic workers, and Kim Il-Sung with farmers are scattered throughout the land.

We love Big Brother!

The oppressive atmosphere was heightened by the eerie and heavy silence that blanketed the city. Pyongyang was the quietest place on earth. There was absolutely nothing to indicate that it was home to two million people. It was a ghost city where the few people who were spotted on the streets walked like zombies, taking slow and deliberate steps as if they had forgotten where they were going. People didn't run in North Korea. No one was in a hurry. And no one smiled—even children walked in silence, with their heads lowered. They paid no attention to the We Are Happy billboard that accompanied a mural of Kim Il-Sung surrounded by smiling children in a flower garden.

Skyscrapers towered over flat, square buildings of monumental size, but there were no signs to identify who or what occupied these grand spaces. Not a soul was seen going in or out of any building. The roads and wide boulevards were kept spotless by women who swept them day and night. But there were no garbage cans, no mailboxes, and no fire hydrants. Pyongyang wasn't exactly a user-friendly city.

Every few blocks I came upon a public telephone booth, and beside every booth was a long lineup. People stood single file, as if they were waiting their turn, but no one was actually on the damn phone. They just stood there. No one moved and no one talked. It was like watching an Asian version of *Waiting for Godot*.

Then there was the amusement park. A crowd of senior citizens and children stood outside the gate as if they were waiting to go in, but it was obvious the park was closed. The roller coaster and the Ferris wheel stood forlorn and shut off. When we drove by an hour later, the crowds were still standing there. Meanwhile, my hosts were cheerfully chattering away about how the people could go to the amusement park and ride all the rides free.

The greatest thing about Pyongyang was its traffic. There were no Stop or Yield signs, no cars, and no speed limit. My driver cruised the city streets at 120 kilometers per hour with ease. Traffic cops were employed, but only for effect. The girls stood in the middle of intersections like models, wearing crisp white-and-blue uniforms with shiny silver whistles in their mouths. When they saw the car of the day approaching, they blew their whistle and waved their arms, frantically directing an imaginary traffic jam. The car would stop at the empty intersection and wait for the young woman's permission to go. Stepping on the gas pedal, the driver would honk the horn to warn imaginary cars as he made a left-hand turn.

# VI

My very first official tour in Pyongyang was to Mangyongdae, the birthplace of Kim Il-Sung. This "cradle of the revolution" was a recreation of the original village and comprised three thatched-roof shacks and a few clay pots. It was delicately nestled in Nam Hill by the River Taedong. Mangyongdae was where the Great Leader had learned to fight, wrestle, and become "the world's greatest and most envied leader."

The tour guide waited at the entrance to this North Korean version of Bethlehem. She wore a navy blue polyester dress and an old pair of pink translucent plastic sandals. Her knee-high stockings had slid down to her ankles, and the heavy layer of foundation on her face had started to melt in the sun. Resolutely, she began reciting the legend of Kim Il-Sung, as she had every day for the past twenty years.

"Our Great Leader Comrade Kim Il-Sung's grandparents lived here ...They were too poor to have a house of their own ... Generation after generation, they lived here and all their family members devoted themselves to the country ... Our Great Leader Comrade Kim Il-Sung spent his childhood here, and at the tender age of fourteen ... his revolutionary struggle started ..."

I squeezed my eyes shut and gritted my teeth. I had already heard all this in the morning and yet I was expected to endure it again.

"For eighty years, our Great Leader devoted himself to the revolution and the happiness of our people. A month ago, the Great Leader passed away. Since that sorrowful day, Mangyongdae has been crowded with those people who are firmly determined to follow and support the leadership of our Dear Leader Comrade Kim Jong-Il ..."

The tour guide's voice was strained, as if she was speaking an octave higher than her normal pitch. When Young-Hee asked if I needed a translation, I shook my head vigorously. The tour was going to take two hours to complete and I had no desire to prolong it.

Looking at the artifacts, Young-Hee and the tour guide broke down in tears, their hearts bleeding with nostalgia. Of course none of the objects was genuine. The straw mat supposedly used for decades by Kim Il-Sung had no hair of straw out of place, and the century-old clay water jug didn't have a scratch on it. But I nodded and snapped pictures of the sacred objects, for lack of something better to do.

"This is the table used by Kim Il-Sung ... He was gifted with the revolutionary spirit that inspired him to write the words *independence of Korea* when he was only four years old ...

"The family was poor but rich in spirit ... The revolutionary exploits of Comrade Kim Il-Sung will be alive forever in the hearts of our people and that of the world's progressive people."

During the tour, I learned that the Great Leader is also known as the Beloved Leader, the Outstanding Leader of the Revolution, Ever-Victorious Captain of the Korean People, and the Greatest Genius

Humankind Has Ever Had. North Koreans spared no adjectives in their efforts to deify both the Great Leader and Junior. These were the most honest rulers, the bravest fighters, and the most generous human beings the universe had ever created. Even natural phenomena were freely used to explain their larger-than-life status. When Kim Il-Sung died, the very heavens above cried, expressing their sorrow with booming thunder and torrential rains. On the day of his funeral, the skies cleared miraculously and a flock of birds circled the Bronze Statue, refusing to forsake the loving arms of the Great Leader. The story of Dear Leader Kim Jong-Il's birth even sounds like the birth of Christ. He was born on Mt. Paekdu, the highest mountain in Korea, on a snowy night in a humble little cabin. And when he entered this world, the largest star the human eye has ever seen shone brightly above the modest wooden shack.

Through all this the guide conveniently left out Kim Il-Sung's real name: Kim Song-Ju. Though it is widely known among many Koreans on both sides of the border that Kim Il-Sung was the name of a famous warrior who died fighting the Japanese in Manchuria, the reason behind this name change remains a mystery.

The guide also neglected to mention that contrary to North Korea's many legends, Kim Il-Sung did not single-handedly defeat the Japanese invaders. In truth, the Korean liberation was possible mainly because the Japanese were weakened and defeated at the end of the Second World War. But voicing that would interfere with the state's official version of the truth, which also claims that it was "the people's unanimous will" that Kim Il-Sung be their leader. In fact, he was personally chosen by Stalin, with the support of Chairman Mao.

Another tour guide greeted us at the next site: the Tower of Juche Idea, also known as the Juche Top. The tower, erected to mark the Great Leader's seventieth birthday in 1982, was a proud symbol of the nation's determination to survive on "self-reliance."

"Our Great Leader Comrade Kim Il-Sung didn't want such an extravagant gift for his birthday," the guide began. "He said the biggest gift is the people's happiness, but it was the unanimous will of our people to build the Juche Tower. Our Dear Leader Comrade Kim Jong-Il took valuable time from his busy schedule to help design and build the tower ..."

She then started to recite numeric details: "The Juche Tower is 170 meters high. The red torch on the top is 20 meters high and it weighs 45 tonnes. The stone tower itself is 150 meters ... The statues of the three men around the base of the tower are 30 meters high and weigh 33 tonnes ... They are a worker, a peasant, and an intellectual, holding a hammer, a sickle, and a pen.

"The tower has eighteen steps in the front and rear, and seventeen steps on its right and left. In total, there are seventy steps, to equal the Great Leader's seventieth birthday. The steps are built of granite. There are 25,500 pieces of granite to equal the days lived by the Great Leader since his birth ..."

The guide took a break from burping out numbers to explain that the site of the tower was chosen by the Dear Leader, who always thought of people's happiness. After many "sleepless nights" of thinking and worrying, he finally decided to build the tower by a beautiful park. Releasing a slow sigh of admiration, the guide explained that the park was visited by hundreds of citizens daily. There was no one in the park that day.

"Where is everybody?" I asked.

"They are mourning the tragic death of our Great Leader Comrade Kim Il-Sung," she replied solemnly.

By the tower entrance, two teenage girls appeared out of nowhere and started to polish the brass door handle.

Young-Hee explained: "It is the unanimous will of our people to clean and polish our nation shiny and clean."

"They came here just to clean?" I asked in disbelief.

"No, no. They were probably taking a walk and were inspired by the Juche Idea."

Good thing they were both carrying dishrags.

The girls also shined the plaques covering the entrance wall. These had been sent from all corners of the world in approval and support of the Juche Idea. The inscribed plaques were mostly from Third World countries like Gambia, Pakistan, Bangladesh, Malaysia, and Uganda.

These were joined by plaques from "Juche followers" in England, Australia, and France.

I was ushered inside the tower for the elevator ride to the top. The lobby was dark and empty. The souvenir shop had a collection of post-cards and books bearing Kim Il-Sung's face, but no miniature models of the Juche Tower. There was no one behind the counter.

The panoramic view of Pyongyang from the Juche Top would make a liar out of anyone who said North Korea was a backward, underde-veloped Third World nation. The cityscape looked futuristic, like the set of a sci-fi movie. A building in the shape of a pyramid jutted out from the ground. This was the 105-story Ryugyong Hotel, which was sup-posed to be the tallest building in Asia but remained unfinished because the money had run out in the middle of construction. I wasn't supposed to know that, of course, and had to listen attentively while my guide listed the building's many attributes. "The hotel has three thousand guest rooms … five revolving restaurants …"

Looking out at the Taedong River, I saw a big chunk of silver float-ing in the middle like a flying saucer. It was the May Day Stadium, with its parachute-shaped roof. "The stadium can seat 150,000 people and has an area of 90,000 square meters …" Then there was the Pyongyang Indoor Stadium, which seats 20,000 people and has floor space of more than 70,000 square meters. And of course, there's the Kim Il-Sung Stadium. A hundred thousand seats.

How did she remember all those numbers?

"The man-made Potong River, which flows through Pyongyang, was completed in only fifty-five days in 1946. We call it the River of Tears."

Mr. Lee stretched out his arms as if to embrace the city and announced, "This is the city built by Juche. It was built by our own two hands with our own resources. Not one piece of steel was imported."

I must admit that I was impressed with North Korea's achievement and shared Mr. Lee's pride. After all, Pyongyang had been reduced to a pile of ashes during the Korean War. Not a single shack was left stand-ing. The Americans had reportedly dropped 428,000 bombs during 1,400 raids on Pyongyang.

"As Reporter Teacher can see, we are a very modern city. South Koreans think we still live on dirt floors, but that is not true," the guide said. "Please tell the people in Canada what a beautiful country North Korea is, and how happy we are."

# VII

After yet another tour, this one to the Memorial Tower of the Victory in the Korean Liberation, I was finally granted the opportunity to see people rather than statues and empty buildings.

On the top of Mansu Hill, the Bronze Statue of the Great Leader stood in all its glory. At its feet, people fell on their knees, kowtowing and crying hysterically. Bouquets of flowers were neatly arranged on Kim Il-Sung's toes. I looked on in awe. This was like watching CNN all over again. I still couldn't believe the tears were real.

Kim Il-Sung was the father of the nation. He was a god to be revered. Every citizen dutifully wore a Kim Il-Sung lapel pin, and the portraits of the two Kims were mounted on the wall of every home, classroom, office, and store, even in the subway cars.

Still, as I watched this display, something was gnawing at me. Not everybody was crying. Mr. Lee, for one, was dry-eyed and the soldiers walking around the square were definitely not crying. Not even the people waiting their turn to come up to the statue were crying. But once they laid their flowers, tears spilled like a waterfall. These people cried on cue, and they had help to get them in the mood.

The saddest, most morbid music was blaring out from speakers that were mounted on the roof of a small van. A woman wearing a Korean traditional dress spoke into the microphone. "Our Great Leader Comrade Kim Il-Sung has left us. Oh, the cruel heaven. How can this happen? Our father, our father, who sacrificed his life and happiness for our nation ... gave everything ... suffered for the people. The Great Leader Comrade Kim Il-Sung will live forever in our hearts." The woman's voice quavered dramatically and echoed through the square, while people howled and frantically beat their chests.

When I asked to interview some of the mourners, Mrs. Lee discouraged me from randomly choosing the subjects. She insisted that she would ask the mourners on my behalf. A ten-year-old girl and an old lady were chosen. The girl looked at me as if I was an idiot when I asked why she was crying. Young-Hee and the two minders huddled around the girl, anticipating her answer.

"I'm here because our Great Leader is no longer with us. We have failed him ... We could not give him happiness," the girl cried.

To my horror and shock, Mrs. Lee recorded the girl's answer in her notebook and asked for her address and the names of her parents.

When I turned to the grandmother, she plopped down in a faint and started to pound the earth with her frail fist. "I received so much love from the Great Leader," she wailed. "I want to come here every day, but I can't because of my high blood pressure so I have only visited about six times." Mrs. Lee scribbled away. "If he was still here, I know reunification would take place ... I thought he would live at least ten more years. I can't believe he's gone."

Young-Hee gave me a bouquet of flowers and motioned for me to walk up to the statue. I instinctively looked around for a camera. I couldn't oblige, but I couldn't just shake my head in outright refusal either. This was a delicate situation. I had no choice but to involve the CBC.

"My superiors would not approve. It's against CBC policy for journalists to participate in activities that we're supposed to be covering," I said gravely.

Young-Hee didn't understand. "But of course Big Sister is sad at the death of our great father Kim Il-Sung," she said, looking at me with her sad brown eyes.

I stood by my CBC policy and shrugged, wondering what price I would have to pay for failing to fall on my knees before their god.

Behind the statue, a man with a briefcase slung over his shoulder was sweeping the grounds. Young-Hee said he was taking time from work to perform his civic duty—voluntarily, of course. Under a nearby tree, three men were talking on a telephone with their eyes fixed on the weeping civilians. The telephone wires were looped around the branches like Christmas lights. Mr. Lee stopped me from taking a picture of it. "It is forbidden to take pictures of government activities," he snapped. I wondered if they were reporting the names of those who didn't display enough grief. I was also scolded when I took a picture of some military men with flowers in their hands. "No one is allowed to take a picture of men in uniform," Mr. Lee barked.

These restrictions didn't leave me too much choice, since two of every three men I saw were in military uniforms, and everything in the country was considered a government activity. Not knowing what else to do, I snapped more pictures of the statue. When a tour guide greeted us, I looked at her with fear in my eyes. I knew what was coming. I wanted to fall on my knees like the mourners and beg her to stop. No more tours, please. No more numbers, please. But I knew it would be useless. She pointed to the bronze statue and began her speech:

"Welcome to the Grand Monument on Mansu Hill. It was the people's unanimous desire to build it. The monument was built in April 1972. The statue shows our Great Leader Comrade Kim Il-Sung looking far ahead, with his left hand resting on his waist and his right hand raised to show the road for the people to follow.

"Behind the statue is the mosaic figure of Mt. Paekdu, the tallest mountain in Korea. The mosaic is 70 meters long and 12.85 meters high … The sculptures on the right side show the anti-Japanese revolutionary struggle … They are 5 meters high, 50 meters long, and 200 meters wide. In total, there are 119 sculptures. Then there's the memorial to the socialist revolution to the left …"

# VIII

Driving back to the villa, I slumped down thoroughly exhausted. I was convinced that if I threw up, I would vomit bits and pieces of undigested numbers. Unfortunately, there was no end in sight. Mr. Lee picked up where the other guides had left off, and this time I needed a road map to follow.

"This street we are driving on is Kwangbok Street. It was built in 1989, in honor of the Thirteenth World Festival of Youth and Students, and it's one of the biggest streets in Pyongyang. It's six kilometers long and one hundred meters wide," he said. "There are twenty-five thousand families living on this street. The street that we were on earlier today is Chollima Street. That was built in honor of the Fifth Congress of the Workers' Party of Korea in 1970."

As if this stupefying recital of numbers wasn't enough, my senior minder then turned his attention to the dangers of Western society. This lecture, however, was intended more for Young-Hee's virgin ears. She had never traveled beyond Pyongyang, and God forbid that her young, impressionable mind should become corrupted by Canadian filth.

The driver, obviously bored with the present company, amused himself by driving down the wrong side of the street. Since our car was the only vehicle on the road, an accident wasn't even a concern. The driver, sporting a pair of cool, dark sunglasses and wearing a tank top that revealed his smooth biceps, had yet to utter a word since my arrival.

"Canadians may look like they're wealthy, but they're not," Mr. Lee, paying no attention to the chauffeur, announced. "They are selfish and they don't open their doors to strangers. That's why there are so many homeless people. This is not just in Canada, but in the United States as well. It's like that in all capitalist societies. If it were our people, we would give them food and let them stay the night and even live with us. But in capitalist society, there's no such thing. If you have no money, you die."

Young-Hee listened with great interest, fascinated by the tales of my adopted home. Encouraged by his receptive and gullible audience, Mr. Lee then told a story about how he saw some poor Canadians so strapped for cash that they were forced to sell their own clothes and furniture right on their front lawn. "The whole family stood outside their house, and little children, poor children, were counting coins," he recalled.

I smiled, amused at the foreigner's interpretation of what was a uniquely North American experience. "They're called garage sales," I said.

"Still, they do it for money," Mr. Lee snapped.

I sank deeper in my seat. I knew I had made him lose face in front of his inferiors. Humiliated, Mr. Lee took more potshots at Canada.

"Canadians don't stop to give rides to passersby because they regard them as strangers, not family members like we do in our country," the senior minder said. "Why, North Koreans would escort them to their front doorstep and even invite them in for dinner."

"Then why don't we give them a ride?" I suggested, pointing to a group of girls on the side of the road. The Young Pioneers were wearing their school uniforms—a white blouse and a red handkerchief tied around their neck.

"No. Our people prefer to walk because it's better for their health," Mr. Lee said. "When I am driving alone, I always stop and offer senior citizens and students a ride, but they say they like the fresh air and exercise."

Ignoring his poor and blatant attempt to backtrack on his previous comment, I asked why the students were wearing their school uniforms during summer vacation.

"Our children insist on wearing their Young Pioneers' uniforms all year round to show their revolutionary spirit," Mr. Lee explained. The uniforms were "presents" from Kim Il-Sung, handed out to mark his birthday.

"Don't misunderstand. It's not because they have no other clothes to wear. No, no. They are spoiled in that they have too much of everything."

## IX

Day Two was a movie day. I felt as if I was at summer camp, at the mercy of zealous teenage platoon leaders in khaki shorts. Everything was planned—the meals, the tours, and the extracurricular activities. But I didn't get a copy of the schedule, so I never knew what was coming up next.

I was supposed to phone Max as soon as I got to Pyongyang, but for some reason my minders were balking at the one call, stubbornly insisting that it would upset the day's schedule. So I sat pouting through seven hours of movies.

To be fair to my minders, watching movies was originally my idea.

It was a plan that had backfired. When I told Young-Hee that I wanted to see a film made by their Dear Leader, it was with the hope that I would be able to watch it in a theater with the public. Instead, I was ushered to an empty conference hall at the VIP compound for a private screening—in the company of Mrs. Lee and Young-Hee, of course.

As expected, the movies were propaganda films. Had they only included scenes of soldiers marching, crowds cheering, and leaders spouting political slogans, I could probably have handled them. But they were much more than that. These films were thinly disguised as dramas, and to describe them as melodramatic would be a drastic understatement. The first was a three-hour epic about the heroic anti-Japanese fighter Kim Jong-Sook, the wife of the Great Leader and the mother of Kim Jong-Il. I watched Madame Kim hunt bears in the middle of winter, sing and dance with other robust women, and walk many kilometers in search of fabric to sew uniforms for the menfolk. She also outsmarted the opposite sex in the planning of battle strategies. It was a North Korean feminist film.

"Reporter Teacher will find this film quite inspiring. Many of our young women decided to become soldiers after watching this movie," my junior minder whispered in my ear.

Eventually, the waiter came in with a trayful of drinks and candies. I persuaded him to stay and watch the next film with me, and he reluctantly sat down. I was curious to see his response to these movies.

The next feature was a North Korean version of *Romeo and Juliet*, with a happy ending. The story takes place in Japan's Korean ghetto. A rich spoiled girl, whose parents were originally from South Korea, falls madly in love with a poor boy from the wrong side of the border. To add to the drama, the boy's father is crippled, a dishonorable state for Koreans, who view physically handicapped people as less than human. Discrimination is so strong that a disabled person can taint the whole family's otherwise good reputation. In the movie, the girl's parents use this as one of their objections to the young couple's romance. The tortured lovebirds are in turmoil. She wants to join her lover and fight for unification. Finally, after endless scenes of crying and parents clutching their chests in disapproval, the girl's family comes around and accepts

Kim Il-Sung as their leader. The happy couple walk along the seashore, holding hands in the sunset. And they, and they … No, they don't kiss. Instead, the boy recites a revolutionary poem: "To fight with the five thousand years of Korean blood in me to free my homeland from the American imperialists."

The waiter dozed off somewhere between a tearful farewell scene at the train station and the bonding scene between the young couple's parents. He had seen the film many times before.

After the movies, I walked back to the house. For a change, I had a few minutes to myself. Taking advantage of it, I tried to strike up a conversation with the kitchen staff. The cooks and the maid, all in their twenties, spoke only when spoken to, and even then, only with one-word answers followed by bashful smiles. But the waiter was different. He acted like more of a confidant.

One afternoon during lunch, I asked him about his future plans. He looked at me as if he didn't know what I was talking about.

"You are a young man, only twenty-four years old. You must have lots of dreams," I observed.

But this was his dream, he said. He loved being a waiter. How else was he going to have the opportunity to meet foreigners? "I don't have this wonderful job because I'm something special," he confessed. "Thanks to our Great Leader Comrade Kim Il-Sung, the state takes care of my every need."

His words didn't betray any emotion. Making a mental note to pursue the subject later, I pulled a stack of photographs from my briefcase and placed them on the table. They were pictures of cultural icons and political figures, including Chairman Mao, Gen. Douglas MacArthur, Jesus Christ, Santa Claus, J.F. Kennedy, Princess Diana, Neil Armstrong, Marilyn Monroe, and Elvis Presley. I had smuggled in the photos in a secret compartment of my bag to test exactly how isolated these people were from the rest of the world. The waiter and the cooks huddled around the table and passed around the photos with bewildered expressions on their faces. In some cases, they weren't sure what they were looking at.

My father during his days working for the U.S. Army in Seoul. When I was growing up, most South Koreans thought of the Americans as the great defenders of their country. Later, with the growth of the student democracy movement, Americans came to symbolize all that was wrong with Korea.

My mother in her mid-twenties, standing on the steps of our "mansion" in Seoul. I was afraid to tell my new Canadian friends that, back home, we had had no indoor plumbing, or that I bathed only once a week, at a public bathhouse.

My family at our new home in Regina in 1978. I'm the one with the turned-down mouth, refusing to smile for the camera, but the real focal point is the piano, a tangible symbol of wealth and superiority.

My brother, Samuel—the youngest of the four children—was only twenty-nine days old when we came to Canada. Eighteen years later, as the baby of the family graduated from high school and prepared to enter university, my parents let out a deep sigh of relief. This was why they had come to Canada in the first place.

A panoramic view of downtown Pyongyang. The city looked like any other sprawling, industrialized megalopolis, but in many ways people were still living an almost feudal existence. The famine of 1997 was only a small indicator of the poverty and destitution that lurked just below the surface.

Reserved for foreign VIPs, the Bong-a-ri villa, my "home" during my visit to North Korea, is forty kilometers from Pyongyang. As a "heroic daughter of Choson," I was obliged to stay there, guarded round the clock by armed soldiers, instead of at the Kyoro Hotel, where most foreign visitors stayed.

My senior minder, Lee Myong-Su; me; the tour guide; and Young-Hee, my translator; at Mangyongdae, the "cradle of the revolution." This birthplace of Kim Il-Sung is the North Korean version of Bethlehem.

Toddlers at the Kim Jong-Sook Daycare gather around a miniature model of the birthplace of the Great Leader. For my benefit, these children sang revolutionary songs and recited facts from the life of Kim Il-Sung—just like trained seals in a zoo.

The streets of Pyongyang are kept spotless by a legion of private citizens who "spontaneously" kneel to sweep up litter with their ever-present brooms and dustpans. "It is the unanimous will of our people," I was told, "to clean and polish our nation shiny and clean."

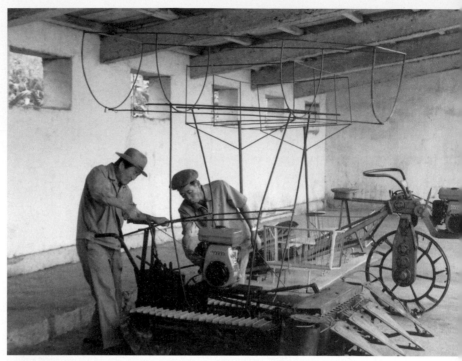

Two farmers attempt to demonstrate North Korea's idea of cutting-edge agricultural equipment, part of the "revolution of technology." In the fields, all the farmhands were bent over, working with their hands.

Young-Hee and Mrs. Lee, my junior minder, weep at the Bronze Statue of the Great Leader at Mansu Hill. In the background, hundreds of dry-eyed mourners patiently wait their turn to come up and grieve.

The Demilitarized Zone from the North Korean side of the border. North and South Korean soldiers stare each other down across the most perilous line in the world, yet I found it very quiet and almost serene.

They were able to identify Mao and MacArthur but no one else. They had never seen pictures of Jesus Christ or Santa Claus. They had heard of Hitler, but this was the first time they had ever seen a picture of him. Still, boys being boys, their attention was immediately drawn to the glossy photos of Rambo, the Terminator, and Bruce Lee. The waiter jumped into the air, striking a kung-fu pose, and one of the cooks held up the Bruce Lee picture to judge the similarity. Then their laughter suddenly stopped. Mr. Lee was standing in the doorway. We were caught. The staff scurried back to the kitchen without a word.

Mr. Lee never entered a room but materialized like an apparition and disappeared the same way. He sat down at the table and slowly flipped through the photographs, nodding at the ones he knew. "I saw this face before. Is he someone famous?" he asked, tapping the picture of Sylvester Stallone. He shook his head disapprovingly when I told him about Rambo and Rocky. I knew that I had broken one of Mr. Lee's rules by smuggling in the pictures, but this was my biggest offense so far. When he didn't give me a reprimand, it made me feel even more nervous. I knew he was keeping score.

Dismissed with a wave of his hand, I went upstairs and fooled around with the radio, which was brought to my room promptly on request. All three stations played socialist songs. Bored, I turned on the TV set. Both channels started broadcasting at three in the afternoon with a military chorus singing "Without You There's No Nation." They signed off at ten in the evening.

There was a knock on the door. The waiter stood there with a sheepish grin, holding a package of North Korean cigarettes. I gave him a couple of packs of Canadian brands in exchange, and we sat there smoking. He inhaled deeply and with satisfaction, enjoying the light, smooth taste of Western tobacco, while I nearly choked on the harsh smoke that filled my lungs.

I also gave him several postcards of Toronto. Pointing to the SkyDome and the CN Tower, he asked about the numeric details. How tall? How big? How many seats in the stadium? I looked at him blankly and shrugged. He frowned, finding it odd that I didn't have the numbers at the tip of my tongue, and even more odd that I didn't seem to care. He then asked to see the photographs again, stopping on the famous photo of Neil Armstrong floating in space with an American flag in his hand. "What is this?" he finally asked. He looked shocked when I told him. "A man on the moon," he repeated in disbelief.

# X

I was finally granted my phone call. International calls were made at the Kyoro Hotel, a hub of activity. It was the liveliest place I'd seen in Pyongyang. There were people everywhere, mostly foreigners accompanied by their minders. They were going up and down the escalator, drinking coffee in the lounge, and exchanging foreign money at the currency counter. I became envious of the hotel guests, who had the pleasure of the company of people other than their minders. Meanwhile, I was helplessly isolated forty kilometers outside the city limits and was expected to give forty-eight hours' notice if I wanted to use the phone. The novelty of the mansion and all its luxury had already worn off.

In the corner of the hotel lobby was the communications center: three telephone booths and two fax machines. The woman behind the counter asked for the country I wished to call and wrote down the phone number in the registration book.

Max and I kept our conversation brief. I told him there was nothing to worry about, describing the guest house and the Mercedes, the clean streets and the fresh air. "And I also have two guides," I said with false enthusiasm. "They are very nice and considerate. They're *always* here with me to make sure I am okay." Max acknowledged the double entendre with laughter.

I spoke clearly and slowly because the connection was bad and the phone was tapped. I wanted to make sure that whoever was listening to the conversation understood that I was praising North Korea. Perhaps my kind words would even win me some brownie points.

"Did you interview a lot of people?" I was afraid he was going to ask that question.

"No, not really," I answered. "But I went on some very nice tours. The few people I did interview all said they were very happy. It is the unanimous will of the people of North Korea to be happy, and thanks to the Great Leader Comrade Kim Il-Sung, everybody's very happy." I had been waiting all day to use that line on Max.

There was a brief pause on the other end. "Sunny, are you okay?" I was all choked up. I quickly said goodbye, hung up the phone, and broke down in tears. I knew Max was counting on me to come back with a wealth of information, but I had a feeling that was going to be harder than either of us had expected. I ran past Mr. Lee and Young-Hee to find a bathroom. There was no Kleenex and the stalls were empty of toilet paper. I kicked the door in frustration. Given that crying was a national hobby, I thought it was only fair that the state provide the hankies.

Mr. Lee tried to cheer me up by suggesting I get married in North Korea. He seemed to have women and marriage on his brain. "White men aren't as attractive as Korean men. But white women, especially Russian and Bulgarian women, are beautiful. I think Canadian women are too fat," he said. Mr. Lee suddenly let out a forced laugh, as if to warn his audience that he was going to say something very funny. "What I am about to tell you is the truth. If you don't believe me, ask your parents and they'll tell you I am right. Women in North Korea are more beautiful than South Korean women, but men in South Korea are more handsome. For you, we'll try to find the most handsome man in our country."

Refusing to dignify his nonsense with a reply, I stormed outside to the parking lot, where all eight spaces were filled with Mercedeses. I noticed that ours was the only car with a big red star on its license plate. It was clearly marked as a government vehicle, which probably explained why so many people, including soldiers, had stopped to stare at us. Of course this moment of reflection was short-lived. Soon my minders appeared in the parking lot and started hustling me back into the car. Distraught, I pressed my head against the window and stared at the empty stores and restaurants as I was escorted back to my isolated home.

# XI

Get in the car, get out of the car. Listen and learn. Numbers and dates, numbers and dates. I stood under the Arch of Triumph, listening to the tour guide boast about its size and point out that it's bigger than the one in France. The arch is 60 meters high and 50.1 meters wide. It was made with more than ten thousand pieces of granite …

"The Arch of Triumph is a monument to the immortal exploits of our Great Leader Comrade Kim Il-Sung … who liberated the country leading the glorious anti-Japanese revolutionary struggle to victory."

Under the blazing sun, I patiently listened to the stories behind every one of the twenty-some statues at the Monument to Fallen Soldiers of the People's Army. I even pretended to look interested at the Revolutionary Martyrs' Cemetery, built on Mt. Taedong, praying that the guide would not walk me past the graves of all two hundred martyrs who had "fallen tragically and heroically, liberating our homeland from the Japanese." Apologetically, the tour guide pulled out a notebook from his back pocket. "I know most of the martyrs and their stories by heart, but there are so many that sometimes I have to refer to the notes," he admitted.

I had decided not to tape the tours anymore, but Young-Hee, who had quickly learned how to operate my tape recorder, offered to do it for me.

A group of students were also walking through the cemetery. Their blue uniforms with brown belts were filthy and their torn runners were covered in mud. Their small faces were grubby and their fingernails full of dirt. They were on a field trip from the countryside and their ambition was to become soldiers. They sauntered through the aisles of the cemetery taking notes with short, stubby pencils.

"They are writing down information about their favorite heroes so they can grow up to be just like them," the tour guide explained.

I took out a handful of pens to offer to the students, but Mrs. Lee grabbed my hand and led me away from the group. She was upset that I had approached them without her permission and offered them "American filth." She said, "Our people get insulted when foreigners come here and give them presents. We don't want them because we have better things in our country."

On the way to the next tour, on the outskirts of the downtown core, we drove past a group of women with babies on their backs. They were down on their hands and knees with a bucket of water and some rags, washing and polishing the guardrails. My senior minder explained that they were idle housewives who volunteered to "shine the nation clean." Farther down the road, farmers with shovels and hoes were being transported in the back of an army truck like a herd of cattle, and others were having meal breaks. They sat on the edge of the highway with their stainless steel bowls and pots spread out on a big, square cloth as if they were having a picnic. My driver honked as he sped toward them and purposely swerved the car in their direction. The farmers jumped up, picked up their bowls of rice, and ran into the field. They regrouped after the car left a trail of dust on their kimchee and other side dishes. The driver got a kick out of this. It was like a game he was playing to stay awake on the road.

The next stop was the Patriotic Martyrs' Cemetery, for those who had died heroically fighting the American imperialists. Mrs. Lee got angry with me again, this time for taking pictures of women who were sweeping the ground. "They're not properly dressed. They don't want to give a bad impression of North Korea to the outside world," she said.

At the end of the day, my ears were ringing from the constant recital of numbers and dates and more numbers. It was excruciatingly painful. After four days, I had more than ten hours of tapes of people saying, "Thanks to our Great Leader Comrade Kim Il-Sung, we are happy ..." and "This building is fifty-eight meters tall and ..." They were going to extremes to prove that everything in North Korea was bigger and better, but I tried to accept that as an inherent Korean trait that my minders couldn't help. Everything was exaggerated and overdramatized in Korea, and moderation was a concept they had a hard time grasping. Added to this was a serious inferiority complex. Despite their insistence on their own independence, North Koreans wanted nothing more than a nod of approval from foreigners. I had to keep in mind that I was dealing with a country that took out full-page advertisements in European and North American newspapers to promulgate the greatness of Kim Il-Sung and his Juche Idea. They then displayed them in Pyongyang museums and told both their citizens and visitors that North Korea was the envy of the world.

The tours were ludicrous, and everything else about the country was absurd, and all I could do was take part.

# XII

The timing of my minders was unnerving. They always walked through the door the minute I finished eating. I began to wonder if the house had hidden cameras. One afternoon, the waiter accidentally let it slip that Mr. Lee, who was supposed to be staying in the house next to mine, had been sleeping upstairs the past few days, and that he wrote long reports about the progress of my visit until the small hours of the night to submit to his superiors the next day. I cringed at this invasion of my privacy.

Angry, I decided to spy on Mr. Lee. I went to his bedroom on the top floor and opened his closet, checked under the bed, opened the drawers, and peeked inside the bathroom. The only trace he had left behind was a package of opened cigarettes, a half bottle of whiskey, and a pair of pajamas. Noticing that his bedroom door closed shut (unlike my door), I slammed it behind me with a loud bang. I then wandered through the rest of the house and noticed the water dripping from a big crack in the kitchen ceiling. Behind the kitchen was the staff's living quarters, which consisted of a room no bigger than a broom closet. A large, gaping hole in the wall was haphazardly covered by a torn sheet, and the place was scattered with dirty clothes, ashtrays, and pillows. This was where the two cooks and the waiter slept and lived.

I went back out to the living room and turned down the air conditioner, which was on full blast, giving me the chills. There, I came upon Young-Hee. I'd noticed that she was having a serious dandruff problem. Chunks of it hung in her hair. She washed it once every three days, she confessed, with soap. She touched my own hair enviously and asked if I washed it every day. When she visited my room, she eyed my clothes but didn't dare admit she admired them. She ran her fingers through my black stockings and leaned over to touch my linen skirt, asking if I always dressed so well. I laughed and told her that normally I lived in jeans and T-shirts, but since they were not allowed in her country, I had to bring along a suitcaseful of formal attire—which, by the way, had to be borrowed and purchased just for this occasion.

Young-Hee then became fascinated with my hygiene products, holding up a box of tampons and individually wrapped sanitary napkins and asking what they were for. With horror, I wondered if they still used cloths that had to be washed and bleached. She found it curious that a deodorant, a product unknown to North Koreans, had the word *secret* written on it. Brand names and advertisements were as incomprehensible to her as the tours were to me. I gave her a small makeup kit and a red lipstick, which she wore with pride.

As usual, the car ride was the time for a lecture by Mr. Lee, who always concluded with the sensible advice: "Don't listen to a government agent like myself because Canadians will think it's just advertisement. Listen to the people and they will tell the truth."

"I would love to talk to the people," I said, wondering if he was mocking me.

"There are two million people in this city!" Mr. Lee exclaimed. "Talk to anyone you want."

For the whole week, I had tried to speak to people, but that seemed to be the most difficult thing to do in this country. When I asked him to stop the car so I could walk around the city, he became annoyed.

"It's so hot outside. Why would you want to go out and leave this nice, air-conditioned car?" And we kept on driving.

# XIII

Young-Hee was holding my hand. We were back at the Kyoro Hotel to have our pictures taken for the annual Pan National Rally, which I assumed was some kind of sports event. We sat in the lounge waiting for our driver, who had gone to fill the car with gas. I fought the urge to call Max. It was three in the morning in Toronto. Instead, I distracted myself by asking Young-Hee a question, already knowing the answer.

"What's the price of gas here?"

"It's free, like everything else in our country," she answered.

I did a quick mental calculation. The distance from the VIP compound, Bong-a-ri, to downtown Pyongyang was forty kilometers. We drove back and forth at least four or five times a day, and then there was the distance from one tour to the next. We were driving more than two hundred kilometers every day. That was a lot of gas, which I knew there was a shortage of in North Korea. But I also knew that Young-Hee would never admit to one of the country's many deprivations. To her credit, she was trying her best to play the part of a coddled child who knew nothing of hard work, thanks to the Great Leader. She even confessed that she pitied me not only because I was deprived of Kim Il-Sung's love, but also because the evil, capitalist society I lived in had forced me to work for a living. In sympathy, she held my hand and squeezed it affectionately.

Young-Hee and I had bonded during our makeup session. Now that we were alone again, she asked more questions about Canada and about my university life.

"Big Sister must have been very studious in university," she observed.

"No. I was too busy rebeling," I said. She asked me what that meant. "I'm sure North Korea has many rebels," I said slyly. "You know, people who defy their parents, their teachers, the government …"

Young-Hee looked horrified. I was pushing the limit by even suggesting that such people existed in her country. "No. Our people are not like that because the people's mind is one. We all think the same and want the same thing. It is the unanimous will of our people to be happy and desire unification." Her voice quavered, as if she was frightened for both of us.

Young-Hee lived in a university dormitory and studied languages. She spoke English, German, and a little French. She loved Shakespeare, and she eagerly asked if I had read all his works. *Romeo and Juliet* and *Julius Caesar* were her favorite plays, and I was taken aback by her knowledge and felt ashamed for underestimating her.

"Don't you find his work difficult to understand?" I asked.

"No. He uses Middle English, so it's much easier to read than Old English, which is what I study." Her English was flawless. Unfortunately, her vocabulary didn't extend beyond the propaganda text assigned to her by the state.

I lit a cigarette. "Why do you smoke?" Young-Hee asked.

"Out of habit," I said with a shrug. Then, as an afterthought, I added, "It's no different from the North Korean habit of starting every sentence with 'Thanks to our Great Leader ...'" I looked at her and smiled, and she smiled back. I began to wonder how many of the state lies she was exposed to she really believed. At the same time, Young-Hee was young and impressionable. At the age of twenty-three, she was naive and didn't seem to question a word of the "truth" being fed to her. She was a perfect little consumer of manufactured lies. Tears filled her eyes at the mere mention of the name Kim Il-Sung, and she echoed the state message with conviction and enthusiasm.

I wouldn't have been surprised to learn she was being trained to become the next Kim Hyun-Hee, the terrorist who had planted the bomb that killed 115 passengers on a Korean Air Lines flight in 1987. Kim was just Young-Hee's age when she got caught by the South Korean authorities.

The thought of Young-Hee as a terrorist sent shivers down my spine, but after a visit to a daycare, I began to understand how people could actually believe the words they were told to speak.

The Kim Jong-Sook Daycare was the most prestigious nursery in the country. Named after the first wife of Kim Il-Sung, it was a show-case for dignitaries and other visitors. Free daycare services were provided by the state, and were available in every workplace, factory, and neighborhood. When it came to hard labor, factory work, and military training, men and women were treated equally.

Before we entered the nursery, I was asked to hand over my video camera. Mr. Lee had decided that I had my hands full with my tape recorder, so he asked the Pyongyang TV station to lend us a cameraman for a few weeks. I hesitated. "I can't afford to pay a professional cameraman," I said. Pay? Mr. Lee laughed. No, this is a cashless society. They were doing me a favor. I reluctantly handed over the equipment and followed my two minders, Young-Hee, and the cameraman—the Gang of Four—into the daycare.

Only privileged parents could enroll their children in the Kim Jong-Sook Daycare. The children were left in the center all week, and were picked up only on Sundays for a day-long visit with their parents. The little girls were wearing white dresses adorned with lace and had flowers in their hair, and the boys were squeaky clean behind their ears. They sat undistracted by the new faces in their classroom. No one fooled around, started fights, cried, picked their noses, or fidgeted. These weren't normal children.

The toddlers smiled on cue and sang and danced without missing a beat. Sitting around a miniature model of the birthplace of Kim Il-Sung, the students recited his birthdate and other important facts. In the next classroom, the kids were singing songs about the heroic exploits of Kim Jong-Sook.

"What do you want to be when you grow up?" I asked one of the children.

"I want to be a loyal daughter of the Dear Leader," she answered in her tiny voice. The teachers and my minders smiled and clapped at the correct answer. The girl was only three years old. Did she know what those words meant? Did it matter if she knew?

"What's your favorite food?" I asked a boy.

He blushed. He wasn't expecting that kind of question. Mrs. Lee and one of the teachers whispered the answer in his ear. "Apple," the boy whispered, disappointed. He knew the whole history of Kim Il-Sung but didn't have a clue what he liked to eat.

The children behaved like trained seals in a zoo. Even the littlest ones performed in a band that left me flabbergasted. With no music sheets and no teachers directing them, they played accordions, pianos, drums, and sang like pros. A girl in a white dress with puffed sleeves held on to the microphone and closed her eyes dramatically as she confessed her love for her country. It was utterly amazing. How many hours a day were these kids trained?

# XIV

That evening, the waiter greeted me with a big smile, announced that dinner would be ready in a minute, and poured me a glass of strong blueberry wine. The smell from the kitchen caught my attention, and I was suddenly aware of what the staff was cooking.

It was a dead dog.

The Korean words for *dog* and *crab* sound extremely similar and when the waiter had asked me that morning if I liked *gehh*, it never occurred to me that he meant dog. To double-check I wasn't mistaken, I called the waiter over and asked if we were eating *gehh*, a special delicacy that even South Koreans ate with relish. He nodded yes. I drew a picture of a crab. He shook his head. Negative.

"I can't eat a dog," I said, shuddering.

"He doesn't bow-wow anymore," the waiter said earnestly, confused at my panicked state.

The cook came out of the kitchen, having overheard the conversation. Thinking I was rejecting his cooking, he was hurt. Dog meat—broiled with hot peppers, garlic, and green onions—prevents colds and other illnesses, he insisted, defending his selection. The cook then showed me a bowl of shredded flesh. It looked just like beef, and I was told that was what it tasted like as well. But all I could think about was how the dogs were hanged by their necks from tree branches and then were beaten to death to tenderize the meat.

During dinner—a bowl of noodles in anchovy soup—I tried to engage the staff in conversation, but all I got was more propaganda. These people were impenetrable. They wore two faces: a false one for the party and a real one for the mirror. I wondered if they trusted anybody.

Soon it was movie time again. That night's selection featured a North Korean girl who went with her circus troupe to Paris, where she had a chance to be reunited with her father from South Korea. But the meeting never took place because the Angibu arrested the father, beating him mercilessly in front of his daughter.

"Why didn't North Korea simply let the daughter visit the father in South Korea instead?" I asked sarcastically.

"It is the unanimous will of our people to stay in Choson until reunification takes place," Young-Hee replied.

# XV

The next day, I sat surrounded by eleven children who looked as though their dog had just got run over by a car. They were orphans adopted by a woman who wanted to return the love and happiness the Great Leader had given her. She wanted to adopt many more children, but there were no orphans left in the country.

The woman and her husband had been lured to North Korea from Japan during the fifties. They were just two of the more than a million Koreans who were forced to work in labor camps in Japan during the time of Japanese colonial rule. After the liberation, North Korea launched a big campaign to attract Korean expatriates back to the Motherland.

The young couple had adopted children whose ages ranged from toddlers to teenagers. The family of thirteen lived in a three-room apartment that was sparsely furnished with a dresser and a refrigerator, both of which sat in the main room. The walls were bare except for framed portraits of the Great Leader and the Dear Leader, which hung side by side.

The husband hardly uttered a word during the visit. His presence was only marked by an occasional heavy sigh as he looked blankly at his children, who all quietly knelt before him. Neither he nor his wife wore a wedding ring. Then again, I had yet to see a North Korean with any kind of jewelry, except for Mr. Lee, whose heavy silver watch sat prominently on his bony wrist. Either they couldn't afford such luxury or the state forbade any display of personal wealth.

The mother, whose fine, sharp features were highlighted by blue eye shadow and red lipstick, insisted that she hardly lifted a finger as a housewife. It was the Dear Leader and his love that raised the children, and all their school needs, food, and clothes were provided by the state. The state knew when the cupboards were empty, and the grocery man showed up at the door just in time with a box of food. The state knew everything about everybody. She was talking so fast that she was almost breathless when I abruptly interrupted her with a question.

"You cannot have children of your own?"

"Yes I can," she said hesitantly. The mother's face clouded over for a brief moment as she fought back tears, biting her lower lip. Realizing what she had admitted, she nervously tried to repair the damage.

"I wanted to return the love of our great father. We're so happy," She then repeated, "We are so happy. What other country on earth would do this?"

Yes, what other country would rob a woman of her most fundamental right to have her own baby? I answered her silently.

For the sake of this woman's safety, I put myself into a North Korean frame of mind and spoke their language. "I think you are truly a heroic woman. I know of no other country whose citizens would feel this kind of love and loyalty to the state." I held her hand and squeezed it tight.

The ready-made family of thirteen was a propaganda tool designed to advertise the goodness of "the popular masses." In turn, the couple was awarded a refrigerator and probably extra food rations. For their part, the children blankly recited their answers, shed a few tears, and sang socialist songs for their guest of the day. This was my hosts' idea of introducing me to regular citizens. Anyway, given all the lies I had already witnessed, I would not have been a bit surprised to discover the family members were complete strangers to one another.

In addition to my minders and Young-Hee, another woman who didn't bother to introduce herself was present throughout this session. When I inquired who she was, she said she was just a neighbor who had dropped by. The "neighbor" and Mrs. Lee recorded every word spoken by the members of the family.

One by one, the children revealed how their real parents had died—all heroically. Each of them had sacrificed his or her life to save a drowning comrade or a fellow soldier on a construction site. No one died a quotidian death, such as one from lung cancer or a traffic accident. The children did not talk like children, and all their answers were identical, word for word.

"My father also died in a construction accident," a boy of thirteen said. "Our new mother came and said, 'I'll be your real mother' and embraced all of us. I realized then that she was a heroic mother raised by the love of our Great Leader, and I realized how big our Great Leader's love was."

## XVI

It was August 15, the day of liberation. On that day in 1945, Korea won back her independence after thirty-five years of Japanese colonial rule. But the price of freedom was the division of Korea.

Korea must be reunified independently, peacefully, and through unity. This was the message the people carried to the Pan National Rally, an annual event that was conceived when North Korea was excluded from the 1988 Summer Olympics in Seoul and hoped to compete for international attention by staging an event of its own. The rally celebrated the anti-Japanese struggle, the Korean War, the fight against American imperialism, and the great revolution that North Korea was supposedly engaged in.

I was asked to attend the rally wearing the official reunification T-shirt and a skirt. A woman wearing pants just didn't look right, Mrs. Lee declared, scrunching up her face, pointing at my slacks. She also requested that I learn the words to the theme song "Reunification Is Our Wish," and an arm movement that resembled the Nazi salute.

No, no, and no. I adamantly refused.

Every muscle in Mrs. Lee's face tightened. "You're Korean," she declared. "How can you betray your people like this? You will not only lose face but also disappoint your parents."

My parents? My junior minder then broke the astounding news to me. My parents, she claimed, were closet Communists, but they wouldn't reveal it for fear of malicious South Korean agents. I would make them proud, she assured me, by fighting on their behalf. It was my duty to carry the torch.

When I didn't budge, Mrs. Lee went back to scribbling away in her blue book. Angry and fed up, I demanded my passport back. Only if I wore the T-shirt and a red banner across my chest, she responded. Then we bargained. I offered to broadcast the rally for the CBC instead. She agreed and handed me the passport the next day.

The next morning, both my minders greeted me with reproachful glances as I climbed into the back seat of the car wearing a CBC T-shirt and a pair of slacks. We drove to the rally in silence.

As they had done in the previous five years, tens of thousands of marchers paraded down the streets of Pyongyang wearing the official T-shirt with red sashes hung across their chests. Crowds of spectators cheered them on and joined them in the chanting.

More than a thousand expatriates from Russia, China, Japan, Canada, and the United States come for the three-day rally. They stand out from the crowd by the natural, carefree way they conduct themselves—chatting idly with their neighbors, laughing, joking, chewing gum, and complaining loudly about the hot weather. The true North Koreans are the ones looking down at their feet.

The opening ceremony is nothing like the ones in North America, with floats and children and balloons. There are no spectators with drinks in their hands, no crowds milling about, no vendors selling ice cream, and no police with roadblocks. Civilians line up along the side of the street in an orderly fashion, and strangely enough, there are no soldiers present anywhere. According to the rally organizers, fifty thousand people attended that year's event.

Without a single drop of water or bite of food, the people march, march, march, their voices hoarse from chanting and singing. They start at ten in the morning and don't stop until eleven at night. When the day's excitement is over, and more than a hundred thousand people return to their homes, not a single piece of garbage is to be found on the streets. I didn't have a clue where all these people came from and where they disappeared to—quickly and quietly—after the rally. Even on a day like that, I didn't see a single person enter or leave an apartment building in the city. Just like my senior minder, the people seemed to materialize out of nowhere.

I admit, however, that I was swept away by the energy and the strength of the crowd. Running on pure adrenaline, I zigzagged through the waving arms, invigorated by the excitement, the fever, and the passion in the people's voices. I ran as though I was in an obstacle course, dodging human pylons. I ran in vain, hoping to lose Mrs. Lee in the crowd.

The participants claimed that Korea had been one nation for five thousand years, separated for only fifty. Reunification was inevitable, they shouted. "One people! One nation!"

These people were asking for a miracle. They might as well have been doing a rain dance in the middle of the Sahara Desert. They didn't have a clue about the drastic changes that had taken place in South Korea, and they didn't understand that unification wasn't on its priority list. They simply did what they were told and that was enough.

# XVII

The American president, Bill Clinton, sent a letter to North Korea to mark the occasion of the Pan National Rally. A public reading of this letter was the highlight of Day Two of the ceremony. President Clinton had expressed his support for the reunification rally, and a *New York Times* editorial had condemned the South Korean government for its crackdown on civilians. With this unexpected surge of interest and support from the Americans, North Koreans were beside themselves with joy.

Since the death of Kim Il-Sung, South Korean riot police had been arresting labor organizers and student activists, accusing them of being

Communist supporters. Furthermore, two hundred university student representatives from both sides of the border had planned, as they do every year on August 15, to march to the border. Though this was widely promoted and publicized in the North, the South marked the occasion with violence and bloodshed. As expected, North Korean students waited in vain at Panmunjom for "their brothers," who never even made it to the outskirts of Seoul.

During the reading of the letter from President Clinton, Mrs. Lee began to urge me to go up to the stage. It was my duty to record the speech and broadcast it to Canada, she said. Before I knew what was happening, Young-Hee, Mrs. Lee, and the cameraman were all pushing and pulling me toward the podium. I fought back in horror. No other media were on the stage, and I didn't want to be the only one sticking my microphone into some official's face. I also thought the accuracy of the letter, which had been translated into Korean, was probably questionable.

But it was too late to turn back. With a big push, my minders practically threw me onto the stage. The North Korean press rushed forward and started rolling their cameras and taking pictures. The lights blinded my eyes. I tried to hide behind the lectern. The next day, my picture was in the *Rodong Shinmoon*, the daily for the popular masses. I had become a star. I was on TV, identified as a Korean expatriate from Canada fighting for reunification. Nowhere did it mention that I was a journalist.

At the end of Day Two, another press conference was called at the Kyoro Hotel. A woman made a tearful plea to the South Korean government to return her brother, who had been captured during the war and was still held as a POW. He was being held in what the woman described as "one of many labor camps" in the South. She held up a black-and-white photograph of her brother. In tattered clothes and with no shoes on, he was trying to lift a boulder with his bare hands. He was staring straight at the camera. The photograph was blatantly posed.

"Who took the picture?" I asked Young-Hee.

One of the inmates had taken it, she professed, and mailed it to North Korea. This claim ignored the fact that there was no direct communication between the North and the South. No phone lines and no mail service. Not even radio frequencies could jump the border.

# XVIII

On Sunday night, I prepared my report to feed to the CBC as I had promised. I scribbled away in a private meeting room at the Kyoro Hotel, while Mrs. Lee paced outside like an expectant father, poking her head in every few minutes. Did I want some water? Was the lighting okay for writing? Was I hungry? Please, she pleaded, do a good job and tell the world about our wish.

Meanwhile, one of the rally organizers was writing in the lobby, and was insisting that I use his version instead. He had written a ten-page essay. I asked Young-Hee to explain that the report could be only a minute and a half long, then I went downstairs and slipped into phone booth number two. Informing Max that the story could go straight to the garbage for all I cared, I read my report (the first report ever to be sent straight from Pyongyang) into the phone.

After I made my report, I sat and watched the international newscast, broadcast every Sunday night: a plane crash somewhere in China, a flood in India, a riot in Seoul, a war in Rwanda. No stock-exchange news, no weather, and no sports. No wonder North Koreans thought they were living in paradise. Images of South Korean student protesters being beaten by the riot police flashed on the screen accompanied by a dramatic voice-over. "Look at this. Poor South Korean students live without knowing the love of our Great Leader. They fight and struggle to come to North Korea, but they're being beaten mercilessly ..."

The newscast also featured a CNN interview. Mike Chinoy, the Asian correspondent, was talking to a university professor and his family who had defected from South Korea in 1988. Apparently, the rumor in the south was that he was kidnapped by the Communists and killed. The professor wanted South Koreans to know that he was alive and well, and happy, thanks to the Great Leader. At least this was the story according to the Korean translation. Mike Chinoy's questions, in English, were bleeped out, so I had no idea what he was really asking.

## XIX

The rally closed with a dinner reception, and I was dragged there practically kicking and screaming. Earlier that afternoon, I had arranged a meeting with CNN's Tom Mintier at the Kyoro Hotel and I had been anticipating it all day as if my life depended on it.

Mintier and his crew had used their deadline as an excuse to get out of the reception. As a result, his promised interview with a high-ranking government official was conveniently canceled. There was a price for everything in North Korea, especially for a few hours of freedom.

Seated in the Kyoro's coffee shop, Tom and I compared notes. I instinctively felt under the table and chair for any recording devices. It made me feel better when Tom confessed that he could hardly wait to get out of the country. Of course all the interviews were staged, he said, and people wouldn't talk even if no minders were around. They knew better than to talk to foreigners, Tom said, never mind journalists. I could feel my confidence growing as I realized that I wasn't alone.

Just then, a friendly-looking man came up to our table, out of breath. He cordially advised Tom that he should've been accompanied to the meeting. Tom had sneaked out of his hotel room when his minder's back was turned. Displeased, Tom's minder took a seat at the bar, ten feet away from our table. On the other side of the room, Young-Hee and Mrs. Lee were watching me like a hawk. Our minders were like bookends, forcing Tom and me to lean closer together and drop our voices to a whisper.

After about forty minutes of griping, we exchanged business cards, he gave me the rest of his American cigarettes, and we shook hands goodbye. I had found an ally and I was heartbroken to discover that he was leaving the next morning. I felt as if I was losing my best friend.

On the way home, Mrs. Lee started her interrogation. What did we discuss? What did he think of North Korea? Did he believe in the unification cause? Was his story going to be positive? She looked away in disgust when I told her, rather gleefully, that we hadn't discussed business. "We talked about holiday plans," I chirped.

That night, to save energy, the streetlights had been turned off. The buildings were pitch dark except for a few neon lights around the Kyoro Hotel. The Bronze Statue on the hill, however, was surrounded by floodlights and seemed to float over the city like a ghostly apparition. Hundreds of people were still waiting at the steps to pay their respects. I couldn't help wondering if people were assigned a specific time to visit the sacred ground.

## XX

Mr. Lee was angry with my CBC report. In it, I had referred to North Korea as a poor cousin to the South, and stated that hopes of reunification were raised by the unification of Germany. But the biggest crime I had committed was failing to give Kim Il-Sung the proper attribution. I referred to him as neither the president nor the Great Leader.

My passport was confiscated again and I was subjected to a brutal, four-hour interrogation that left me physically exhausted.

Mr. Lee was so angry that he could hardly speak. He was tripping over his own contradictions. North Korea didn't need money because it's a cashless society; North Korea is financially poor because of the collapse of the Soviet Bloc. North Koreans could blow South Korea to pieces; North Koreans wanted peace with its brothers. The food shortage was a nasty rumor spread by the capitalist South; the popular masses volunteered to go without food for the sake of the nation.

Mrs. Lee listened quietly while her superior unleashed his fury. Young-Hee kept her head lowered and didn't dare make eye contact with me. I could sense her helplessness. Even my friend the waiter, who poked his head in from the kitchen, looked at me for a brief second, then disappeared until he was summoned for coffee.

It was past dinnertime, and the kitchen staff was waiting for me to show them how to make spaghetti as I had promised. I was fatigued and hungry and the room was cold. Mr. Lee's words echoed in my head but nothing registered anymore. "You're a Choson flower ... a Korean ... five thousand years of Korean blood in you ... Choson flower ... the Dear Leader wanted the best for you ... we gave you our best ... our honored guest ... Choson flower ... reunification, reunification ... do not betray your own people ... do not betray ..."

My stomach was in knots and I felt like vomiting. My right eyelid twitched nervously and my body started to jerk. Smoking was all I could do to stop from trembling. Cigarettes had become my most reliable friend in North Korea; smoking was the only act of freedom I could practice. I smoked until my throat felt raw.

Max was wrong to think I was the right person to be here. I didn't understand these people. We spoke the same language, but we could not communicate. This culture was as alien to me as it would have been to him.

After my ordeal was over, the waiter came out of the kitchen with a hot cup of tea in one hand and a bottle of whiskey in the other. He smiled his mischievous smile and lit my cigarette. Assuring me that my minders had left for the evening, he gently reminded me that the kitchen staff was waiting patiently, and hungrily, for the cooking lesson.

The cooking class was a big success. The staff slurped up the spaghetti, which I made with onions, garlic, and a teaspoon of ground beef. I couldn't imagine where they had managed to dig up a teaspoon of what looked like ground beef, and I didn't want to know. The rusty tin of tomato paste looked as if it might have dropped out of the back pocket of an American GI during the Korean War, but it had to do. Italian seasoning would've been asking too much.

For the first time, the waiter joined me for dinner. We poured wine for each other and clinked our glasses. As we ate, I explained that pasta was usually served with salad and garlic bread. He then became unexpectedly sentimental and tears welled in his eyes. Holding the CBC keychain I had given him earlier, he said he would bring it to the airport the next time I visited North Korea. "That way, Big Sister will know it is me." He smiled.

After dinner he wrote his name—in English. It was his dream to learn the language and become an interpreter, and perhaps even travel outside the country. "Big Sister, I have many dreams, but what can I do? They're just dreams."

We were both startled by his confession, he more than I. With a frightened look on his face, he quickly got up and disappeared into the back room of the kitchen. When I came down for breakfast the next morning, I found a plate of garlic toast and salad on the table.

# XXI

In the car, Young-Hee shared her knowledge of the outside world. We were on our way to a concert of revolutionary songs. It was the North Korean version of MTV. Young-Hee volunteered that she had read in the newspaper that Europeans were beating their children to death for amusement, and that men were poking out girls' eyes in South Korea to sell them for money. For his part, Mr. Lee, pretending that the previous evening never took place, was back to his cordial self and complimented me on my outfit. "Every time I see you, you change. Different outfits give you totally a different look." He smiled. "Last night, you looked like a child. Today, a sophisticated woman."

The cabaret started at the peculiar time of five in the afternoon. The auditorium was filled with soldiers and children who clapped to the beat of the music. I was kept away from them in the empty balcony. Looking down on the stage, I could not ignore North Koreans' taste, or lack thereof, in fashion and interior decorating, especially when it came to their choice of colors—lime green and pink seemed to be their favorites. The stage curtains were lime green, pink, blue, and burgundy and clashed horribly with the musicians' purple tuxedos. One conference room I visited had red Persian rugs with pink flowers, blue vinyl chairs, and mustard yellow sofas. Even elevators were decorated with locker-size mirrors and plastic flowers. Everything was kitsch.

During the concert, Young-Hee mouthed the words to all the revolutionary songs: "Song of Loyalty" (written by the Dear Leader himself), "Only One Mind," "The Leader Is Always with Us," and "Look at the World."

*If you look at the world*
*You can know how happy we are*
*If you look at the world*
*You can know how strong we are*
*If you look at the world*
*You can know we have nothing to envy.*

I closed my eyes, trying not to laugh at the ridiculous title of the next song: "We Have a Bumper Harvest Thanks to the Great Leader." For an hour and a half, I listened to one socialist song after another. At the end of this bizarre spectacle, a man sporting the same permed hairdo as the Dear Leader came on stage and sang "Well-Being of the Dear Leader Is Our Happiness."

# XXII

My alarm went off at 4 a.m. We were going to the mountains southeast of Pyongyang for three days. After my torturous interrogation, I began to wonder if I was really being sent to a prison camp. Still half asleep, I got dressed in the dark and threw a few articles of clothing in my overnight bag.

It was still dark outside, and heavy fog made the driving difficult. I was surprised to see so many people walking to work at this time of the day. They walked into the thick fog and disappeared.

When we finally got outside the urban fantasy of Pyongyang, I began to see scenes that were what I had always imagined the Third World would be like. People slept by the roadside, an occasional ox with protruding ribs worked the fields, and a weather-beaten old grandmother pushed a wooden cart full of debris.

Low, decaying apartment buildings stood in the middle of cornfields;

an old man leaned out a window smoking; boys bathed and women washed clothes in a stream. Unfortunately, taking pictures of the countryside was also forbidden. My junior minder was so paranoid that she grabbed my camera when I tried to snap a picture of a pair of children's running shoes left on a rock beside a worn-out copy of a book with Kim Il-Sung's picture on its cover. The runners were too dirty, Mrs. Lee said. She didn't want North Americans to think that children in her country had filthy shoes.

There was no life here, no energy. The people's weariness was almost tangible. But in a way, the drive through the countryside was revitalizing. For the first time, I was seeing real people. The real North Korea. It wasn't the extravagantly lavish facade of the city, where everything lacked conviction. Out here, there wasn't the same desperation to compensate for the very little they had with gross exaggeration.

I was seeing North Korea naked, and a tiny glimpse of the truth finally emerged. These people were hungry, poor, tired. They were paranoid and terrorized by the state. They had seen their neighbors get taken away by soldiers, or discovered that they had disappeared in the middle of the night without a trace. They woke up every morning to the hopelessness of it all. How long could they suppress the rage? How long could they continue to play the grand charade? Of course, I was never going to find out because I wasn't allowed to talk with them. Besides, we were late. Mt. Kumgang was waiting for us.

I pressed my face against the car window and watched the farmers sleepwalk through their chores. Two little boys wearing identical torn blue runners waved when I stared at them and chased the car down the road until they ran out of breath. I smiled and continued to wave even when they were out of sight.

We stopped for a lunch break by the beach. Mrs. Lee unloaded a trunkful of rice and side dishes, all carefully wrapped in brown paper. The restaurant by the shore was big and empty, and it was obvious the place did not serve food. The souvenir shop, however, did sell Kim Il-Sung books and needlepoint works. Pencils, erasers, and ballpoint pens, all made in Japan, were for sale at the counter, and American cigarettes and bottles of Johnny Walker were safely locked in a glass case. It was odd to see North Koreans selling products of the two countries they regarded as their worst enemies. A Japanese pencil set was more expensive than a hardcover autobiography of Kim Il-Sung.

The two drivers, two minders, Young-Hee, the cameraman, and I sat down to eat. During lunch, Mr. Lee and associates did their best to engage in humor, at Young-Hee's expense. Remarking on her love for bread, the comrades joked that she'd make a good wife for a Big Nose—Canadian, not American, of course. The joke wore thin after a couple of minutes, but the gang insisted on beating it to death, and asked me if I could find a baker in Toronto for the young virgin.

After the meal, the pressure was on for me to swim, and as usual they refused to take no for an answer. Young-Hee borrowed a red swimsuit from the beach house and insisted that I do the same. I reluctantly went in the water with my white tank top and shorts to stop the group from badgering me. The cameraman immediately started to videotape the fun in the sun.

I casually remarked that it was a shame the beach was empty on such a sunny day, and a troop of male students came on the scene minutes later. My minders wouldn't go so far as to stage this as well, would they? This has to be a weird coincidence, I thought. I decided to put it to the test and asked, "Aren't there any girls?" The girls joined the boys minutes later, wearing identical red swimsuits. I looked around the beach, confused. Where did they all come from?

Mt. Kumgang was absolutely breathtaking. Its grandeur and beauty, however, were spoiled by the immortal words of Kim Il-Sung, which were chiseled on the steep sides of rocks and cliffs and splashed with blood red paint. From afar, the mountains looked as if they were bleeding.

Our hotel, the only hotel in the mountains, was built with money sent by Korean expatriates in Japan. There was a big Korean community in Japan that openly supported North Korea and was responsible for contributing millions of dollars to its economy. A ship traveled back and forth between the two countries on a weekly basis, transporting goods and valuables and visiting family members.

That night Mr. Lee and I dined alone in the empty hotel restaurant. There was no menu, and the type of dishes suggested that North Korea was indeed suffering from a food shortage. White rice was supplemented with corn, and the side dishes consisted of shredded cabbage and a small fried fish with hardly any meat on its bones. The soup tasted like dirty dishwater. I concentrated on chewing the coarse grains from my rice bowl but found it impossible to swallow. If this was a special treat for an honored guest, I could only imagine what common people ate.

An uncomfortable silence made it hard for me to digest my food. When Mr. Lee offered to light my cigarette, I knew that foreshadowed another lecture. My stomach was already in knots.

"Everything is political," he began. "Reporter Teacher is naive to think that you could come here on the pretense of doing a story on only our people. Our people and our politics are inseparable."

I could tell by the tone of his voice that I had done something to annoy him again, but I didn't know what.

"You don't deserve to meet our Dear Leader Comrade Kim Jong-Il if you can't even address him in the proper manner," he said.

The penny dropped. He was referring to a letter I had written requesting an interview with Kim Jong-Il. Mr. Lee was offended that I hadn't addressed Junior as Dear Leader, and had chosen to bring it up now, in the mountains. Maybe this was a warning sign. Tomorrow I had to climb a mountain. Suddenly it didn't seem too inviting.

# XXIII

I decided to dine alone the next night. I was fatigued from climbing mountains and the cold I had caught from swimming in the ocean was getting worse, so I told Mrs. Lee that I would not be joining the senior minder for dinner. This set off an alarm bell. Mrs. Lee brought a tray of dinner and asked if I needed a doctor. Mr. Lee was pacing outside my room, and Young-Hee knocked on the door every few minutes to check if I was still alive. No one had dinner; they were all waiting for me to get better.

Seeing that I felt better the next day, Mr. Lee continued his speech from the other night, reiterating that I should never, ever compare the two Koreas. It would be like comparing apples and oranges. "South Korea has money but no one's happy. We're all happy here. Nothing can compare to that now, can it?"

He must have been drunk because he began to get quite belligerent. For days, he had been commenting on my outfits, and now he felt obliged to point out how I stood out from the crowd. "Our people are offended when Choson people come here dressed like Westerners, showing off their wealth," he said and slammed his empty glass on the table. "White people, we don't care how they dress when they come here. But Choson people are different."

He spoke in circles, as usual, leaving it up to me to figure out the hidden message, which was that I was dressed like a Yankee, too flashy. It was attracting too much attention. Civilians didn't know I was from Canada, Mr. Lee pointed out. My clothes would indicate that I was rich, and therefore that South Korea was rich. This would lead to a scary thing called knowledge, and that would be too dangerous for people to have.

He might as well have taken a hammer to my head the way he was pressuring me. He reminded me that he had other foreigners to attend to, but that his specific instructions from the Dear Leader were to keep me happy and satisfied. "Don't let the Dear Leader down," he said. He then threatened that I wouldn't be welcomed back to the country if I did.

"What happens if I say something you don't approve of?" I asked.

Crimson red color spread across his face and down his neck. He said he would always remember those who criticized North Korea, and that they would pay the price once reunification took place. I grabbed my tape recorder to record his words of warning, but with one violent, sweeping motion, he pushed my hand away and disconnected the microphone.

## XXIV

When we finally returned to Pyongyang after our three-day sojourn in the mountains, the city seemed to have been transformed. There were cars on the streets and people were smiling and talking to one another. A mother and child stopped and smelled the flowers (now, that was a bit too much). Women were wearing colorful blouses, with makeup on their faces and heels on their feet. As Young-Hee was eager to point out, there were customers having lunch in the restaurants. All the window seats were full. Young couples were rowing in the pond, and old men were fishing. People were still lined up at the empty telephone booths, of course, but now the city buses were packed with passengers.

I thought I had completely lost my mind. There was no explanation for this sudden change, and when I tried to ask my minders, they played dumb. I had heard rumors that North Korea had actors pose as civilians to impress foreigners, but I didn't think it would go this far. It was as if a whole troop of extras had been called in to liven things up.

At the Kyoro Hotel, while I was waiting for my turn to use the phone, Young-Hee started singing "I Did It My Way." It was her favorite English song, the only English song she knew. Earlier that morning, she had come to my room to look through the photographs of famous people. She thought Princess Di "looked beautiful enough to be a princess." Santa Claus was an old crazy man who had gone senile, and she gritted her teeth at General MacArthur. Her face lit up at the picture of Kennedy. "This is Dustin Hoffman!" she yelped. "I saw him in the movie *Kramer vs. Kramer.*"

Carefully chosen Hollywood movies were shown in English classes. No doubt *Kramer vs. Kramer* was shown to prove that North Americans were selfish and that mothers threw their own children away.

"All round eyes look the same," I said, smiling at the thought of Kennedy as Tootsie.

When I finally got my chance at the phone, I called Max and spilled my guts. I no longer cared who was listening, and could not contain my sarcasm and rage. Pyongyang was Mr. Rogers' Neighborhood.

Everybody was too bloody happy, I screamed into the phone. The city should be turned into a giant theme park called Happyville.

Not wanting to hang up, I told Max about the tours, the smiling children, the propaganda films I was forced to watch, and the brain-numbing lectures. I enunciated each word carefully to make sure whoever was listening understood that I was not happy.

"Max, I don't know if I can last," I finally said, before I reluctantly hung up. The forty-minute conversation cost me $300 (U.S.). Since there was no standard rate for international calls, I had to pay what was demanded.

I was silent on the way to our next appointment. My minders confessed that it was a bad time to be visiting Kim Il-Sung University because it was the last day of classes. There wouldn't be any students for me to interview.

When we arrived, I was led through rooms and rooms of displays to admire stuffed animals that were supposedly hunted by the Great Leader: a bear he shot and killed in 1959, the first fish he caught in 1958, the biggest eel the Great Leader had ever seen, a reindeer presented to him as a gift (by Santa himself, no doubt). We also walked through rooms filled with pictures of the Dear Leader. He always stood alone in the foreground, while his entourage fell away into the background. This gave the impression that Junior was taller than he actually was. Every pencil, notebook, and ruler he had ever touched was enshrined in a glass case.

He attended the university from 1960 to 1964, and of course, graduated at the top of his class.

The tour guide explained that despite countless letters of invitation and pleas from famous universities abroad, the Dear Leader had chosen to study at the most prestigious university in the world, the one named after his father.

I was asked to wait in an empty classroom while my junior minder and an entourage of university staff members went in search of the designated interviewees. Minutes later, two male students came in, declaring their happiness from the outset.

"Is there anything they're not happy about?" I asked sarcastically, annoyed at yet another bogus interview.

"No. They're perfectly happy," Young-Hee translated.

I felt like throwing my hands up and surrendering. I had lost; they had won. I could not persuade the people to tell me the truth, their truth. Any truth.

I spoke in Korean, with utmost deference and humbleness. I was coy with soldiers, friendly with children, direct with tour guides, and gentle with senior citizens. To show respect, I bowed, averted my eyes, and sat with my legs folded under me. To break the ice, I chatted idly about the weather, inquired about their health, offered my condolences at the death of their Great Leader, apologized for my intrusion, and thanked them for their time. I listened attentively and nodded at the right time when they talked about the Korean War and the Japanese colonial years. In an attempt to get answers that weren't already prescribed to them by the state, I tried to engage them in conversation, and subtly, cautiously, dropped questions. I then strained to listen for possible hidden messages, codes, double meanings that might be wrapped in their words, but it was all in vain. They did not stray from their scripts, and I could see their jaw muscles tighten as they spat out the words, their eyes far away somewhere else.

Trying a different tactic, I asked questions in English, hoping to appear more professional, distant, and alien. I tried everything, playing the devil's advocate, a naive foreigner, a gullible girl. Still their stoic faces betrayed no emotion.

## XXV

August 22—only one more week to go. I was no longer worried, paranoid, anxious—or interested. The absurdity of the place and the predictability of these automatons took away my curiosity and my drive to know and to understand. My senses had been dulled. My minders were breaking me down bit by bit, and I was giving in. The brainwashing process seemed to be working. I'd learned to nod and refrain from asking too many questions. There was no point. Young-Hee now operated the tape recorder, pressing the Pause and Record buttons at will. But I had also learned to be aloof and indifferent. It was the only way to cope with the rage that was building inside me.

Like a lobotomized patient, I absentmindedly walked through what was left of the thirty-three official tours. I clapped on cue at the three-ring circus where magic tricks and North Korean beauties on tightrope held the audience's undivided attention, and squirmed in my seat during yet another three-hour cabaret of revolutionary songs. On a subway ride, I listened to a Pyongyang Metro Transit commissioner list the names of the stations—Kaesong (triumphal return), Sungni (victory), Ragwon (paradise), and Yonggwang (glory)—and boarded the empty train at Kwangbok (liberation) station. The subway was adorned with ballroom chandeliers that glittered with a hundred orange-and-purple-tinted crystals, and an impressive thirty-meter mosaic, inlaid with over ten thousand small pieces a square meter. More chandeliers were hung at the Grand People's Study House, a library with a hundred thousand square meters of space but no books or readers visible anywhere.

Obediently, I walked through the Three Revolutionary Museum— where two ushers ran down the hallway to roll out the red carpet for their guest—and observed the achievements of the popular masses. The museum was a potpourri of junk passing as high tech—transistor radios and television sets and polyester clothes that would make Wal-Mart look like a Chanel fashion boutique. A model of a Western-style home was displayed, complete with toilets with fuzzy seat covers and La-Z-Boy chairs. Upright pianos and saxophones were also on exhibit. It was like walking through a Sears catalogue, circa 1964.

Of course no building or museum would be complete without several displays dedicated to the two leaders and their godly achievements and love of the common people. It was there that I learned about the "beautiful trend" in North Korea: young virgins married soldiers who were injured during their army training. Pictures prominently displayed on the wall showed women in colorful Korean dresses dutifully standing by their new wheelchair-bound husbands. Oddly enough, I had never seen a handicapped person on the perfect streets of Pyongyang. The disabled didn't belong on the stage.

I also discovered that no weddings would take place in North Korea for the next three years. With the death of their Great Leader Kim Il-Sung, the citizens had to abide by a Confucian tradition that forbids life's pleasures—including drinking, dancing, and sex—during the official grieving period of at least three years. The death of a parent does not liberate a child from his duties of filial piety.

If North Koreans actually remained faithful to this ancient tradition, the Women's Maternity Hospital would remain empty for some time. And judging by what I saw—or didn't see—during my visit there, it appeared as though the procreating had stopped long before Kim Il-Sung's death. A doctor walked briskly through the dark, empty hallways, and announced that people rarely got sick due to the country's excellent "preventive" medicare system. Apparently, the state knew when people were about to get sick, and treated them before they fell ill.

As at the daycare center I had visited before, I was asked to wear indoor slippers provided at the main entrance. I slid down the halls, trying to catch up with the doctor who pointed to empty beds and examining rooms, boasting of the latest imported X-ray machines from Europe. "Our Great Leader wanted nothing but the best for our new mothers."

Speaking of which, where were they?

There was a small roomful of a half-dozen babies but no mothers to go with them. There were no doctors, nurses, or orderlies. In the whole hospital, in fact, there were only two "new mothers" sharing a room, and one woman being examined by the lone doctor on duty. Her head was haphazardly enveloped with tangles of wires—tentacles sprouted out of the wall and wrapped around her skull. Yet the patient sat there, smiling as if she was having the time of her life.

Ushering me through another room, the doctor then informed me that there were as many as fifteen sets of triplets born every year. The miracle was due to the love and care shown to the mothers by the state, he declared. I couldn't help wondering if genetic engineering had anything to do with it. The North Korean population was only half that of the South. This made me realize that I had not seen a single pregnant woman since I'd been in the country, and I mentioned this in passing to Young-Hee later in the car. Lo and behold, a few days later, two very pregnant women were hobbling down the street.

# XXVI

The next day I visited the Pyongyang movie studio, the North Korean version of Hollywood, but there was no action. It was my guess that the actors were all busy walking around downtown Pyongyang posing as civilians.

So, once again, we walked through the empty movie lot and the studios. On one of the sets, the guide pointed to a big rock. He was eager for me to touch it and see for myself that it wasn't real. Of course, this was the Dear Leader's invention, so no actors would get hurt during filming.

I sat in a sound-editing room while the technicians pretended to work on a movie that needed no editing. Each film was directed, produced, written, or supervised by the Dear Leader. He also designed the sets and oversaw the music. According to the plaque on the studio wall, the Dear Leader had given his guidance to the country's arts and culture some 10,900 times.

After walking through fifteen display rooms filled with old movie cameras, copies of scripts, and pictures of the Dear Leader at work, I met the country's two leading stars for an interview. Both in their fifties, they put on a convincing performance. They explained that acting was not a profession but a revolutionary duty. It was their responsibility to set a good example for the public, to show them what true heroes were all about. Foreign films didn't carry any meaning, they claimed. North Korean films were educational and instructional.

Oddly, in a culture built on the personality of the Great Leader, there were no films or fictional representations of his life and heroic exploits. No actor has been awarded the honor of playing the role of Kim Il-Sung or Kim Jong-Il. Like North American movies based on biblical stories, where God is omnipresent but never seen, Kim Il-Sung was portrayed in the same light.

North Koreans knew Kim Il-Sung and Kim Jong-Il existed, but they never saw them in person. They believed in the myth, but knew very few facts. North Koreans—academics, citizens, soldiers, and even government officials like Mr. Lee—didn't know whether or not Kim Jong-Il was married or had any children. There were countless photographs of the two leaders with farmers, factory workers, and children, but I had yet to encounter a single person who admitted to meeting them.

# XXVII

After days of negotiating and pleading, I finally had a chance to visit a farm for an afternoon. We just happened to arrive during the farmers' lunchtime, however, so I wasn't allowed to go into the fields. My minders were concerned that I might suffer sunstroke or get my white shirt dirty.

The local designated farmer proudly started up three machines that were sitting idly under a shed. I was standing in front of the "revolution of technology." The machines looked like the skeletal remains of the Massey-Fergusons I had seen on the Canadian prairies.

"We have forty-eight machines. With them we can cover 638 hectares of land on this farm. We can finish the harvest in ten days. Thanks to our Great Leader, our people no longer have to work manually!" the farmer shouted over the growling engines.

I slowly scanned the fields, hoping the farmer would catch on to what I was trying to tell him. His farmhands were in the field, bent over with towels on their heads, working. Working with their hands. There were no machines in the field. There had been no machines in any of the fields I'd seen in the country.

I genuinely wondered if they knew that I knew they were lying. But I didn't see the point of making an issue of it. Besides, I was already in trouble—again. I had made the mistake of wearing a white T-shirt with a caricature of Henry Miller's face on it. I should have known I was committing a social faux pas by the way Mrs. Lee nagged at me all morning, scrunching her face and making a fuss about getting the shirt dirty. I found out later that I had offended the popular masses, who thought that I loved the Yankees so much that I had to display one of them on my chest.

## XXVIII

For our next tour, we went to the DMZ. Standing on the North Korean side, I felt the impulse to place one of my feet on the South Korean side and straddle the border. But such a small symbolic gesture was pointless and it might have caused an international incident. "You can start a war if you get too close to the line," one soldier warned. "South Korean soldiers will shoot you."

The soldier then explained that thousands of troops from both sides were strategically and inconspicuously deployed within striking distance of the border, ready to go to war in an instant. With its army of 1.2 million men, North Korea has twice as many as South Korea's 650,000 troops. There are 36,500 American soldiers also stationed in South Korea.

The DMZ is located in the Joint Security Area or the so-called Truce Village, better known to the world as Panmunjom. I was surprised and somewhat disappointed to find the DMZ very quiet and almost serene. With its acres of cornfields, sunny blue skies, and cicadas singing in the trees, one of the most heavily militarized zones on earth looked more like a nice place for an afternoon picnic.

The Demilitarized Zone runs 250 kilometers from east to west and is two kilometers wide on each side of the border. This is bisected by the Military Demarcation Line (MDL), which snakes its way across the Korean peninsula for 241 kilometers. The border is heavily secured by electric fences and barbed wire, except for one area where seven identical buildings are set squarely on the MDL. Here, fewer than a dozen soldiers from both sides of the partition stand within steps of each other.

The buildings, which look more like simple, cozy cottages, are where the United Nations (representing South Korea) and North

Korea conduct their meetings. Inside the main conference building, even the felt-covered wooden table is divided in half with a microphone wire. I playfully walked my fingers across the black wire and made a motion to sit on the south side of the table, but my tour guide gently discouraged me.

Though this building is in theory a neutral place, completely accessible to both North and South Koreans, who can cross the frontier just by walking around the table, neither side treated it as such. South Koreans did not enter the building when North Koreans were conducting their tours, and North Koreans returned the courtesy by doing the same.

Until recently, the DMZ housed the neutral-nations commission, which gave four member nations—the Swiss and the Swedes on the south side of the line, and the Poles and the Czechs on the north—the rare privilege of crossing the border. However, the commission went into diplomatic limbo when Czechoslovakia pulled out of North Korea in 1993, and a year later the North Koreans passed a resolution refusing to recognize the commission altogether.

Once upon a time, soldiers from both sides had moments when they could be "friendly enemies," freely exchanging greetings and swapping cigarettes. One South Korean officer told me that he used to kibitz with North Korean soldiers and give them what they most needed: condoms. In a country where birth control and safe sex were practically unheard of, it wasn't unusual for women to hop around like rabbits after intercourse, thinking that this post-sex ritual would prevent pregnancy.

The friendly atmosphere changed after an American soldier, Capt. Arthur Bonifas, was killed by an ax-wielding North Korean during a tree-pruning operation on August 18, 1976. In his honor, a UN command post where 450 U.S. and South Korean soldiers are stationed was named after him—Camp Bonifas. When the tree was cut down after lengthy international negotiations, it was discovered that it had not been planted personally by Kim Il-Sung, as North Korea had initially insisted.

Though I didn't find out the story behind Captain Bonifas's death until my visit to the DMZ, I never forgot the date of this incident. It was my baby sister's third birthday, only two weeks after my family came to Canada. Oddly enough, I also always remembered my mother's birthday because it was the same as the 6-2-5, the way Koreans refer to the Korean War, which started on June 25. The first assassination attempt on South Korean president Park Chung-Hee was on January 21, 1968, the day before I turned one year old.

# XXIX

The most peculiar part of the DMZ is the two propaganda villages located directly across from each other: Peace Village in the North and Taeson-dong in the South. My North Korean guides avoided releasing any information about the Peace Village, but the South Koreans distributed a press kit about Taeson-dong's 236 villagers. They lived under a strict military curfew and other restrictions, but enjoyed generous government subsidies and land holdings. All 236 residents were either original inhabitants or direct descendants of villagers who were living in the area when the armistice was signed.

Residents of both of these farming communities are subjected to propaganda messages that are relentlessly broadcast around the clock from hidden speakers, turned on full volume and guaranteed to damage the eardrums of anyone within a few kilometers. Standing on an observation post on the North Korean side, I could hear muffled American music flowing across the cornfields and read the painted signs that encouraged North Koreans to defect. South Korea Is Free!, Everyone Gets Summer Holidays, and Come to Free Korea! For its part, North Korea had the usual Victory to Juche and Long Live Great Leader Comrade Kim Il-Sung signs.

Obviously, the two villages were forbidden to have contact, yet they competed ferociously. In a kind of absurd "keeping up with the Kims" pantomime, they struggled to outdo each other with their harvests and the volume of their public-address system. This rivalry reached its apex in the competition to have the tallest flagpole. Like a kind of phallic semaphore, each village would erect a new flagpole every few months, only to find their neighbor had raised an even higher one. In the latest round of mine's bigger than yours, the North Koreans had won.

As usual, my minders rushed me through the tour until they escorted me to an observation post to show me the Concrete Wall. According to the Communist soldiers, the wall was eight meters high and it snaked across the peninsula on the South Korean side of the border just a few kilometers away from the DMZ. However, when I looked through the binoculars, to "see it for myself" as my guides insisted, I could barely make out a faint image of what appeared to be a wall. It was impossible to determine whether it stretched all the way from east to west, as my hosts claimed, or only a few kilometers. Noting my skepticism, some North Korean soldiers showed me a videotape of the wall when it was being erected in the seventies and was then cleverly hidden by trees, man-made hills, and mounds of dirt.

With contempt, my North Korean comrades blamed the American puppet regime for the construction of the concrete wall, a physical manifestation of the divided peninsula. They claimed the South Koreans had absolutely no reason to build the wall except to spite their neighbors.

A year later, when I was visiting South Korea and asked my tour guide to show me this mysterious wall, he looked puzzled and asked, "What wall?" He then explained that the "wall" was nothing more than a series of tank traps, concrete structures meant to halt Communist invaders. "There is no wall that stretches the length of the border," he said, pointing out that it would be hard for me to miss if it was as big as my North Korean sources claimed.

Still confused, I asked other South Koreans if they knew about the concrete wall. In the middle of Seoul, in a poor attempt to conduct a random survey, I asked passersby if they had seen or knew about the wall. Many didn't have a clue what I was talking about, but a few stopped to explain that they had heard about the wall, though they had never seen it, and that it was built to prevent North Koreans from digging tunnels to Seoul and staging another invasion.

# XXX

The very last North Korean tour was of the city of Kaesong, the closest city to the border. An interview was arranged with a woman who had been separated from her brother during the war. Most of the residents in Kaesong had family members living on the other side of the border, but until recently, South Koreans would not acknowledge their North Korean kin. Such an admission had brutal consequences: army recruits could not rise to the rank of officer, citizens with political ambitions could not run for public office, private civilians were prohibited from obtaining visas, and people of all kinds were subjected to police interrogations and false arrests.

The woman and I talked in the darkness of a hotel lobby after a power failure. "In my fifty-six years, I've lived under three significant periods," she began. "I lived during the Japanese occupation until I was seven years old, and until thirteen, I lived under the rule of Rhee Syngman, then the president of South Korea. And since the war, I've lived in the arms of the Great Leader.

"In our home, there were my parents and my older brother. My father passed away in 1950. A few months later, our country was invaded. My mother sent my older brother away because he was her only son. She thought if something happened to us, my brother could at least pass on the family name. We didn't know anything about politics. We were told that if men didn't leave the city, they'd be killed.

"We thought he was going to come back after a week, but it's been forty-four years. I don't know whether he's dead or alive. I was only thirteen years old then. I was too poor to go to school, so I worked for a rich family, baby-sitting their children.

"When friends from the neighborhood brought us rice cake, my mother would think of my brother, who left home without anything to eat, and she would store the rice cake in the cupboard until the mold spoiled it."

I was moved by the story. This might well have been the first true story I heard in North Korea.

# XXXI

With two more days to freedom, I had nothing to lose. It was time to confront Mrs. Lee, one on one.

"I'm not surprised that foreign correspondents come in here and criticize your country," I began. "You know, they all come with an open mind. I did. As a Korean, I wanted to understand your people, but I was fed nothing but lies. Next time you plan to invite a foreigner, you should understand that we're not stupid. We're journalists with incredibly fast *nunchi*. We try and try, but your country doesn't give us very much to work with."

Mrs. Lee looked into the distance. She was determined not to acknowledge my presence.

"Do you really think I'm going to return to Canada and tell everybody what a wonderful country North Korea is? Do you think I really believe people when they say they're happy? Do you think I don't know what's going on here?"

The blood drained from her face, but she sat stoically on an ugly green sofa with broken springs. I was sitting on the edge of a coffee table with my legs crossed, facing her. I knew I would eventually have to deal with the consequences of my outburst.

I had tried to explain to Mrs. Lee, back in the mountains, that North Koreans needn't be so stubbornly proud. The world was concerned with their human-rights record, not trivial things like the dirty pair of runners a child ran around in. I had stressed that they were focusing too much energy on all the wrong things. Farmers got dirty when they worked the fields, I had told her. That's nothing to be ashamed of, so please let me take some pictures and talk to them. Desperate, I had repeated the whole business about "the determination of the popular masses," and how I wanted to capture their spirit and strength in my report. I had told her it was the spirit of the people I wanted to record, not empty museums. But nothing had worked.

Now I was reduced to playing the role of interrogator. I told her that I knew about the labor camps in the northern regions of the country, and that international human rights organizations had records of them.

"I was refused a trip to the north because they were afraid I might see something. Isn't that right, Mrs. Lee?"

"We have no jails," she said. "Our people ask to be reeducated if they've done something wrong because they can't live with their guilty conscience."

I was stunned by her answer. For a brief moment, I really thought she believed her own lies. My minders had manipulated the truth to conform to their own reality. It was their way of surviving, the only way to cope.

My whole trip had been about image and appearance. To their credit, my minders had gone to extraordinary lengths to put on a spectacular show for me. True, I never had the freedom to walk around or talk to civilians, but I realized that my hosts were only doing their jobs. They didn't know any other way to treat a foreigner.

Despite my childhood preconceptions about North Korea, I had come with an open mind, willing to learn and understand. But I never imagined it would be such a struggle. At first, when I couldn't get a straight answer out of people, I blamed my own inexperience as a journalist. Then I thought that maybe I wasn't hearing what they were trying to tell me, so I listened to every word over and over on my tape recorder, trying to read between the lines. I even listened to the silences, to see if the pregnant pauses held any significant meaning. But I couldn't make sense of the propaganda. Finally, my frustration turned to anger, and it released all the prejudices I harbored against my own people. Never before had I wanted so desperately to understand my fellow Koreans, but they weren't willing to help me, not even a little. I was being fed lies by my own people, and it made me angry. I couldn't help wondering if I would have felt less insulted had I been a Canadian who had no emotional ties to Korea.

# XXXII

The day before I was due to leave, Mrs. Lee and Young-Hee took turns asking me to write a letter to Kim Jong-Il. I had been a guest in his home, so it was only polite to thank him, they argued. After some hesitation and consulting Max, I finally sat down to write—in English.

Everybody in the house tiptoed around as if I were preparing for a law exam. They expected me to labor for hours over each word. But to Mrs. Lee's disapproval, I wrote the letter while I watched TV, sprawled lazily on the couch. "This is a very important letter," she said, with a certain artificial sweetness to her voice. "Wouldn't it be better to write sitting down at the desk in the study room?"

To avoid any misunderstanding, and keeping in mind Young-Hee's English skills, I used the most elementary and basic English grammar: I've been a good girl and I didn't fight with my minders and I studied hard to understand the state ideology. My only remaining wish is to meet you in person so that I know you really do exist. It was like a letter to Santa.

Examining the English version of the letter with his superiors, Mr. Lee came back insulted. They objected to the use of the familiar "you" in the letter. How did I dare refer to somebody so enlightened and wise as Kim Jong-Il as "you," he raged. It was disrespectful and rude. He wanted me to write the letter again.

For the first time, Young-Hee protested and came to my defense. "That's how the English language is," she said curtly. "There is no other way to do it." Young-Hee spoke with confidence and authority, and assured her brooding boss that this offensive pronoun would be replaced with *Chi-nae-hanun-jido-ja-Kim-Jong-Il-dongji* (Dear Leader Comrade Kim Jong-Il) in the final translation of the letter.

That night, the whole group assembled for a farewell dinner. The Big Boss presented me with the most precious gift a foreigner could ever receive: a Kim Il-Sung button. My promise to take good care of the sacred object was misunderstood by my minders, who immediately assumed it would be enshrined in a Canadian museum. I did nothing to dispel the misconception.

There were heartwarming toasts and speeches by the Big Boss and the Senior Minder, but the dinner menu was a sharp contrast to the first feast. In place of the tender beef and caviar were watery soybean soup and cabbage. I took this to be a subtle sign that I'd overstayed my welcome.

The Big Boss asked if I had achieved all that I had hoped during the visit, but before I could answer, the Senior Minder interjected with a sarcastic snort. "Of course not," he said. Sipping his soup, Mr. Lee casually remarked that he knew all about my discontent and frustration, as if he had been my confidant in the past few weeks. He challenged me to explain the problems with their country as I saw it, but the Big Boss interjected before I could begin. I was the first North American journalist to have been invited to their country for a generous three weeks, he reminded me. That alone deserved good press. "If the reports are critical, we'll have to assume that is because you are still young and ignorant about our country," he said patronizingly. "All we ask is that you tell the truth. Nothing more and nothing less."

After dinner, the two men requested a private meeting. The Big Boss advised me not to breathe a word about my minders. They were just there to guide and help me, he explained, not to influence my judgment. Giving me a fraudulent receipt from the Kyoro Hotel, he then suggested that I shouldn't disclose any information about the villa. That was a secret, he said. Dumbfounded, I asked why. Naturally, no answer was given. "Just do what we say," they ordered. Unsure of what game they were playing, I explained that I had every intention of discussing the villa in my radio documentary. They nodded impatiently. Yes, they knew. What they meant was, Just don't tell other Koreans.

When I gave them a white envelope stuffed with American money to pay for the accommodation and food, they refused to take it. I had been informed by Mr. Chun before the trip that a total of $2,000 (U.S.) would cover the expenses, but now I was being scolded for insulting my hosts. With a wink and a nod, the two men insisted that I pocket the money for myself.

"Don't tell your boss at the CBC or Mr. Chun," Mr. Lee said. "Go and buy yourself something nice. We will tell Mr. Chun that you paid us."

"This is bribery," I said firmly, pushing the envelope across the table.

They pushed it back in my direction. "North Koreans don't need money," the Big Boss said angrily. "This is a cashless society." They finally won.

I gave my copy of *War and Peace* to Young-Hee and asked her to let me know how it ended. It had sat on my night table, untouched, for three weeks. When I had prepared for the trip back in Toronto, I deliberately chose to bring along a book written by a Russian, reasoning that it had a better chance of passing through customs than one by an American. Young-Hee accepted it without a thank-you, as if it was rightfully hers. I slipped the waiter a $100 bill and wished him luck with his plans to study English, though we both knew that would never happen. A bag of gifts was distributed among the house staff, and I thanked my minders empty-handed.

The morning of my departure, the waiter handed me a carefully wrapped bundle of food to eat on the plane. The Junior Minder had already left in the burgundy Mercedes with my luggage, my passport, and the plane ticket. All I could do was pray that she didn't have another flat tire. I was eager to get the hell out of the country and could hardly hide my agitation when the car pulled up at Mansu Hill. Young-Hee and Mr. Lee suggested I lay a bouquet of flowers and pay my final respects to the Great Leader. These people never gave up. Afraid of missing my flight, I compromised and agreed to stand at the foot of the statue—without laying any flowers. As we drove away, I could see a television crew packing up their cameras to leave.

# Back in Little Korea

A year after my trip to North Korea, a hundred questions were still gnawing at me. I finally decided to go to the other side of the border and search for some answers by interviewing North Korean defectors. That was easier said than done, however, as with everything related to Korea. Considered government property, the defectors were under constant surveillance and were subject to strict rules and regulations. They were used for South Korean propaganda, and ordinary citizens were not at liberty to approach them. The only way for me to have access to the defectors was through the government, via the Korean consulate in Canada, and needless to say they were wary about granting permission.

In their eyes, I had made a grave mistake by entering North Korea without their consent. It was their job to monitor the movements of any Korean trying to enter the forbidden North. As far as the South Korean government was concerned, mine was a defiant act, and they couldn't help feeling deeply betrayed. To add insult to injury, they had first learned about my trip through a Canadian newspaper long after I was already in Pyongyang. To them, my Canadian citizenship didn't matter much and my journalistic credentials even less. They saw me only as a traitor.

The pressure was on to investigate the matter. The South Korean government came down on its embassy in Ottawa, who passed the buck to the consulate in Toronto. At the bottom of the pecking order was one Mr. Lee Kee-Woo, a press attaché who was not amused by what he considered a ploy on my part to make him lose face. So when I later came knocking on his door for help getting access to the North Korean defectors, he seized the opportunity to make my life as difficult as possible.

Aware of his motives, I was as sweet and courteous as I could be when he requested a "debriefing on North Korea," and I readily agreed to meet with members of the South Korean government and the press to answer their questions. In the end, all they wanted was reassurance that North Korea was as poor as they had hoped and that I hadn't turned into a Communist spy.

Any refusal to cooperate would have led to false accusations and gossip in the community, which I would have been only too happy to ignore; but I had to consider my parents and their concern with the opinions of their friends and associates. I had to play along with the consulate if I wanted to spare them the guilt-by-association factor.

Though I found these games with the consulate quite amusing, my parents were of a very different mind. The South Korean government still intimidated them and they didn't want to get involved. They had suffered through the aftermath of the Korean War and Park Chung-Hee's brutal military regime. They were there when the government gave birth to the Korean CIA, called the Angibu, which arrested, tortured, and murdered innocent civilians. Understandably, my parents didn't share my delight when I told them about "the file" that officially put me on the blacklist, along with others who had also visited North Korea or were suspected Communists. The potential banishment from South Korea wasn't a particular concern of mine, but I couldn't jeopardize my parents' chances of visiting their homeland in the future.

So once again, I put on my best Korean face and paraded through the community and met its expectations. For about three months after my return from Pyongyang, I became a celebrity in Korean enclaves across Canada. My picture was on the front page of community newspapers. I gave speeches and interviews, and graciously received compliments on my polished Korean. I was showered with invitations to private gatherings, dinner parties, and other social functions where I was coaxed to praise South Korea and denounce the North. The only person to quietly dismiss my unflattering reports on North Korea was Mr. Chun at the *New Korea Times*.

Max and I met with Mr. and Mrs. Chun only once after I came back from North Korea, and that was to give him the $2,000 that Senior Minder and Big Boss back in North Korea had refused to accept. I then explained exactly what had transpired back in Pyongyang when I tried to pay for my accommodation and food.

As it turned out, it took some time to sort out the confusion because everybody was given a different version of the story, and no one knew where the money was supposed to go. According to Mr. Chun, the money was to go to him in the first place. Apparently Senior Minder was to have instructed me to hand it over to the *New Korea Times* as a secret donation. I told Mr. Chun that Senior Minder and Big Boss insisted that I keep the money for myself and advised me to keep the whole affair secret, especially from him. Mr. Chun raised his eyebrows and shook his head skeptically, concluding that I must have misunderstood. He then announced that he had been talking to Senior Minder on the phone the night before, and he had told Mr. Chun that I never presented him or anybody else with the money. Backstabbing, deceitful Koreans, I cursed under my breath. It sounded like a sweetheart deal gone sour between Mr. Chun and Senior Minder. Somebody was trying to rip somebody off and it looked as though they were both going to blame me. Exchanging a knowing glance with Max, I pushed the envelope of money toward Mr. Chun and left his office. As I walked out the door, I could hear Mrs. Chun laughing and saying, "She's so honest!"

Though Mr. and Mrs. Chun were disappointed to learn that my experience in North Korea wasn't exactly enlightening, they never showed it. When my documentary was broadcast, I nervously anticipated an angry phone call from them, but I heard nothing. Several months later, Mrs. Chun finally admitted that she and her husband had "faced some embarrassment and difficulties" with North Korean officials. As my link to North Korea, they found themselves caught in the middle: they couldn't very well defend my criticisms before their comrades, but they couldn't fully dispute my claims either.

When I asked why she hadn't told me of their difficulties, Mrs. Chun shrugged and said, "You're free to say what you want. My husband and I didn't want to pressure you."

In the midst of all the stress of dealing with the South Korean government and its lackeys, I really appreciated these words from Mrs. Chun. She and her husband were the only ones who left me to go on with my business. Perhaps after decades of being ostracized by the community and harassed by the government, they knew better than to meddle. Their absolute refusal to even acknowledge the political shenanigans was quite admirable.

I was saddened when Mr. Chun passed away in February 1995, and

I regretted that I didn't have a chance to thank him or say goodbye. A year later, I dropped by the *New Korea Times* and found Mrs. Chun sitting behind the reception desk, looking lost and scared. In her late sixties, Mrs. Chun was learning to cope on her own for the first time in her life. In a gentle, self-deprecating way, she described herself as a baby learning to walk.

"It's pathetic, I know, but my husband used to take care of everything," she said, tears welling in her eyes. "I just followed. Do you know that I never had to open the door to my own home? In forty-some years, we were never apart. Never! Now I have trouble remembering to take my keys everywhere."

Over lunch, she explained that she had been no different from other Koreans in the beginning. "I didn't like Communists, and just hearing the words *North Korea* used to terrify me. So when my husband wanted to go there in the seventies to meet his sister, I seriously considered leaving him.

"Back then, we were actively involved in the church. Did you know my husband started the first Korean church in Canada? Of course when he went to North Korea, the church demanded he resign as an elder. Oh, the church hates communism."

When I asked Mrs. Chun if there really was a church in Pyongyang (which I wasn't allowed to visit), she nodded. She and her husband had attended it and she even had an old copy of the Bible from the service to prove there was freedom of worship in North Korea.

Mrs. Chun thoughtfully munched on a hot pickled radish and continued with her story: "I had to choose between my husband and the community, and of course I chose my husband. I lost all my friends after he went to North Korea."

The Chuns were political pariahs, on the fringes of the pro–South Korean community, but they handled it with grace and dignity, immune to the community's pressure. When I asked if she had ever thought of moving to Pyongyang after her husband died, she laughed and reprimanded me for asking a stupid question. She declined to explain why it was stupid. As soon as I pressed her for information on North Korea, she became tight-lipped.

"I'll tell you anything you want to know about my husband's life except that," she said sharply.

"But you are the only one who really knows anything about the country," I insisted in vain. "You've been there dozens of times and met with both Kim Il-Sung and Kim Jong-Il. Can't you at least tell me what kind of men they were?"

She shook her head impatiently and gave me a stern look. "I don't know very much. You know how secretive that country is. When we went, my husband and I used to stay in a house like you did and talk to designated people. We didn't talk to the public."

I knew she was lying. She was sitting on a gold mine of valuable information and I had the feeling she was going to take it to her grave, just as her husband had done.

Mr. Chun had written a memoir that was published shortly after his death. I sent a copy to my mother for her to read and summarize for me, since it would have taken me months to wrestle with the language. As suspected, Mr. Chun didn't reveal anything about North Korea other than what I already knew. My mother reported that the book was full of compliments about the country and was largely about his reunion with his older sister. There was no mention of his personal meetings with the two leaders, or of the political intrigue between Mr. Chun and North Korea, the South Korean CIA, and the Canadian Security Intelligence Service. He also didn't confirm the decade-old rumor that he was a double agent, a story that supposedly led Kim Il-Sung to terminate his financial support for the *New Korea Times*.

## II

I had hoped to learn more about the Chuns through the consulate, which undoubtedly had a whole filing cabinet of information on them, but instead the consular staff was asking me for the latest news. Each meeting with the consulate was a pointless fishing expedition that became increasingly frustrating.

My lunch meeting with the consulate's press attaché was at a fancy

Japanese eatery in downtown Toronto. Korean diplomats preferred to treat their guests to Japanese restaurants to avoid the suspicious eyes and curious ears of the Korean community. Their choice also reflected an unspoken admiration for the Japanese culture. Koreans, especially women, are secretly flattered when Westerners mistake them for Japanese but are insulted if they're called Chinese. They will rarely serve Chinese food in their restaurants, but go out of their way to prepare delicate sushi and call their establishments Korean Japanese.

Mr. Lee, the press attaché, was short and stout, and his forehead was unusually shiny, as if it had been polished. In his early forties, Mr. Lee was a typical Korean ultraconservative, who spoke quietly, as if he was almost embarrassed to be seen with me in public. Unable to ignore my professional status but uncomfortable with my gender and age, he had a hard time deciding whether I should be addressed formally or as his inferior. He eventually settled for the latter.

Throughout lunch, he concentrated on his beef teriyaki and seemed quite content to ignore me. To fill the awkward silence, I informed him of my hope to go to Seoul and meet some North Korean defectors, as research for my book. A grimace surfaced on his face. Swallowing the last morsel of his food, he asked, "You think you can do it?"

He wasn't shy about expressing his doubts and immediately discouraged me from writing about a subject that concerned my betters. Shaking his head, he asked what my parents thought about my venture and warned me that Koreans would mock my courageous but foolish pursuit.

Blatantly patronizing, Mr. Press Attaché reveled in his power over me and demanded the following: copies of my published articles, my radio documentaries, my résumé, and any letters of support. I was also asked to forward a transcript of the *Ideas* documentary and any press clippings on it. A week later, I was told that the government was still hesitant about granting me access to the defectors because I was "a nobody in Canada."

"You have to understand," Mr. Lee explained. "We don't think you can do a good job."

Biting my tongue, I told him that a Canadian publisher was confident enough to ask me to write a book on the subject. Still unconvinced, Mr. Lee then asked how big the publishing company was, how many books it had published and sold, and what the company's annual profit was. He demanded a copy of the book contract, as well as a personal letter from the publisher.

Later I discussed the humiliating encounter with my mother. Her casual response only fueled my contempt for Koreans. She thought my anger was unjustified, and insisted I had completely misunderstood Mr. Press Attaché's paternal concerns.

"He just doesn't want to see you embarrass yourself," she said. "Frankly, I'm a bit worried, too."

"Thanks a lot, Mother," I huffed.

"You never wrote a book before," she pointed out. "Does the publisher know that?"

"Yes," I answered. "They gave me a contract and money to write it."

"Really?" She paused. "I don't know what I find more frustrating, my daughter who thinks she can write or the publisher who believes her."

"Mom, cut it out," I protested. I knew she didn't mean any harm. Oddly enough, this was her way of expressing concern for a daughter who had just quit yet another job after a record two and a half months.

"If you write this book, it has to be a best-seller or else Koreans aren't even going to acknowledge you."

"Jesus Christ! Of course it's not going to be a best-seller, but that's not the point!"

"Then why are you wasting your time writing? Why can't you get a job and stay with it and let your mom live in peace? You're probably going to say bad things about Koreans again. I don't have to read your book because I can already see clearly what you're going to say."

"Mom, I have to go," I said, defeated.

"Do you have money? Are you eating? Can you pay the rent? You're not evicted yet, are you?" she asked, neither waiting nor wanting to hear the answers.

"No! I'm dying of starvation and I've been living on the street for the past three months!" I screamed impatiently.

Two weeks later, a box of food with a check for $1,000 arrived at my door.

## III

The incredible frustration of arranging the North Korean trip paled in comparison with the aggravation I had to endure tackling the South Korean government. With North Korea, one naturally expected the usual obstacles of dealing with a totalitarian regime, but what was South Korea's excuse? It was supposed to be a free, democratic country, and the way I was treated was intolerable.

My relationship with the consulate became more convoluted when a senior member of the community felt compelled to volunteer to be my mentor and personal agent. To no avail, I tried to refuse his help, which I knew would inevitably lead to more hassle.

Mr. Kwon belonged to an obscure organization called Advisory Council on Democratic and Peaceful Unification of Korea in Canada, a make-work project for Korean men who pined for more prestigious roles in the community while they tended to their corner stores. Mr. Kwon considered himself a man with friends in high places, such as the consulate and the government. Boisterous and falsely modest, Mr. Kwon had a certain reputation among some members of the community, who thought he was a serious brownnoser, even by their standards. They questioned his ever-shifting allegiances and called him "Sunflower" because he enjoyed basking in the reflected glow of power—wherever it was coming from.

"Don't worry," he said confidently. "I'll talk to the consulate. I'm good friends with them."

Mr. Sunflower promised to talk to Mr. Press Attaché and his colleagues and superiors, and launched a personal campaign to send me to Seoul. He was sympathetic to my frustrations and consoled me over lunches and dinners. "Koreans are so conservative. They don't understand the younger generation," he said. "Leave it to me, I'll talk to them."

Surprisingly, he was as good as his word. A few weeks later, interviews with several defectors were granted. Then, as I had anticipated, Mr. Kwon started to try to control the whole affair. Without consulting me, he managed to convince the Korean Businessmen's Association (KBA) to pay my airfare, and he began contacting Korean newspapers to inform them about my book. When Mr. Sunflower found out that I had refused the KBA's offer, he screamed into the phone. In turning down the money, I had made the KBA president lose face, and he, in turn, embarrassed Mr. Kwon.

"After all I've done for you," he said, hurt. "I talked to the KBA president personally, asking for his help on your behalf."

"Thank you," I said. "I appreciate your help, but I cannot take any money from the Korean community. It would be called bribery and ..."

"What?" he shouted, and quickly changed the story. "You don't understand. They weren't paying your airfare, they just wanted to give you a few dollars to buy yourself lunch when you're in Seoul."

A $2,000 lunch? Exasperated, I explained to Mr. Sunflower that I had refused the KBA for the same reason I had withdrawn my initial request for a discount from the Korean airline. But "conflict of interest" wasn't a phrase familiar to Koreans. This was a country where journalists earned a large part of their income from the sources of their stories.

"Now be a good girl and take the money," he advised.

"I'm sorry but I can't," I insisted. I had never had to work so hard to refuse money before. The angry silence on the other end of the line made me nervous, and I wondered how I had got myself into this mess in the first place. Mr. Sunflower was really furious.

"So this is how you want to play," he snarled. "You think you're so good you don't need me? If it wasn't for me, the consulate would never have agreed to help you. I gave you those interviews and I can take them away. Your trip will be canceled just like that."

Then he hung up the phone.

But apparently Mr. Sunflower didn't hold a grudge. A few days later, he called and pretended everything was business as usual, happily wishing me a good trip. A few days before leaving for Seoul, I went to the consulate to pick up the list of my interviews with the defectors and discovered yet another surprise. Sitting in the office of Mr. Press Attaché was his colleague, Mr. Song, a good friend of Mr. Sunflower's and a member of the Angibu. Mr. Song was responsible for arranging the interviews. I looked at the official itinerary for my trip, arranged by the government, and gasped.

After all this, one bloody interview with a defector! And that was strategically sandwiched between meetings with academics, who would no doubt preach South Korean propaganda, and tours of Samsung and the Daewoo auto factory. This looked too much like the visit to North Korea, and I shuddered at the thought of more tours and lectures.

"I'd like to meet more than one North Korean," I said. "After all, this whole trip is about …"

"There's the interview with the spy. Other than that, there's really no time to meet anybody else. Just look at the schedule. You are going to be very busy," Mr. Press Attaché said.

"Why do I have to go to an auto factory?"

"I think you'll be very impressed by South Korean technology. It's very important for you to see how different we are from North Korea."


# IV


Nineteen years after I emigrated, I was finally going back to visit my home country. It was hard to believe I had waited so long. When I first came to Canada, all I wanted was to go back. Now I was surprised to discover that I wasn't looking forward to it. I was weighed down by my emotional baggage, and I knew my bias would taint everything I saw and heard in Seoul. I was also scared that I'd find myself falling in love with Korea and deciding to stay, which would only confirm what I always knew: I was more Korean than Canadian. What I dreaded the most, however, was the possibility of hating my country and having that hate shatter the idealized Korea I had created as a child and preserved all this time.

# My Hometown

A day after my arrival in Seoul, I found myself sitting in the backseat of a car, escorted by an Angibu man.

"Hankuk is richer and better than North Korea, isn't that right?" the driver asked sheepishly.

"That's a stupid question," I snapped. "Especially coming from the Angibu, who should know better than to ask something so obvious—"

"Weren't you scared?" he interrupted.

"Of course," I admitted. "But there really was no reason to be."

"When I was in school, I thought Communists had red faces and devil's horns," confessed the driver, a junior Angibu recruit. "The first time I saw a real North Korean was on TV a couple of years ago, and I was so surprised to see that he looked no different from us."

"Then maybe he wasn't a real Communist," I teased.

The driver smiled, but stole a suspicious glance in the rearview mirror. For the most part, South Koreans knew as little about North Koreans as the Communists knew about them. So they asked endless questions: Did South Korea have more cars, buildings, and money than North Korea? Did South Korea have more freedom? Which country did I like better, the North or the South? If I had to choose, would I live in the North or the South? Did North Koreans have white rice, or was it supplemented with barley or corn? Did women wear makeup? Did they carry leather purses? What about shoes? Did men wear tailored suits? Did children have fancy toys? Did homes have refrigerators and television sets, and did they work or were they props?

South Koreans were desperately seeking assurances that their country was indeed superior to the Communist North. When I confirmed that South Korea did have more cars, money, and buildings, a look of relief washed over their faces. With a contented sigh, they stated with authority, "Of course, of course. I knew it." When I toyed with their insecurities and pointed out that North Koreans drove Mercedes-Benzes, they became alarmed and demanded to know how many I had seen.

These petty displays amounted to little more than clumsy one-upmanship. All my life, I had been a witness to this relentless competitiveness in Koreans. Everything had to be better and bigger—and more and more and more. Enough was never enough.

Eager to change the subject, I asked my driver if the Angibu still arrested and tortured people.

"No," he replied. "We don't have that much power anymore. That was long before my day."

He was only a year older than me. He had a haircut that made his head look perfectly square and he walked bow-legged, but he had a dazzling smile. He was also tall, with an attractive physique for an Asian man. When I offered him a cigarette, he politely declined. He was a university student by night, majoring in sports.

"I have a black belt in tae-kwon-do," he said, blushing. "But please, go ahead and smoke. It doesn't bother me at all."

"So that's how you catch bad boys—karate chops," I joked. "How many North Korean spies have you caught lately?"

"That's a secret," he said, suddenly alarmed by my question.

Inching our way along in the bumper-to-bumper traffic, the driver pointed to a bridge that was missing its whole middle section, as if it had been neatly sliced and lifted out like a piece of cake.

"The bridge collapsed recently," the driver explained. "The middle part just fell."

The collapse of the bridge had killed thirty-two people, only one in a chain of recent tragedies in the past few months. The biggest was the collapse of the Sampoong Department store in Seoul, which killed five hundred people. Then a ruptured gas line exploded during subway construction in the city of Taegu, claiming more than a hundred lives. This was the price South Korea was paying for an economic growth spurt that came hand in hand with government corruption, bribery, and cutting corners.

After about an hour of circling the city, the driver finally found the right place for my interview with the self-confessed spy. In front of an inconspicuous unmarked building stood a young woman wearing a turquoise dress suit and a pair of white pumps. Rushing over to greet me, she stuck her head in the car and told the driver to come back in an hour.

Angibu agent Hwang Yoon-Jung welcomed me to Seoul and escorted me up several flights of stairs. I eventually found out that buildings with fewer than five stories didn't use elevators (many didn't have them), to save on electricity.

Agent Hwang opened the door to a dark, empty room that looked more like a storage room than an office. There was no computer, no filing cabinets, no fax machine, and the bookcase was bare. A man seated behind an empty desk cheerfully greeted us and phoned the office girl for tea. After a cordial introduction, I gave Agent Hwang a polite smile that said, Thank you but you can leave now. To my surprise, she said she was staying and took out a small notebook. It was blue, the same color as the one my North Korean minder had had.

"You're staying?" I asked in disbelief.

"Yes, just in case you have trouble communicating in English." Agent Hwang, who didn't speak English, never lost her smile.

It took a moment for me to regain my composure. This was not Pyongyang, I reminded myself, but a parallel universe. Taking out my tape recorder and my notebook, I started the interview—for what it was worth.

Oh Kil-Nam went to North Korea in December 1985 with his wife and their two young daughters to teach economics at one of its universities. Born in Pusan, South Korea, and educated at Seoul University, one of the country's most prestigious institutions, Dr. Oh had earned a Ph.D. in economics. In the early seventies, disgusted by the military dictatorship of Park Chung-Hee and threatened with political persecution if he spoke out against the government, Dr. Oh and his wife fled South Korea and immigrated to West Germany, where he became a member of the Socialist Democratic Party. Both their daughters were born there.

In Germany, Dr. Oh was approached by some North Koreans who offered him a job in Pyongyang. "I went without anxiety," Dr. Oh said in English. But "the sky fell" as soon as he and his family arrived. They were taken to a secret camp buried deep in the mountains and were forced to undergo three months of intense propaganda reeducation. "I was a hostage," he said. At Headquarters Number Three, he studied ideology and revolutionary history and watched propaganda films. The only North Koreans he met were secret agents, his minders.

"This sounds very similar to my experience," I volunteered.

He then asked me where I had stayed, and his mouth fell open when I told him. "That sounds like the place I stayed at. Was there a lake there?"

Dr. Oh explained that I had been a guest at a "brainwashing" compound where people were trained to be North Korean agents. "You were extremely lucky they let you go," he said, with a fearful look in his eyes. "You were foolish, very foolish, to go there at all." I tried to ease the tension by telling him about my frustrations of not seeing the "real" North Korea. He practically jumped out of his chair and said, "If you did, they would never have let you go. The reality is too horrible for words and they would never want you to tell the world the truth."

Dr. Oh claimed that there were several camps and villas scattered throughout the city where Korean expatriates were held hostage. They were lured to North Korea from Japan and Europe, like him, with false promises of personal and financial security. No one knows how many hostages there are, but according to international human-rights organizations, both Koreans and foreigners are held prisoner in North Korea.

To date, Amnesty International has published only one full account of political imprisonment in North Korea. Ali Lameda, a member of the Communist Party of Venezuela and a poet, was arrested and held for a year without charge or trial. He was invited to the country by the North Korean government in 1966 to work at the Department of Foreign Publications, where he translated the collected works of Kim Il-Sung, a work that was to be promoted throughout the Spanish-speaking world. Two years later, he was arrested and sentenced to twenty years' imprisonment with forced labor. Public Security agents informed him that he was an enemy of the state. No other explanation was given for his arrest. Lameda was finally freed in 1974 after Amnesty International campaigned for his release.

Dr. Oh was convinced that I had been invited to North Korea to be trained as a spy. After I assured him that I was not brainwashed, we exchanged a couple of stories from Pyongyang, and he clarified the "public phone booth" mystery for me. As I had suspected, the phones were placed there for the benefit of foreign guests, and the "telephone people" would pose at just the time the guest was scheduled to drive by. Only young men and attractive women were chosen for the assignment. Dr. Oh was in Pyongyang when Fidel Castro visited the city, and he remembered months of North Koreans practicing their greetings and memorizing their lines so they could play the role of happy civilian.

Dr. Oh said he was surprised by how many people were kidnapped from abroad and forced to work at the radio station where he was sent after his reeducation. He met about twenty to thirty expatriates, many of whom were from Europe. Their job was to read propaganda on air and to expose the evils of South Korea to the masses.

"How do you kidnap somebody to North Korea? I asked.

"The same way you got in," he said. "You're curious, so they let you in, but they don't let you out."

At the radio station, Dr. Oh had a glimpse of the real North Korea, where people dozed off from fatigue and hunger, fought for extra pieces of meat in their soup, and cried in gratitude when Dr. Oh offered them his. Of the two to three hundred people employed at the station, only four to six had managed to bring their own lunches. Many ate in the cafeteria, which served noodles that broke into tiny pieces because there wasn't enough starch. Only one cow was butchered a day, and that meat was reserved for government officials and foreign guests. (I never did have a chance to ask how Dr. Oh knew that only one cow got butchered a day.) Aside from the severe shortage of food, there were no toothbrushes, toothpaste, or underwear.

"That was in 1985, and North Korea still hasn't crumbled," Dr. Oh said incredulously.

In March 1986 Kim Il-Sung buttons were bestowed on Dr. Oh and his wife. The family was also given a three-bedroom apartment in downtown Pyongyang, on the twelfth floor of a residential building next to the Kyoro Hotel. Compared with other North Koreans, the family lived like royalty, receiving two beers every month and an annual ration of a quarter of a watermelon. His day started at four-thirty in the morning, sweeping the ground though there was nothing to sweep. Every morning, for thirty minutes, he had to polish and shine the portraits of the two leaders which were hanging on his office wall, and attend a service where "revolutionary workers" sang and praised the two Kims. He said he didn't really work because there was nothing to do. A shortage of ballpoint pens meant there was nothing to write with.

On December 13, 1986, when the North Koreans thought he had been safely converted, they decided to send Dr. Oh to Germany via Moscow to "recruit" South Korean students. He had a week to find two students to bring back with him, and his prize would have been a personal handshake from the Great Leader. Instead, Dr. Oh planned his escape. A week later, during a flight change in Copenhagen, he ran, leaving his wife and children in the hands of God. They're still in North Korea, and to this day he doesn't know whether they are alive. Dr. Oh suspects his wife was sent to a labor camp. He heard that she was gravely ill and had attempted suicide several times. This information was delivered to him by two defectors, one of whom (by coincidence, I'm sure) was the very same one I was scheduled to meet later in the week.

"Two defectors from the Yodok Camp told me," Dr. Oh said, as if he was reading my mind. "At first, I didn't believe them, so I questioned them over and over—for two years."

After his escape, Dr. Oh returned to South Korea and asked the government for forgiveness. "I did wrong," he said. "I wanted to be put in jail and I still want to go to jail, but they won't arrest me."

"You were the victim here," I said.

"But I went to North Korea and denounced the South Korean government," he insisted. "This country has laws. It may not suit my personal needs, but I broke the law all the same. The law is there to protect society and I must accept that."

"Fine, but why do they call you a spy?"

"Because that's what I was," he said.

He then praised South Korea for embracing democracy and freedom of speech. "I can badmouth the president, and I do, and it's okay." He laughed. To prove his point, Dr. Oh looked straight at Agent Hwang and started to criticize President Kim Young-Sam's recent decision to send rice to North Korea when the country's crop was wiped out by a flood. He pointed out that the ordinary citizens of North Korea, who needed help the most, would never see a single grain.

Dr. Oh then turned his attention back to me. He reminded me again how lucky I was to escape and that I must be very careful, even in Canada. There were North Korean agents all over the place, he warned, and now that they had my passport on file with my picture and name, it would be easy to track me down. I also had to be careful in Seoul because there were North Korean spies, many of them, roaming the streets, constantly trying to entice students to go to "the paradise without the sun."

Dr. Oh laughed a lot during the interview, and I assumed it was because he was nervous. But I wasn't sure if it was me or Agent Hwang who had made him uneasy. I noticed he made a lot of eye contact with Agent Hwang, and at one point asked her if she was bored, implying that she had heard his story one too many times before. The fact that he showed absolutely no emotion when he talked about his family really struck me. I couldn't help wondering how much of what he said was fabricated by the South Korean propaganda machine. I had to assume the passage of time had perhaps soothed his sorrow, but still, his display of detachment left me a little mystified.

## II

As instructed, the driver was waiting outside to take us to our next appointment, at the Hanyang University with Professor Choi Sung-Chul, a specialist on North Korea. Once we were five minutes into the interview, it turned out that he had more questions for me than I had for him, and it was hard to say who was interviewing whom. Agent Hwang scribbled down every word.

"I know almost everything about North Korea," Professor Choi declared. "How much it's changed, I don't know, but I generally know everything." Professor Choi was born in North Korea and had moved to the South with his family at the age of four. Obviously, he hadn't been back since.

Though he couldn't estimate how many defectors had entered South Korea in the past few years, he spoke of the massive "refugee problem" at great length and stressed the generosity of the South Korean government in indiscriminately welcoming the defectors with open arms. I found it extremely odd that Professor Choi, one of the country's leading experts in this field and the editor of *Human Rights in North Korea*, had no statistics to back up his claims. When I insisted on an estimate, he waved his hands in front of him and muttered, "It's around here somewhere," waving his arm to indicate shelves of books and reports. "Ask the government—it will have the information."

I was surprised to learn that Professor Choi had never personally met any of the defectors. I'd naturally assumed that he would have conducted endless hours of interviews with them for his research on North Korea, but that wasn't the case at all. He really didn't seem to know much about the country, and if he did, he certainly didn't feel compelled to share it with me. I became highly suspicious and began to question the credibility of my interviewee—handpicked by the government—when he admitted that he hadn't even met or talked to Kim Hyun-Hee, the most famous North Korean terrorist, who has been living under house arrest in Seoul since 1987.

As the dean of social sciences and the secretary general of both the International Human Rights League of Korea and the Center for the Advancement of North Korean Human Rights, Professor Choi sounded too much like a mouthpiece for the South Korean government.

After we quickly exhausted his limited store of knowledge on North Korea, Professor Choi began comparing human-rights records in the two Koreas. He claimed that North Korea had committed every atrocity while South Korea had a clean record. He also declared that South Koreans didn't crank out propaganda about North Korea the way it did about them. "I wish it was propaganda, but we just tell the truth," he said. I could only admire the way he lied with such a straight face.

"Professor Choi, the whole world knows about South Korea and its corrupt governments and military dictatorships and student protests."

"Of course, of course." He nodded. "There must be opposition and we let them oppose. They're free to do that because this is a free country."

As far as the radical students were concerned, they expressed pro–North Korean sentiments only because they didn't know better, he said. They'd feel differently if they, too, had lived through the war. "We tell the students, 'You like North Korea so much, go and live there,' but no one ever does. They're just being idealistic."

Feeling completely discouraged, I left the professor's office. The car was waiting for me, just steps from the building, just like in Pyongyang, but I was intercepted by a strange man. He ushered me to a bench nearby and started firing questions at me. He didn't bother to introduce himself, and it was taken for granted that I knew who he was. Angibu.

He asked me about my father's occupation, when I had been to North Korea, and several other questions I had already answered many times. Either they were testing me to see if I was lying or they had a serious communication problem in their department. Then he started in on the book. When was it going to be published? How many pages? Were there going to be pictures of North Korea in it? What about South Korea?

When I asked for his business card, he said the Angibu didn't carry any ID, and when I asked his name, he just grinned and bade me farewell.

# III

For years, my parents had attentively listened to extravagant praises of their homeland from other Koreans who could finally afford to return for a visit. My parents' friends would slump in our living room in near agony as they described how much Hankuk had changed. It had become a wonderful and rich country: everybody in Seoul was a millionaire and Canada's wealth paled in comparison.

My parents could only gasp when they were told that $1,000 was mere pocket change to South Koreans, who couldn't spend it fast enough. The cost of living was so high that it was cheaper to send children overseas to North America to study English than it was to hire private tutors in Seoul. The price of a golf-club membership was more than my mother's annual salary, and the rent on a one-room apartment surpassed the mortgage for a big house in Regina. "Korea is wonderful," they would conclude. "So rich, rich, rich …"

They would then begin to bemoan their fate. They had come to Canada to seek better opportunities and now Korea was the place to make money. If only they'd stayed for a few more years, they could also have reaped the benefits of the new, rich Hankuk. Now it was too late. Caught between the two worlds, they felt as if their hearts and souls were still in Korea while their bodies carried on mechanically in Canada.

"We've turned into country hicks in Regina," a bitter voice rose from the group. "Koreans know how to live in style. And look at us, so frugal and worried."

As the evening passed, the men continued to nurse their wounded pride in the living room with multiple shots of Johnny Walker, while their wives huddled around the kitchen table, picking at the leftovers from dinner. In a chorus of melancholy voices, they declared that the world had changed while they were faithfully embracing the old values and traditions. Now that was out of date even in their homeland.

Then, in a sudden change of mood, the women would exchange stories about their homecoming reception, where "poor cousins from Canada" are whisked off to beauty salons and dress shops for a complete makeover as soon as they land at the airport. They would slap their knees and laugh as they mimicked the terror on the faces of their nieces and best friends, who scorned them for sporting outdated hairstyles and wearing shabby-looking dresses that were never in style in the first place.

It was getting more and more difficult to buy presents for families back home because everything was better in Korea, the women complained. In the old days, back in the seventies, jars of honey and cotton underwear and socks were considered appropriate gifts, but not now. Korea had everything that Canada had, and more.

My mother listened quietly, pretending to be preoccupied with slicing fruit for dessert, but I could tell by the way she twisted her lips, trying to bring a smile to her face, that she was disguising the pain that sat in her heart like a stone. From where I stood, in the corner of the kitchen doing the dishes and scraping off the rice that stuck to the bottom of the bowls, the women seemed to be taunting my mother in their sweet, sympathetic voices. They were wives of university professors, corner-store owners, and other businessmen in the community. My parents were the only ones still holding down blue-collar jobs, and the only couple who had yet to visit Korea. Though they never admitted it, I knew this bothered them.

Nearly two decades later, wandering through the streets of Seoul, I was trying to figure out exactly what it was that was supposed to impress me. What were my parents' friends referring to when they boasted about the new and better Seoul? Was it the gray, concrete skyscrapers, or the smog and the pollution? Was it the heavy traffic, the loud noise of construction at every street corner, or the soldiers that blocked the subway entrances and ranged the alleyways as if the place was under military siege? It certainly couldn't have been the aggressive city dwellers who pushed and shoved their way through the crowds with a grunt, or the hustling cab drivers who didn't know where they were going any more than their passengers because there were no street signs or numbers on buildings. With new roads, bridges, and buildings, Seoul was constantly changing, bursting at the seams, and no one knew where anything was.

Seoul was a maze of alleyways, where deteriorating shacks the size of matchboxes hid in the shadows of modern buildings. There were more company signs in English than in Korean. The few that didn't use English were in Kolish, English words pronounced with Korean phonetics. An American fast-food chain, Hardee's, became *Hadee's*; plaza became *praja*; Real Car Garage Service was *Leal Car gara-gee sevice*; and a beauty salon was written as *booty saron*.

When I came back from Pyongyang, one of the first things Korean Canadians wanted to know was how North Koreans dressed. When I told them, they clicked their tongues in pity. "Go to South Korea and you'll see that everybody dresses well," they said proudly. So I made a special note of it and looked for the well-dressed people in Seoul, but it turned out that South Koreans didn't dress that differently from North Koreans.

Men wore navy-colored trousers with white dress shirts; they all had identical haircuts—short and clean. No perms or sideburns or ponytails, and no mustaches or beards. There were a few rebellious middle-aged men who challenged the fashion status quo by daring to don loud-colored (pink and red were the favorite choices) shirts with white pants, but the majority of the city's population dressed more or less uniformly. Women wore cotton blouses with floral-patterned polyester skirts that fell freely below their knees, and their short hair was permed. Many senior citizens still chose the traditional Korean *chogori* over Western attire: full-length dresses that wrapped tightly around a woman's chest and flared out like a tent at her feet, disguising her figure, were worn with short jackets with sleeves wide enough to hide a small puppy. The style was similar for both men and women, except men wore pants like a genie's. Of course, as always the younger crowd was the exception to the rule.

Myongdong, in the heart of Seoul, was the city's fashion district, where young anorexic women paraded from shop to shop sporting designer outfits and cosmetic surgery. Some were accompanied by their boyfriends, who strutted about in knock-off designer shades and jeans. The sight of young couples holding hands signaled to me how much Korean society had changed. Public displays of affection had been severely proscribed for so long that it was startling to see people spooning in the most innocent of ways. These were not teenagers, but young people in their twenties. Still, to the eyes of a Westerner, they were acting like adolescents.

Although I was amused by the primness of their attempts at courtship, it was at odds with the surgical mutilation of their faces, expressing an almost fetishistic obsession to look American. Their flat noses were delicately raised, their smoothed eyelids cut and folded, and their lips chemically injected to give that pouty, voluptuous look. Every inch of their young faces could be cut with a scalpel, molded with extra skin and fat, and sanded down. Artificially suntanned, they appeared both glamorous and freakish. They were clones of an American-made ideal of Caucasian perfection. In physically altering their features through modern surgical techniques, they were taking an ancient culture based on conformity to post-modern extremes.

Surrounded by these fashion victims, who so slavishly paid homage to Western notions of beauty and consumerism, I felt perplexed. I was never embarrassed to be Korean. I never envied blue eyes and blond hair, and never resented my slanted eyes. I never wanted to be Caucasian; I just wanted the freedom my Canadian friends had. But I felt defeated and betrayed by my fellow Koreans' apparent acquiescence in the corruption of some of their most basic values.

I remember hearing a story from an expatriate who had just returned from a visit to Seoul. While there, he had stayed with an attractive couple who had had so much cosmetic surgery that they no longer resembled their own children, whom he described as "ugly as pumpkins." Then there's the story of a man who married a woman so beautiful that he couldn't believe his good fortune. Yet when their first child was born, he was confounded to discover the child had none of his wife's comely features. His first thought was that his wife had been unfaithful, but she finally admitted that her unnatural beauty was the product of one of Seoul's premier cosmetic surgeons.

Meanwhile, the clones marched in and out of Club Monaco, the Gap, and other trendy fashion boutiques that boasted exclusive designs from Italy and Paris. Sitting in a café, I observed several girls coming in for a break from their shopping spree. Any facial feature that may have been spared the surgeon's knife was disguised by tons of makeup. Pounds of face cream and half a tube of lipstick were applied with care through false eyelashes that obstructed the view. This was their way of presenting themselves as young and single. In a few years, these excessively fashionable girls would abandon their heels and hip-hugging dresses for the polyester frumpery of the traditional housewife.

Reaching into their Gucci bags and Christian Dior purses, the girls checked their beepers, which wouldn't stop beeping. All the customers and waitresses beeped as they moved. I looked out the window and noticed that every passerby also had one, including a group of construction workers across the street and the old lady selling rice cakes between two alleyways.

I was told that the pager was the latest trend in Seoul, and anybody without one would almost attract suspicion. They might get accused of being a North Korean spy. I couldn't believe Koreans were still playing this silly game. Back in the seventies, when I was an eager little patriot on the lookout for spies, it wasn't unusual to hear people remark, "You must be a spy from North Korea if you don't know that." That might refer to the current inflated price of rice, or to the name of a famous actress or a pop star, or to a certain brand of cigarettes or beer.

The combination of the beepers and the hiphop music playing in the café gave me a mild headache, and the $3 cup of weak, lukewarm coffee was no help. Taking out a couple of Aspirin, I tried to get the waitress's attention for a glass of water, which was achieved only by barking at her from across the room. Taking her time, she finally sauntered over to the table and eyed me with slightly annoyed indifference. I understood why no one tipped in Korea.

I went to the washroom and discovered that it was shared by both sexes. In a small booth, a woman squatted over a urinal while on the other side of the panel a man stood zipping up his pants. They were total strangers taking care of their bodily functions within inches of each other without a hint of embarrassment. I eventually learned that most restaurants in the city had unisex bathrooms, with the exception of those in hotels. What made it worse was that the main door of the bathroom stayed open, depriving the occupant of any privacy. From my table, I could see a man urinating, and a woman's pants around her ankles in the next stall.

Leaving the café behind, I stumbled through the narrow, twisting streets of the city, trying to decide what to have for lunch. I had a craving for Korean food, but ironically, it wasn't the easiest thing to find in the midst of McDonald's, Kentucky Fried Chicken, and the other North American fast-food chains.

The few Korean restaurants I did find were little shacks tucked in

alleyways where old men sat idly by the entrance, discouraging any customers from going in. Some noodle places had rolls of toilet paper on
the table for serviettes, and open kitchens that exposed more than the
public needed to see. Piles of dirty dishes, garbage on the floor, the
cook's hands pawing four dishes at once, and the nonchalant way she
blew her nose on her apron were almost enough to encourage me to
grab a Big Mac. When I did finally find a clean and presentable place,
it turned out to be a Japanese restaurant—run by Koreans, of course.

# IV

I stayed with my mother's friend at the Olympic Village in Seoul, in a
two-story condominium that was originally built to accommodate
thousands of athletes during the 1988 Summer Olympics. Mrs. Bak had
a round, cheerful face that radiated contentment. As a favor to her old
high-school buddy, Mrs. Bak was more than happy to shower me with
hospitality and treat me as if I were her own daughter—and that was a
problem. Since my mother couldn't be there to check up on me, Mrs.
Bak worried enough for both of them. She fussed and panicked when
I was late coming home; she coaxed me to eat more and quizzed me
about my personal life. She even went as far as asking me if I'd stay and
live in Korea if she found me a good husband with a well-paying job.

"And quit my work?" I asked.

"Of course. You don't need to work in Seoul," she answered. She
scrunched her face in disappointment when I gently shook my head.

Mrs. Bak was a typical Korean housewife who had too much time
on her hands. When her bank-executive husband left for work, she listened to English instruction tapes and studiously copied down nouns
and verbs on pieces of paper and stuck them on the bathroom wall.

"I memorize and study and read, and I still can't speak English," she
said. "I bet your mother speaks fluent English by now."

"No, she still finds it very difficult," I said. "Besides, you can't learn
English like that. My mother tried for years, but you can't learn English
by memorizing the dictionary."

Discouraged by my comment, Mrs. Bak turned off the tape player and turned on the TV, to the special English channel for the American military in Korea, and watched MTV. Listening to Madonna's "Like a Virgin," Mrs. Bak concentrated on her morning exercises, which consisted of doing the twist on a small, rotating disk.

The Baks knew about my work—thanks to my father, who had enthusiastically sent newspaper clippings about his daughter to every living relative and friend on the south side of the border—but they didn't quite understand what it entailed. Mrs. Bak didn't know the extent of the Angibu's involvement in my affairs. She was under the assumption that I was working with the Korean Foreign Affairs Department (because that's what the Angibu had told her), so when my driver came to pick me up one morning and accidentally revealed his true identity on the intercom, Mrs. Bak's heart started to flutter in fear and paranoia. For days, she walked around the house muttering, "We don't want to cross their path. We haven't done anything." Mrs. Bak was also worried that my Western values would rub off on her twenty-four-year-old virgin daughter, Sook-Hee, who was patiently waiting for the right suitor to come along and take her hand. With a growing sense of guilt, I could only watch as Mrs. Bak transformed herself into a tightly wound ball of nerves before the week was up.

Sook-Hee reminded me a lot of my North Korean translator, Young-Hee, not only in her age but also in her vulnerability. They were like empty vassals who blindly accepted, obeyed, and submitted to the rules of life. After a lifetime of being dictated to by authorities, the girls were incapable of thinking for themselves, let alone making independent decisions.

Like the majority of young unmarried people in Seoul, Sook-Hee lived with her parents. I was amazed to learn that she not only was bound by a nine o'clock curfew, which she accepted without protest, but the thought of moving out on her own never even crossed her mind. Of course, she was a product of her culture, which balked at such an act of independence, but still, I had a hard time imagining such a lifestyle. When I asked her if she didn't feel suffocated, the blank look on her face was no different from that on Young-Hee's when I had asked her if she ever got tired of state propaganda.

Sook-Hee greeted her father at the door when he came home from work and quietly sat on her haunches on the floor as he was ensconced on the sofa watching the evening news. She had never worked a day in her life but managed very nicely to keep up with the ever-changing fashion trends on her allowance. Her only ambition in life was to find a rich husband capable of increasing her present income. She had a boyfriend, but she was keeping the relationship secret on the chance she might meet someone better. She didn't want to gain a reputation as a used woman, she admitted.

After years of hearing how much Seoul had changed, I was disappointed to discover that the people's conservative attitude and feudal mentality had not progressed since the day I left Korea. And as usual, my parents' friends had greatly exaggerated when they described their homeland. Everybody was not rich. Like everywhere else in the world, Seoul had only a small minority of people who enjoyed the wealth, while the rest still struggled to make ends meet. But then again, when a country goes from outhouses to indoor plumbing, and a month's salary doesn't have to be sacrificed to buy beef for dinner, people can't help getting excited about their economic achievements. Sadly, the obsession with money seems to have bankrupted the nation's spirit.

## V

August 15, 1995, was the fiftieth anniversary of Korea's liberation from the Japanese imperialists. South Korea marked the occasion with a week-long series of parades, concerts, and television specials. The highlight of the nationwide celebration was the demolition of the National Museum, which had been the headquarters of the Japanese colonial government during its rule.

I was one of fifty thousand guests invited to attend the demolition, held at the Kwanghwamun Gate in central Seoul. More than a thousand Korean expatriates (mostly from the United States and Canada) had received special invitations from the South Korean government, along with free airfare (I was not one of them), to attend the historic event.

Seoul was dominated by soldiers—thousands of them. They lined the main streets, huddled in alleyways, and filed out of army trucks and buses. Some climbed into their black-and-blue riot gear, adjusting their helmets and body shields. For someone from Canada, whose exposure to men in uniform was limited to RCMP officers riding their horses during parades, it was like walking into a war zone. But Koreans were used to it; the soldiers were a permanent fixture of the city.

The American embassy, a few blocks from the Kwanghwamun Gate, was surrounded by riot police and their trucks. They were stationed there all year round, ready to fight the student protesters who made frequent visits to the embassy with their anti-American banners and Molotov cocktails. Today, the security was greater than usual as the government anticipated the mass student demonstrations that peaked in the summertime, especially on this memorable date. The civilians whose lineup snaked around the embassy waiting to apply for visas didn't seem put off by the possibility of impending danger. They were only mildly irritated at the thought that they might lose their place in line if trouble started.

The security team at the gate took my camera apart to look for hidden explosives and frisked me before they let me walk through one of a dozen portable security checkpoints. Inside the square, I gazed over the sea of white hats with "50th anniversary" badges sewn to the peaks. It was still early morning and the sun was already scorching hot.

I found my way to the press section, where a dozen chairs were reserved for foreign correspondents who were already bored and eager to get the whole ceremony over and done with. They had been summoned to cover a nonevent that would be of very little interest to the world. I think they were almost hoping student protesters would come crashing through the gate, disrupt the ceremony, and at least provide them with a lead for their stories.

Cynically, the journalists thumbed through the press release and cracked jokes. The press kits were all in Korean, as the speeches would be, and there were no translators. If the government was hoping for any international media coverage, it was in for a big disappointment. In fact, it seemed that the organizers had gone out of their way to make it impossible for journalists to cover the event. So, bored and restless, they kibitzed noisily among themselves.

"Hey, what's in the building now?" a British reporter asked.

"A bunch of stuff from the Jap years. It's a museum," an Associated Press correspondent yelped from a few seats down.

"What are they going to do with all the stuff after the building's demolished?"

"Have a garage sale!" another voice shouted, and everybody broke into laughter.

This exchange was typical of the journalists' response to the destruction of the National Museum. Many of these same reporters had just finished covering the collapse of the department store and the bridge in Seoul. They could only shake their heads at the irony. Leave it to bloody Koreans to destroy what is still left standing in the country, they said.

After an hour of listening to five hundred drums beating and watching a troupe of folk dancers, the reporters were disappointed to discover that the building wasn't being demolished after all—not that day, anyway. Only the spire was being removed. Feeling cheated, some journalists tried to escape, but they were warned that they couldn't come back inside once they had left the grounds, for security reasons. The president was going to make his appearance soon. On the off chance that something newsworthy might happen, they fell back into their seats.

The AP correspondent was doodling in her notebook, and two other newspaper men were discussing the O.J. Simpson trial. The British journalist suggested we march to the Foreign Press Bureau and watch the ceremony from the bar on the top floor of the building, but the idea was quickly dismissed. All the windows of the buildings within a ten-block radius were blackened by paint or boarded up to prevent any assassination attempt on the president. So, with absolutely no interest in hearing what President Kim Young-Sam had to say on this occasion, I sneaked out.

## VI

The ongoing political turmoil in South Korea had played an important role in my career choice.

Throughout the eighties, like many North Americans I identified Korea with violent anti-government student demonstrations. I no longer saw the country through the propaganda prism and fantasies of my childhood. The real Korea was in my living room, on the TV screen, not in my head. This was a turning point in my life. A revelation.

The news images of people screaming and running from the tear gas, students being beaten and kicked by the police, and reports of civilian deaths made Korea look like the Philippines and every other tinpot dictatorship. Some students committed suicide by setting themselves on fire and jumping off campus buildings. Many cut off their fingers and wrote their messages to the government in blood. Thousands were arrested, and there were stories of many being beaten and tortured to death by the police.

The Kwangju Massacre in May 1980 shook the nation and forced the world to pay attention. The ten-day confrontation between the Republic of Korea troops and anti–martial-law demonstrators in Kwangju resulted in the death of several hundred (some sources estimate as many as five thousand) civilians opposing Chun Doo-Hwan's rise to power through a coup d'état. The Kwangju Massacre was Korea's Tienanmen Square. It changed Korea irrevocably.

When the president and military dictator Park Chung-Hee was assassinated on October 26, 1979, by the Angibu director Kim Chae-Gyu, the then-general Chun Doo-Hwan used his role as the chief investigator to purge the army and replace its leaders with his colleagues from the Military Academy. Chun intensified martial law under the "purification campaign," closing down all the universities, banning political activities, dismissing thousands of government officials, and barring more than eight hundred politicians, including the leading opposition leaders, Kim Dae-Jung and Kim Young-Sam.

The city of Kwangju, in Cholla province, was Kim Dae-Jung's political power base. Chun Doo-Hwan was from the rival province,

Kyongsang. Former president Park Chung-Hee, who came to power through a military coup in 1961, was also from Kyongsang province. During the Park regime, Cholla province was deprived of its share of economic development, as Park concentrated on pouring money into his home constituency, Kyongsang-do. All the South Korean presidents have come from Kyongsang-do, and I grew up hearing that the province would perish if the country ever saw a Cholla-do man come to power.

The intense hatred between the two provinces had its roots in ancient tribal rivalries. Discrimination and prejudice ran so deep that a wedding between a person from Cholla and one from Kyongsang was bitterly opposed. This was Korea's version of interracial marriage. Even at harmless dinner parties of Korean expatriates in Canada, the underlying tension between those from Cholla and those from Kyongsang was palpable.

During the Kwangju Massacre, Koreans had hoped for American intervention, since the ROK army was basically under U.S. command. But that never happened. The Americans watched passively, turning a blind eye when Chun sent in the ROK special forces and the men from the Twentieth Division, deployed under American command, opened fire on the helpless citizens.

This set the stage for growing anti-American sentiment.

Student activists began to hold the United States responsible for the Kwangju Massacre, the division of Korea, and pretty much everything else that was wrong with the country. The activists became increasingly radical and militant, and many came to regard the pro-democracy movement in the same light as anti-government and anti-American ones.

Despite Chun's efforts to suppress the opposition by firing professors and expelling students suspected of anti-government activities, and even planting secret agents throughout the campuses, the students remained unshaken. The universities became an oasis for their struggle for democracy.

In May 1982 university activists set fire to the United States Information Agency building in Pusan; in 1985 hundreds of thousands of riot police were deployed to suppress the student protesters; in

October 1986 more than two thousand students were arrested after twenty thousand police broke up a mass meeting of students at a university in Seoul. Then, in January 1987, the police tortured and killed Park Chong-Chol, a student from Seoul National University, during an interrogation. Many students had died at the hands of the police before, but this time the death didn't go unnoticed. The public outcry forced Chun to dismiss the head of the national police as well as a cabinet minister.

Meanwhile, the mass rallies continued and the opposition parties demanded a direct presidential election. When Chun refused, the students, joined by businessmen, laborers, and even housewives, took to the streets of Seoul and other major cities in the country. This time, Chun could not suppress the public through military force. The 1988 Seoul Olympics were just around the corner, and the president had received a direct warning from the Americans that they would not tolerate any more military intervention.

In February 1988 Chun finally caved in under the relentless public protests, orchestrated by student activists, stepped down as president, and called for the first presidential election in the country's forty-year history. But for the students, this was not enough. They still wanted the American troops out of Korea and demanded unification with the North.

In 1989 Lim Soo-Kyung, a South Korean university student, defied the government ban on travel to North Korea and visited Pyongyang via several Third World countries. Representing Chondaehyop, the National Association of University Student Representatives, Lim participated in Pyongyang's World Festival of Youth and Students. She returned to South Korea by crossing the border and was immediately arrested and sentenced to five years in jail for violating the National Security Law. Lim Soo-Kyung had set a precedent for other students.

I couldn't think of the Korean students' anti-American sentiments without reflecting on my own childhood in Korea and those handsome, blue-eyed GIs who had delighted me with Hershey chocolates and Juicy Fruit chewing gum. Koreans loved them then. They used to cheer, "America okay! American number one!" Now they shouted, "Yankee go home!"

My father had worked for the U.S. Eighth Army in Itaewon and that had made him the most envied man in our neighborhood. Even my teachers worshiped the ground he walked on, and treated me like a star student. They knew they could benefit handsomely by using me to reach into my father's wallet.

In the seventies, when I enrolled in elementary school, teachers routinely accepted bribes. On the first day of class, they'd carefully scan the sixty-some students and divide them into two categories: rich and poor. The rich sat in the front of the classroom, and the poor went to the back; the well-dressed children were spared from corporal punishment, and the others were slapped around; the students with white rice and beef for lunch had the privilege of sharing it with the teacher, and those with barley and cabbage were chastised for eating too slowly.

My parents never admitted to slipping the "white envelope" to my teachers, and as proof, my mother always said that was why I got beaten up in school. But I know my parents were guilty of bribery when they sent me to a private kindergarten, because I often received mysterious awards for artwork I had no memory of having created.

My mother must have been telling the truth to some degree, however, because something terrible happened when I was in Grade 3. I got demoted from being the teacher's pet to being her slave. I was moved from the front row to the back of the class, and she often ordered me to walk to her home and fetch her lunch. I remember running there during my own lunchtime, in the winter, and running back with her meal before it got cold. If I didn't do it, I'd get beaten up for disobeying the teacher. She made arbitrary decisions to punish me, and there was nothing my parents could do. Korean teachers had the right to beat their students black and blue.

There were two kinds of corporal punishment that were especially painful and humiliating. The most common one involved hitting the student's open palms with a wooden stick. If the teacher was in a particularly nasty mood, she would strike across the knuckles instead, though she used a ruler to avoid breaking bones. My teacher reveled in

her power. She'd hit us harder if our hands shook nervously in anticipation of the blow.

The second method of punishment was even worse. I had to kneel
in the corner of the classroom, facing the wall, and hold a wooden chair
above my head. If my arms got tired and the chair wobbled, my teacher
got angrier, screaming at me until tears stung my eyes.

Teachers beat students; parents hit children; children kicked the dog.
The old slapped the young; the powerful crushed the weak; the government shot civilians. This was Korea's way of maintaining order.

In three short years, from ages six to nine, I had been a witness to
bribery, corruption, physical violence, lies, and injustice. When I recalled
my childhood, the political turmoil of modern South Korea didn't
shock me at all. My school had been a microcosm of the state.

As the student protests continued throughout the eighties and into
the next decade, even the most avid supporters were getting tired of the
unending violence and disruption. In my own family, though I remained
faithful to the cause and cheered the students on, my parents gradually
lost their sympathy for the activists and dismissed them as troublemak-
ers. The Korean press portrayed the students as an extremely small
minority of radicals who were influenced by their professors and by
Communist propaganda, and many Korean Canadians accepted and
supported the lie. At home, I was told the student activists were militant
thugs who took their problems out onto the streets because they had
failed their university entrance exams and couldn't find employment.

Although many Korean Canadians blamed the students for giving the
world such a bad image of their country, I had never been so proud
to be Korean. The people were fighting back and I wanted to be a part
of it. I wanted to be one of the students throwing Molotov cocktails
in the name of democracy. I pleaded with my parents to let me go to
Seoul and join the student movement, to no avail. Nevertheless, I had
been inspired by the students to help change Korea and all that was
wrong with it. If I couldn't do it from within, I would do it from the
outside. I would tell the world the truth that the Korean press clearly
refused to reveal.

So, in distant but somewhat meaningless solidarity, I marched over to the students' union at my own university and wrote for its paper. Within a year, I was so engrossed in student politics that I was elected to office. I boycotted a variety of products, including Chinese beer and South African wines. Then, as my ultimate act of sympathy for the Korean students and a symbol of my renascent patriotism, I sewed a Korean flag on my jean jacket and wrote my first political-science paper on the democracy movement.

Still, I developed my interest in Korean politics accidentally. Or perhaps it would be more accurate to say that I kind of bumped into it along the way.

Throughout my Canadian schooling, my teachers and fellow students assumed that I knew everything about Korea, from ancient history to religion to contemporary politics. I thought it was unfair that I was expected to be an expert on all things Korean when my Canadian friends didn't even know the words to the Canadian national anthem. But the questions were simple at first. What did Koreans eat? Did it snow in Korea? Was I from North or South Korea? Did Koreans speak Chinese? Japanese? What was the difference between us and them?

As I got older, however, the questions became more challenging. What was the country's population? What was the nation's GNP? What was the difference between the Vietnam War and the Korean War? How often were Korean elections held, and how many parties participated in the process? What was Shamanism and did people still believe in it? How the hell was I to know?

Too proud to admit ignorance, I ran to my parents and to encyclopedias in search of answers. What's Korea like? Why are the students demonstrating now? Korea, Korea, Korea. I spent hours in the university library digging for information and soon realized how little my country mattered in the West. There were only half a dozen books written on Korea, and two of them were about ancient ceramic art. The two slim volumes on Korean history and politics were out of date, and their contents reflected the biases of the Korean authors. Old and dusty, the books leaned against the shelf like forgotten carcasses, rubbing against fat volumes on Japan and China, which crowded many shelves.

Newspaper clippings were no better. Aside from a few stories and photos of student protests, the Canadian dailies chose to ignore Korea altogether. I wanted to help change this Western indifference to my country.

# VII

Although I felt I did my part to agitate Koreans from afar, I really wanted to meet some student activists who were trying to change the system from within. Through Steve Kim, a contact in Toronto, I was hooked up with a secret informant, a former student activist named Park Hyun-Jun. Hyun-Jun had spent a few weeks in Canada with Steve one summer, and to return the favor he was willing to stick his neck out for a complete stranger. As a recent journalism graduate, Hyun-Jun was more than happy to talk to a foreign journalist, but he couldn't hide his paranoia about the Angibu.

"Were you followed?" he asked, looking suspiciously around the restaurant where I met him.

"I don't know." I shrugged. Seoul was the world's tenth-largest city, with more than ten million people. I wouldn't have noticed if the whole secret service was following me.

Hyun-Jun fidgeted in his seat and instinctively looked over his shoulder every few minutes. He confessed that he was breaking the law simply by talking with a Korean whose feet had touched North Korean soil. He suspected that I was being followed and watched around the clock, and that my phone was probably tapped. "Always use a public telephone," he warned.

Hyun-Jun had a smooth moon-shaped face with bright, eager eyes. He wore a baseball cap, a pair of faded jeans, and a white T-shirt, which was partially drenched with sweat. When I noticed that he didn't carry a beeper and that his shirt didn't bear any trendy, corporate logos, I knew immediately we'd get along. If he was right in his theory about the secret police, Hyun-Jun had every reason to be nervous as he told me about his years as a student activist. The Angibu routinely posed as journalists, university faculty members, and seniors to spy on student dissidents. They also tapped phone lines, intercepted faxes, and had access to the computers in both the universities and the private homes of suspected students.

When Hyun-Jun was convinced that I wasn't an agent, he phoned his friends to meet us. At the request of the other three students, I didn't record their names, and to distinguish between them I noted them as Kim, Lee, and Chung. And of course Park.

We were in a teahouse in a bohemian village quietly tucked away in the city, away from the traffic and the American fast-food chains. Artists and their works spilled into the alleyways leading up to the café, and I eyed ceramic bowls and vases, oil paintings and charcoal sketches in the hope that I could come back later for a shopping spree. Inside, the teahouse was dimly lit and decorated with works by local artists. It was like a sanctuary—until we showed up. The cozy ambiance of the café was disturbed by this group of opinionated students who loudly vented their discontentment.

Park's first exposure to student activism was guarding the corpse of a Yonsei University student shot and killed during a protest.

"I watched the student's mother and sister shake the body and scream at it to wake up, but for some strange reason I wasn't really affected," Park admitted. "I guess I was in shock. But after a while, I started to get angrier and angrier, and that's when I decided to fight."

"South Korea has free elections now, so what are you fighting for?" I asked.

"We want the thirty-seven thousand American troops out of Korea, we want the government to abolish the Angibu, and we want the government to allow direct communication between North and South Korean students on reunification." Lee spat out the demands.

After this opening statement the others joined in, talking and bantering as if I wasn't even there. For two hours, they floated from topic to topic, touching on Korean anti-American sentiment, their admiration for Kim Il-Sung, their fear of the secret police, and their days in the army.

"Korea isn't democratic," Kim cried. "The world thinks South Korea is rich and free just because we export Hyundais, but there's still a very big gap between the rich and the poor."

Kim was the only girl in the group. She was as thin as a willow, but she had a harsh edge to her voice that made her appear tougher.

"We take one step forward and ten steps back," she said. "The more things change, the more they stay the same. My friends are still getting arrested and thrown in jail. People think everything's changed, but there's still censorship, oppression, and police brutality. What has changed is that the government does a better job at covering things up now."

The students told me that one of their colleagues was confined to a wheelchair after he was beaten up by the police; that one of their friends had lapsed into a coma right after he came out of a police interrogation; and that a classmate poured gasoline over his body and jumped off the roof of a campus building during a protest. All four students had friends still in jail. Yet as they described what happened to some of their friends, they stayed calm, unmoved.

"I was proud as a student when I saw my fellow student set himself on fire for our country," Chung said quietly.

"Do you know what it's like to inhale tear gas?" Kim asked.

"No," I said almost apologetically.

"What is North Korea like?" Chung asked quickly, changing the subject. "It's not as bad as people think, is it?"

I didn't know where to begin. These students didn't know anything about North Korea, and their heads were filled with idealistic but naive views about the Communist North. They believed it was a socialist state, and not a totalitarian regime. Some were even under the impression that everyone enjoyed equality in North Korea because that's what they thought communism was all about. Many of them really didn't understand the differences between Marxism and Stalinism. But that wasn't their fault.

All books on communism and socialism were officially banned in South Korea until a few years ago. Even schoolteachers and university professors were prohibited from reading Marx and other left-wing literature. It was hard to imagine what the students were taught in their history and political-science courses, and how on earth the teachers could have justified condemning North Korea when they couldn't provide any historical context.

"The teachers just tell you that North Korea is bad, bad, bad." Park and his friend mimicked their teachers and laughed. "We didn't know that they didn't know, so we believed them. But when we started university, something smelled funny, and that's when we discovered everything was a lie."

What little information they had accumulated over the years came from reading the books circulating underground. They read, without suspicion, the biased words and descriptions of North Korea written by Korean expatriates from China and Germany. Many students also bought into North Korean propaganda, including the pamphlets and letters that were placed inside helium balloons and floated across the border. North Koreans also had special pop guns that shot out messages enclosed in little canisters. And there were North Korean spies who entered the country and infiltrated the student organizations. Some people believed Communist spies were behind all the student protests.

The students I was talking to assumed life was better on the other side of the border because "it couldn't be as bad as or any worse than here." Chung was even a great admirer of Kim Il-Sung and his Juche Idea.

"Kim Il-Sung kicked out all the Japanese and Korean traitors after liberation. He was a true patriot," Chung said. "But in South Korea, the same bastards who helped to kill and destroy the lives of their own people were promoted. Just look at Park Chung-Hee. He was trained by the Japanese army and he became the president."

Chung and his colleagues also spoke indignantly about the reunification issue.

"In the Second World War, Germany was the aggressor and it was divided, and rightly so, I think," Kim said excitedly. "The same thing should've happened to Japan, not Korea. Why is Korea divided? We were the victims, not the aggressors. We didn't do anything wrong, and what's more, we were divided by our allies."

Everybody around the table vigorously nodded in agreement, cutting each other off in their haste to get their ideas on the table.

"How does it look to the world when we can't even work out our own problems …"

"Yes, so we must be unified and sort out the problems …"

"We're not saying North Korea is perfect, but its government looks out for its people's welfare, unlike South Korea. We're just proposing taking the best things from the two countries and putting them together to work toward …"

"North Korea is much more patriotic and more Korean than we are …"

"Yes, we're so American influenced. That's not good. We want to be pure Korean …"

Lee, who was deep in thought while his friends threw out their incomplete ideas, began to reminisce about his days in the army. All Korean men, with very few exceptions, served three years in the army.

"I was assigned to the DMZ and I really liked it there. It was so peaceful," Lee said. "I got to read the propaganda papers and listen to the North Korean broadcasts. In fact, when I was in the army, two soldiers defected to North Korea. Not because they thought North Korea was necessarily better but because army life was so brutal.

"For three years, we're trained to obey like dogs. They break us down. We go through a reeducation process where we watch three hours of propaganda videos every day, and we receive six weeks of training about the evils of Kim Il-Sung. We are told about cases of South Koreans who turned into spies and of other defectors who are miserable in North Korea.

"I was a university philosophy major when I joined the army, and I was told that I was a dangerous person because I spent too much time thinking. So they made me forget to think. They assigned mindless tasks. For example, I had to run and pick up pebbles, one by one, and run back and arrange them in whatever shape my commander directed that day. When that was complete, I had to repeat the process, arranging the pebbles in a different shape. Once I was made to kick a tree until it fell.

"The army knew I was involved with the student movement, so I had to write essays on my thoughts on the student organizations and repent. Every day, I wrote the same thing and answered the same questions. It was the worst torture, worse than any corporal punishment I got. There are many soldiers who try to commit suicide and some succeed. Many more try to run away. I know I almost did."

The students then exchanged notes about the soldiers who were assigned to fight the protesters.

"They're not the bad guys," Chung said. "I feel sorry for them. They're our brothers and friends and classmates. During one of the protests, I was punched by a cop in riot gear. As soon as we each recognized who the other was, we started laughing. That day, we spent most of the time joking and goofing around."

It seemed that everyone took turns fighting for both sides. Student activists joined the army and were often assigned to crush their fellow students. Once they were discharged, they crossed the line and joined the students again.

"Don't you think there's something wrong with that picture?" I asked, confused. "I mean, when you fight, you supposedly stand for something you believe in, so how can you change sides just like that?"

"You try saying no to the authorities. You'll die," Kim said. "It's the system that's wrong, not us."

"So what happens after you graduate? Do you continue protesting?" I asked.

"No. It's finished," Lee said.

"What's finished?" I asked.

"Our job," he answered.

"So what do you do then?"

"We get a job, get married, and have children," Lee answered casually, as if it made perfect sense.

"So that's it? All that screaming and anger and frustration go away, just like that?"

"We want stability, too," Chung said quietly. "In South Korea, you die without money. You have to make money."

"But I thought it was hard to find employment if you participated in antigovernment protests," I said.

"If that was true, no one in Korea would have a job," Lee said with a laugh. "You have to understand that the majority of university students take part in antigovernment activities. It's a big part of a student's life."

Most students washed their hands of the movement once they joined mainstream society, and it was their turn to look at the next generation of student activists with the same disapproval as the generation before had looked at them. Some of them joined the Angibu, a branch of the government they had tried to destroy as students, and some were even elected to government and helped to implement laws designed to suppress opposition.

The predecessors of these students had rallied against the Park regime, the generation before that had brought down the Rhee Syngman government, and before that the people had marched in protest against the Japanese occupation. Round and round they went.

I offered Canadian cigarettes to the smokers at the table, lit one for myself, and inhaled deeply, reminding myself not to take Korea to heart from here on. I had spent my whole life caring about a country that I really had no ties to except for the fact that I was born there. Like these students, and the generation before them, I had allowed myself to be governed by emotion when it came to my country—a place I barely knew.

I was disheartened to discover the students' pragmatic attitude toward the struggle for democracy, and in my anger came to the conclusion that this country was full of hypocrisies and contradictions. Students attended anti-American protests wearing Levi's jeans and Gap shirts, and many hoped to immigrate to the United States in search of better opportunities. They rebelled against the establishment and detested those in power but aimed to join them on graduation. They wanted reunification with North Korea but neglected to consider the political and economic implications of such an act.

But I couldn't tell them that. I had no right. My observations and opinions didn't belong here, not when I knew that the students were instrumental in changing South Korea. They had helped to bring the country closer to democracy. South Korea would still be a fascist nation run by a military dictator if it weren't for the millions of students who risked their lives to fight for justice throughout the past five decades. I knew all that. Yet I still couldn't help feeling disappointed at the discovery that their sense of commitment came with an expiry date.

A few days later, when I visited Yonsei University and talked to some student activists, they were hard-pressed to find convincing arguments to justify their planned demonstrations for the week. Some freshmen simply regurgitated what their seniors had told them about North Korea, while many more frowned and confessed to feeling apathetic about the whole movement. One of the organizers admitted they weren't as well organized this year because the student leaders had a hard time reaching an agreement on their mandate. Many wanted to protest under the banner of reunification, and others voted to protest the presence of the U.S. troops in Korea. Another group thought the most important issue was to call for a public trial of former president Chun Doo-Hwan for the Kwangju Massacre, and still others wanted to fight for changes to the labor laws and call on the unions for support. In the end, protests were poorly organized and scattered throughout the city.

The students no longer knew exactly what they were fighting for. Issues weren't black and white anymore. It wasn't the eighties, when the Chun government openly fired on innocent people. It wasn't the seventies, when the Park regime jailed civilians without trial. President Kim Young-Sam was elected by the people, and the two former presidents, Chun Doo-Hwan and Roh Tae-Woo, were facing trial on bribery and corruption charges. The general public was quite content with the economic boom and no one was going hungry. Of course there was still censorship and corruption, but these weren't as blatant as they had been before. Injustice came in a more subtle and sophisticated package now, and it was harder for students to take it to the streets and win public support as well.

# VIII

The young man leaned over the table awkwardly, cautiously avoiding touching my hand with his, to accept the light I offered him for his cigarette. He sat down and pressed his back firmly to the chair, as if he were trying to get as far away from me as possible without actually getting up and walking out. Like a fugitive afraid of detection, he kept his eyes lowered and spoke in a soft voice that was hardly audible. This was Kang Chol-Hwan, the infamous defector.

Now in his mid-twenties, Mr. Kang had all the features I had come to identify as North Korean: thin weatherbeaten face and sunken eyes with murky brown pupils that didn't stop shifting. A look of weariness suffused his face.

We met at the Sejong Hotel coffee shop, and the ever-present Agent Hwang made sure we knew we had a time limit. Mr. Kang had another interview later in the day. Since he had entered South Korea in the summer of 1992, Mr. Kang had told his story a thousand times over, and he was still making the media circuit to carry out his South Korean agenda.

His testimony about escaping from a labor camp was published in several of the propaganda books I was given by my interviewees and Angibu agents. Though South Koreans claimed there were so many defectors that they couldn't keep count, I couldn't help noticing that Mr. Kang's story seemed to be the only one that was published in these books.

I started to get a little suspicious of these publications when I realized they focused only on Yodok Camp, the labor camp where Mr. Kang had been imprisoned for ten years, but didn't mention anything about the dozen other slave-labor camps that allegedly "incarcerated 200,000 political prisoners." And it was quite a coincidence that the wife of Dr. Oh, the self-confessed spy, was also held at Yodok Camp, and that Mr. Kang had just happened to witness Mrs. Oh's arrival and her subsequent suicide attempts. According to the official source, Yodok Camp had about fifty thousand inmates.

The published accounts of Mr. Kang's ordeal—which were full of errors and discrepancies—highlighted his experiences of raising rats for food and fighting other inmates for pig bones. Some books stated that he had spent ten years in the camp, and others claimed it was eleven. Most seemed to agree that he was sent there in August (or October) 1977, when he was nine years old. A few books stated that he was arrested in the middle of the night; others claim it was morning.

Officially known as the No. 2915 Korean People's Guard Unit of No. 15 Control Office, Yodok Camp is in South Hamgyong Province, about a hundred kilometers northeast of Pyongyang. Mr. Kang recalled the prison as being nestled in steep mountains. He said he and his whole family were sent there because his grandfather was accused of being a traitor to the country.

According to one publication and my own notes from the interview, Mr. Kang defected to South Korea via China with a fellow inmate in the spring of 1992 (August in other books). When I asked him how he had managed to run away, he shrugged. Taking a thoughtful drag on his cigarette, he said he had bribed one of the guards, but he didn't say with what. When I pressed for more information, he said it was a long, complicated story, and pointed out that everything was explained in the pile of books sitting before me. Later I searched in vain for an answer in the pages.

We continued our interview over sushi at a Japanese restaurant. Mr. Kang explained that underground organizations did exist in North Korea, especially in the universities, but they remained powerless. If caught, you would be brought before a firing squad. He then explained that people got arrested if they failed to save the front page of the newspaper and return it to the state in mint condition. It was against the law to deface pictures of Kim Il-Sung, let alone use newspapers for toilet paper, as North Koreans still did.

North Korean civilians were also forbidden to visit Mt. Kumgang because it was too close to Panmunjom. And when Korean expatriates from Japan came to visit their family members in Pyongyang, minders and officials routinely demanded bribes. The family reunion was always cautious because all apartments are bugged and visitors are rarely left alone. Kang recalled one incident where a government agent slept between a daughter and her mother, visiting from Japan, to prevent them from passing information in the middle of the night. "The mother looked years younger than her daughter, so we knew which country was richer and better," Kang said.

For every forty households in an apartment complex, there were a few informers whose job was to spy. Children denounced their parents, parents denounced their friends, and students denounced their teachers. Still, as in every other society, capitalist or Communist, there was no shortage of prostitution or crime.

# IX

Feeling disheartened after all these interviews with government mouthpieces, I tried to cancel my meeting with Kang Induk, a North Korean expert and the publisher of the *East Asian Review*. But after a series of panicked phone calls from the Angibu, who insisted that I couldn't possibly insult a man of Kang's stature by canceling, I went.

Agent Hwang was already at the Sejong Hotel when I arrived. While waiting for Mr. Kang, she and I bonded. Her face, as soft and smooth as tofu, was buried under layers of cream, which glowed most unflatteringly under the fluorescent lights. Ms. Hwang was my age, married, with a child. When she told me that her husband was also with the Angibu, I was most tempted to joke about their "pillow talk." She cautiously admitted that her days as a career woman were numbered because she was expected to leave her job voluntarily to take care of her home. But in a way, she was looking forward to it because working for Angibu was just an ordinary job with very few perks. She then surprised me by admitting to the time she spent as a student activist during her university years.

"How can you work for the Angibu when you protested against them?" I asked.

"Protesting was my job as a student. Angibu is my job now," she answered matter-of-factly, emphasizing that she wasn't a leader or a Communist rebel, so it didn't work against her when she applied for her job.

When Mr. Kang arrived, we all moved to a bigger table in a corner of the restaurant. Kang Induk was an articulate and animated speaker who gave as fair an assessment as his pro-government sentiments allowed him to when it came to criticizing both the political system and the student movement in South Korea.

Student protests were a healthy sign of progress, he stated. It was a true sign of democracy when freedom of assembly was guaranteed. Still, he hastened to add, young people today were spoiled. "Their bellies are full. They have the luxury and the opportunity to concentrate on the wrongs of our country. You can't do that if you are scrounging for food."

According to Mr. Kang, the South Korean government was too confident of its mission to be hindered by student protests or threatened by North Korean spies. "We can teach about socialism now because the world has changed ... and we won economically. North Korea is no longer a threat," he said. He then cited an example where one spy openly talked to thirty or forty people and no one had bothered to report him.

"North Korea can't bring South Korea down," he said. "It would've been possible thirty years ago when North Korea was ahead economically, but not anymore. North Korea is so far behind that it can't possibly catch up to South Korea. It'll take at least twenty years just to get to where China is today."

I thought it was very unfortunate that even a learned man like Kang Induk could speak only in terms of dollars when discussing the spirit of a nation divided.

# X

After my out-of-town visit to the Daewoo auto factory, in Inchon city—four hours of total driving time and fifteen minutes for the tour itself—which was scheduled to coincide with a citywide student demonstration in Seoul, I went to an interview that was arranged by the Angibu at the last minute after a lot of pleading on my part. It was with excitement that I entered another unmarked building hidden away in a back street to meet Kim Hyun-Hee.

An attractive woman in her early thirties gracefully entered the room, wearing a soft kitten gray dress suit and a heavy gold chain around her slender neck. Her shoulder-length hair was tied with a black velvet bow. Her voice was seductively silky. She was accompanied by three government agents, who took up strategic positions. One stood on guard by the door, one sat right behind her, and the third sat next to her with a notebook and a tape recorder.

We were in a room that was starkly empty except for a few hard wooden chairs and a big table carelessly thrown in the middle. Poorly lit, with fluorescent lights that blinked every few minutes, it looked more like an interrogation box. It was then I noted that all my interviewees had met me outside their homes. As in Pyongyang, I never had a chance to see how the North Korean expatriates really lived in their new country.

Sitting across the table from her, I was momentarily entranced by the young woman's delicate features. The most striking was her sad, remorseful eyes, which cried out for forgiveness for the murder of 115 innocent people. Kim Hyun-Hee was the North Korean terrorist who planted a bomb in Korean Air Lines flight 858 in 1987, in an attempt to sabotage the 1988 Seoul Summer Olympics.

Having failed in an attempt to take her own life by biting into a poison capsule, Kim was arrested and put on trial in South Korea. Despite the public cry for revenge, her life was spared by the South Korean authorities, who decided she was more useful to them alive than dead. Heavily guarded around the clock, Kim lived "freely" as a prisoner under house arrest, and eventually became a best-selling author.

With her hands folded in her lap, Kim prepared to tell the story she had told a million times since 1987. I was allowed only forty-five minutes, and I didn't know where to start. Luckily Kim did. She was one of the most polished interviewees I had ever come across. Words rolled off her tongue in perfectly executed soundbites. She knew when to pause for dramatic effect, and she didn't stumble over her words once.

At the age of sixteen, Kim Hyun-Hee was chosen by the North Korean Communist Party for special training in foreign languages, the highest honor imaginable for Kim and her family. Three years later, she became a pupil at the North Korean army's elite espionage school and underwent rigorous training. At twenty-five, she was given her first major international assignment: Kim was ordered to travel with a senior comrade through Europe and several Third World countries, using the most circuitous routes, to plant an explosive device on a KAL plane. She and her partner posed as a Japanese father and his daughter. She had learned to speak fluent Japanese during her special training.

As I scribbled Kim's words in my notebook, Agent Hwang occasionally glanced over my shoulder to see if I was getting the information right. Annoyed, I wrote illegibly and only hoped that I could read my own writing later on. One of Kim's security men took pictures as I continued with the interview.

Like every North Korean child, Kim Hyun-Hee had believed that Kim Il-Sung was a god. "He was immortal. As a child, I believed he'd live forever. He was always in our hearts," she said softly.

On learning of the death of Kim Il-Sung, Kim Hyun-Hee was probably the only North Korean who didn't shed a single tear. Instead of being sad, she was angry. Kim Il-Sung had denied any responsibility for the KAL bombing and had accused the South Korean government of killing its own people and trying to put the blame on North Korea. The government had even denied Kim Hyun-Hee was a citizen of their country.

Two years after her arrest, Kim became a faithful Christian. Many North Korean defectors stay away from the church because it reminds them too much of the cult they left behind. But, for Kim, it was a way to find peace within herself. She said she now believed in God, not Kim Il-Sung, and put her faith in Him and prayed for unification.

Though many letters came her way, thanking her for telling the truth about North Korea, Kim said most people still didn't really understand how North Korean society functions.

"When did you realize that your life in North Korea was a lie?" I asked.

"Two, three days after I was in South Korea," she answered. Tears welled up in her eyes when she spoke of her family, who most likely had been arrested and sent to a labor camp, or executed.

"What surprised you most about South Korea?" I asked.

"The voting system, the elections," she answered. She said she was baffled by the freedom of choice when it came to presidential elections. "Here, you can criticize the president and nothing happens. In North Korea, men drink and say something, the whole family disappears the next day."

# XI

As part of the tour arranged by the Korean consulate, I took a field trip to the DMZ from the south side of the border—after first making a pit stop to walk through a few of the underground tunnels North Koreans had dug in their attempts to invade the South. When you come from the south, the DMZ is less than fifty kilometers from Seoul. Still it took almost two hours to fight through traffic and report to several military checkpoints along the way. Unlike the Communist side of the border, the south side of Panmunjom is a tourist site. About a hundred thousand visitors a year walk away with bags of souvenirs—North Korean liquor and coins, Swiss army knives, and beach towels and handkerchiefs stamped with a map of Korea—and wander through the small outdoor war museum. For most visitors, this was where their tour ended. Only a very few people had the dubious privilege of continuing their journey inside the DMZ, to which South Korean civilians were forbidden access.

I boarded the official DMZ tour bus and joined a UN delegate and a few other Westerners. Before departing for the border, the guests had to sit through a brief slide presentation of Korean history and sign a release form that stated we understood the danger and the risk involved in venturing through a military compound, and that we would not hold the ROK and the U.S. Army responsible in case we got shot by Communists.

We sat in the bus wearing visitors' armbands that were big enough to wrap around our heads, and attentively listened to the American soldier do his spiel. I was touched by the way he put his heart into his recitation of dull facts and military trivia. In a deep, authoritative tone, tinged with a southern accent, he asked us to close our windows just in case the North Koreans felt compelled to throw rocks across the border, as they were apparently known to do. He then quickly reassured us that we were protected by a team of highly trained troops strategically spread throughout the area.

I soon found myself at the border once again, fighting that same temptation to step over it. My picture had now been taken by both North and South Korean soldiers for their files, probably proof enough to charge me as a double agent.

Staring at the thin white line that separated North and South, I tried to imagine what it would be like to stand there day in and day out, knowing that it was emblematic of millions of lives destroyed. It really was like standing on the edge of freedom. Although it was just an arbitrarily drawn geopolitical boundary, the 38th parallel provoked intense and deadly hatreds, and had become a deep psychological scar that even a united Korea could not heal. You could say that my own family had fled South Korea because of the threat implicit in this border.

Like the nation itself, I was divided, caught in an emotional paralysis. By walking away from this simple white line, I felt as if I was betraying my country once again, but to stay would have been futile. I was barely capable of handling the petty politics of the Korean community in Toronto, so how could I even contemplate staying to fight bigger battles? If truth be told, I had enough trouble sorting out my own loyalties and duties to my parents, who were secretly hoping that I would cross back over the invisible line between my Korean and Canadian lives.

As I turned my back on the 38th parallel and walked away, years of suppressed memories overwhelmed me. The incessant fears and worries of my parents no longer seemed groundless or innocuous, and for the first time I felt full import of their words "We came to Canada for your future."

# XII

I finally had my first date with a Korean man, and I decided not to make a habit of it. In Canada, it was almost against my principles to date Korean men because of their Neanderthal attitudes, their unhealthy attachment to their mothers, and their inability to grow up. The gossip factor in the community also discouraged me from going near them, not to mention my parents' nagging about marriage. A breakup with a Korean man would be the scandal of the year and the woman would be ruined forever. So when I found myself agreeing (quite willingly) to have dinner with my driver, Mr. Kim, a Chuck Norris—worshiping secret agent who still lived at home with his parents, no one was more surprised than I.

Agent Kim had flirted with me from the first day he'd come to pick me up for an interview. I thought it was sweet that he blushed every time he paid me a compliment. On the second day, he pulled the car over to the side of the road and asked me to ride in the front seat. He was trying to be cool about it, but it sounded more like an army order. Somewhat amused, I obeyed.

We had dinner on Saturday, the last day of my interviews and official visits. He said he wanted to take me to a war museum just outside of Seoul and grab a bite to eat afterward. The mere thought of walking through a museum made me sleepy, but I agreed. I was curious to find out what constituted a first date in Korea.

We left in the early afternoon, just after he finished his half-day shift at the office, and got on the highway. The traffic was bumper to bumper, so that what should have taken thirty minutes took three hours.

In the car, Agent Kim showed me pictures of himself in a taekwon-do uniform, doing various kicks and chops, and played a tape of himself singing at a karaoke bar with his friends. He then suggested I take a nap, assuring me that he was a safe driver. He was charming and sweet, in a boyish way, and his smile was impossible to resist.

We started talking about mundane things like the weather and traffic. I told him how I got into journalism and he explained how he became involved with the Angibu.

"How do you become a secret agent?" I asked.

"People come around the campus to recruit, and then you take exams," he answered.

"Whatever possessed you to do it?"

"I wanted to defend and protect my country," he said.

We then inevitably exchanged notes on each other's personal life. I lied about mine, as I was sure he did about his. He said that he didn't have a girlfriend, and that his mother and the matchmaker had tried several times to find him the perfect girl, without any success. And, oh, by the way, he was a virgin. Without shame or embarrassment, he just blurted out this information, and I wasn't sure if he was confessing or boasting. When I accused him of lying, he looked confused. "Why would I lie?" he asked, quite innocently.

Perhaps this was a classic pickup line that guaranteed getting laid, I thought. I looked out the car window and laughed, thinking, My first date with a Korean and it had to be a thirty-year-old virgin who chased North Korean spies in the daytime and went home to be tucked in by his mother at night. To top it off, he was a Cholla-do man, the rival province of my father's home, Kyongsang-do.

Unable to think of a clever comeback, short of offering my condolences for his state of purity, I quickly changed the subject and asked him if his family and friends knew what he did for a living. He said no one knew. Being coy, I told him how impressed I was by his career. I found all this spy talk exciting. Wow!

Encouraged by my enthusiasm, he told me that the Angibu was spread throughout the city, in unmarked buildings, to spy on suspected Communists and antigovernment activists. When I asked how many spies had been caught lately, he said none. He then added, "They're hard to catch. That's why they're called spies, but we know they're everywhere."

When a police cruiser passed by on the shoulder of the highway, Agent Kim smiled proudly. "I feel a close kinship with the police because we're in the same line of work," he said. "We help each other and work together. We're like a family."

Agent Kim was just itching to impress his date by demonstrating his power over civilians, but trapped in traffic, all he could do was pick on the other drivers, who weren't even violating any rules. He honked at one driver for not driving in a perfectly straight line, and cursed at another for something just as trivial. "If you weren't here, I'd get out and give that driver a severe tongue-lashing," he said. Put off by his macho posturing, I wanted to dare him to go ahead. But remembering that he actually had the license to beat that driver and anybody else he wanted, I distracted him with another question.

That's when he revealed that my "file" had been circulating in his office for the past couple of months. The file had told him a lot about me and even included pictures. Acknowledging that I already knew about the pictures taken at the DMZ, I asked Agent Kim if there were any others. Photographs of me taken in Toronto, perhaps? He answered with a smile.

Agent Kim never planned to take me to a museum. It was a ploy to get me out of the city to prevent our being seen by one of his colleagues, who would no doubt disapprove of our little rendezvous. He knew the weekend traffic would make it impossible to get to the museum before closing time, and just to make sure we didn't, he took the wrong exit on the highway, which conveniently brought us to a hotel in a small city outside Seoul. I held my breath and savored the dose of reality I was going to give him if he even dared to go near the hotel lobby to reserve a room.

With the collapse of the Sampoong Department Store still fresh in his mind, Agent Kim was reluctant to park his car in the basement garage of the hotel. But after unsuccessfully circling the block a few times, he finally drove into the underground parkade, and that's when he announced we were having dinner at the hotel restaurant.

The restaurant was brightly lit and decorated sparsely with silk flower arrangements. The pianist was playing elevator music on the grand piano, which was on a raised platform in the middle of the room. My dinner companion sat across from me at a round table that was big enough to seat all the members of a small conference, and a young waiter, who moved stiffly in a tuxedo, came by to take our order. The place was empty except for a family with small children who didn't stop chattering and burping all through their meal. It didn't exactly set the mood for a romantic dinner for two, but better this than room service and having to fend off sexual advances.

Agent Kim talked very little while he ate, and he accepted half of my dinner when I offered it to him. Eating is a serious business for Koreans, and they don't fool around with polite, idle chat while they methodically shove food into their mouths. After the main course, our date quickly turned into an inquisition, as Kim questioned me about North Korea. "Look in the file," I said, with a hint of annoyance in my voice.

Over coffee and dessert, Agent Kim's final motive finally surfaced. He wanted to emigrate to Canada, and he thought I was his ticket. I could use my (nonexistent) professional clout to convince Canadian sports figures to help him set up a tae-kwon-do school and then could influence my sports-journalist friends (also nonexistent) to give him the exposure he needed to recruit students. From there, he could move to Los Angeles, where his relatives lived, and expand his business.

"I don't know any sports writers," I said, trying to be as polite as possible. "I know what you're thinking, but things don't work like that in Canada. And believe me, I have absolutely no control or influence over anybody."

Unperturbed by my remarks, Agent Kim became more excited about his fantasy. "What would you do," he asked, "if I dropped everything and followed you back to Toronto?"

"You'd be very disappointed," I said. "Let me tell you something. You're an Angibu agent and I am a journalist. It's your job to arrest civilians, and it's my job to expose people like you. The very nature of our careers alone would prohibit us from being friends, and we're both making a great exception by having dinner together."

He quickly backtracked, and I was stunned by what followed. Without blinking an eye, he began smothering me with patronizing comments. He told me to keep up the good work I was doing for his country and said he was very proud of my "brave achievements." Leaning over the table, he softly advised me not to read anything into the evening. I shouldn't misunderstand his intentions, he said. He was just trying to thank me for cooperating with the Angibu. Then he begged me to keep the date a secret.

We drove back to Seoul through torrential rain. I was most perplexed by Agent Kim's behavior. He was cunning and deceptive, yet he wasn't too bright. He was a bully whose naiveté made it hard for me to regard him as an equal or dignify his idiotic ideas and patronizing words with any kind of reaction. But I couldn't let him off the hook completely, so when we said goodbye, I kissed him on the cheek (not an acceptable Korean social custom), just to excite his libido, and watched his knuckles turn white where his hands tightly grasped the steering wheel.

# XIII

The day before I left for Canada, I decided to check into a hotel so I could roam the streets of Seoul free of curfew and the Angibu. Also, I could no longer bear watching poor Mrs. Bak and her family tiptoeing around the house in a state of barely contained panic. I knew I had overstayed my welcome when Mr. Bak, an even-tempered man of very few words, angrily dismissed the country's leading social activists and student protesters one evening. But the final crunch came when Mrs. Bak pleaded with me to let my mother read my book before I sent it off to the publisher. "She'll know if you have gone too far and said things you weren't supposed to," she said. "You'll be in Canada, safe, but we'll still be here."

Free of the Baks, I decided to spend my last remaining hours in South Korea with my informer, Hyun-Jun. We sat under a tree, drinking beer and listening to people sing and play their guitars in the park. The park was like an enchanted forest in the middle of a concrete jungle for young bohemians who knew the world had more to offer than Hyundais and beepers. Near the entrance to the park was a big billboard plastered with risqué posters promoting stage plays. It was a beautiful summer night and the perfect way to end my nine frustrating days in Seoul.

After so many years of pining for Hankuk, I'd never imagined I'd come back to my home country under these strenuous circumstances. The Angibu had frightened away my relatives and my parents' friends, whose paranoia got the better of them. When they phoned, eager to see me, I made a point of telling them about the Angibu. I had to. If there was even a tiny fraction of truth in people's theories about the nation's bogeymen, I had to at least give them the chance to decide whether they wanted to be implicated in my affairs.

One of the most vivid memories I have of my childhood in Seoul was an unspoken fear as omnipresent as Kim Il-Sung portraits in North Korea. I remember my mother constantly worrying about my father's missing the midnight curfew whenever he went out drinking with his friends. She feared he might talk nonsense in his drunken stupor and criticize the government and get himself arrested. Things like that happened in Korea. People got locked up for even mentioning North Korea. The paranoia didn't go away when we moved to Canada. Living on a different continent, my parents and their friends were still cautious about expressing their opinions, and my father was constantly warning my mother to watch her words. Freedom of speech did not exist in our country (it still doesn't), and it wasn't easy to shake off decades of fear and intimidation.

Enjoying the music that echoed through the park into the deep of the night, and mellowing under the influence of alcohol, I was uncharacteristically moved to indulge my sentimental thoughts. I wanted so much to take something good away from this whole experience, but I didn't know what. I'd seen things in both Koreas to make me realize that they were too much alike to get along. Underneath the banner of two different ideologies were a people trembling with anger, insecurity, and fear.

Hyun-Jun interrupted my drunken reverie with his. His cheeks were rosy from drinking, and his words came out slightly slurred. He wanted reunification, and when it happened he hoped the museums and statues in North Korea would be preserved, for the sake of history. But until then, he wanted to go to Canada again, to live this time. He liked Niagara Falls and the jazz bistros in Montreal.

He pointed to a few girls who were dressed up as if they were on their way to a cocktail party. Their hair was seductively swept up and their sequined dresses with spaghetti straps clung to their bodies. "They watch American soap operas and think North American women dress like that all the time," he said, laughing. Aroused by the sight of pretty women, Hyun-Jun felt compelled to talk about his last girlfriend, who had dumped him for no apparent reason that he could see. "We didn't even sleep together," he stated. "I'm still a virgin."

"Stop!" I said. "Why do Korean men admit to this? In North America, men lie out of shame if they're still virgins past the age of sixteen."

Hyun-Jun explained that it wasn't unusual for a man to stay a virgin for a long time. "Marriage is the most important thing for women and virginity is a must, so the choice is very limited for men. Besides, there's no place to have sex. We all live at home."

"You're twenty-something!" I cried out. "It's not healthy unless you plan to be a monk."

"I know, I know," he said.

"Maybe if you guys got laid more, you wouldn't protest so much," I joked. "The student protesters are probably taking all their sexual frustration out to the streets."

Finishing our beer, we watched a loud argument turn into a fistfight across the street from the park. Within minutes, it had become a mini riot, as passersby debated among themselves, took sides, and threw punches freely at whoever stood in their way.

As the park emptied out, my emotions were in turmoil. I wanted to stay in South Korea just a little longer. Despite the unpleasantness of the whole Angibu affair, I couldn't ignore the sentimental attachment that I felt on returning to my birthplace. In a way, this was still my home, where I was supposed to belong. But I also couldn't dismiss a little tugging in my heart as I brought myself to admit that I was an outsider. It was painfully obvious that I could never fit in. I felt like a Canadian in Korea, and a Korean in Canada. I couldn't decide where I belonged anymore. All I knew was that Sun-Kyung wished she had never left Korea while Angela counted her blessings and thanked her parents for sparing her from all the injustice and prejudice of the old country. True, I wanted to help change Korea, but I couldn't do it from within. Picking up my jacket, I left the park alone.

# XIV

My farewell dinner with the Angibu men was uncannily reminiscent of the one I had had in North Korea with my minders. While they had vented maliciously about the capitalist South, the Angibu mocked the Communist North. In Pyongyang a nameless man, whom I called the Big Boss, had joined us for dinner; in Seoul another nameless man, whom I shall call Big Boss No. 2, honored us with his presence. No. 2 was so high up in the Angibu that even Agent Hwang didn't know his name, just as my North Korean translator Young-Hee didn't know the name of her Big Boss.

As a parting gift, I had received a Kim Il-Sung button in North Korea. In Seoul I was given something of equal social and personal significance: a miniature clay model of the traditional Korean wedding procession, with the bride and groom encased in a frame.

My North Korean minders had instructed me not to reveal their identities or where I had stayed; the Angibu advised me to keep their involvement in my affairs confidential. Neither group wanted credit for their "covert assistance," and they pointed out that I'd lose credibility if the public learned of their involvement.

Neither side fully understood the consequences of talking to a journalist, and they failed to recognize that Canadian journalists enjoyed a degree of freedom alien to both countries. (Perhaps it was easy for them to forget I was Canadian because I looked just like them.) I don't think it ever occurred to any of them that I would resist their attempts to sabotage my work.

In their own perverse way, both North and South Korean secret agents had done everything they could to accommodate their guest and fulfill their respective government's agenda. And whether they realized it or not, both my minders and the Angibu had failed in their mission by putting themselves at center stage. They embodied all that was wrong and terrible about the two Koreas.

Big Boss No. 2 and his two cronies sat cross-legged on the mat while Agent Hwang and I took an inferior, more ladylike position and sat on our haunches. And once again, I was assaulted by the same questions about North Korea I had answered a thousand times. In North Korea, I had gone out of my mind listening to the same thing over and over again, and now I was going mad repeating the same answers over and over again.

Sitting to the left of No. 2 was Mr. Yoon Kwang-Su. Mr. Yoon, who had once been assigned to a Toronto consulate posting, had pulled strings to arrange my interviews and tours as a favor for his friend Mr. Sunflower. Raising his glass to make a toast, Mr. Yoon announced that he knew all about my reputation as a hell-raiser in Toronto's Korea Town, and playfully cautioned his colleagues to "be on their guard with this one." Mr. Yoon was reassigned to the Toronto consulate several months later, and when he started to pressure me to hand over a copy of my manuscript for government approval before publication, I knew his return to Canada was more than a passing coincidence.

Sitting on the other side of No. 2 was Mr. Na Jin-Sung, a short, balding man whom I had met several days before outside a university campus. He had declined to give me his name when I asked, but his identity was accidentally revealed to me by one of the drivers, who didn't know it was supposed to be a secret. Mr. Na was the designated stenographer. He ate with one hand and transcribed the evening's conversation with the other.

As the final, wrap-up question, Mr. Na asked, on behalf of the Angibu, "South Korea is richer than North Korea, right? You saw it with your own eyes, right?"

Before returning to my hotel, I visited a Korean-style hot-dog stand, where a lady served noodles heated by a lamp underneath a tent, and ordered my favorite childhood dish, one I had craved ever since I left the country in 1976: white rice cakes smothered in spicy chili sauce. I looked around the city for the last time and devoured the *duk-boki* with relish.

# Epilogue

# I

The news came.

My North Korean senior minder, Lee Myong-Su, had been sentenced to a "reeducation" camp after American money was discovered in his home. His arrest came only weeks after my trip to Pyongyang, and I wondered with guilt and sadness if I had played a role in the tragic events. Though I did not give him any money, my widely publicized criticisms of North Korea would surely not have helped his cause. The authorities must have been looking for a scapegoat.

Mr. Lee had been North Korea's main link to the United States and Canada. He had had the rare privilege of making frequent visits to the West, where Korean expatriates like me pursued him doggedly in hopes of getting inside the Hermit Kingdom. His occasional glimpses of the outside world were what gave him that special power over his comrades back home and made his pitiful existence in North Korea bearable. But his desire to be more modern and progressive became evident even as he continued to pay lip service to the greatness of the Juche ideology. While he spat on American imperialists and Japanese colonialists, he smoked Japanese cigarettes, drank Johnny Walker, and complained about the improper way North Koreans served coffee—in teacups instead of big mugs like the ones he'd seen in L.A.

Like many senior officers, Mr. Lee probably wasn't immune to bribery. But this man wasn't naive or stupid. No one knew better than he the dire consequences of keeping "filth"—anything connected with the West—in his home and the danger that posed for him and his family. And yet, American money found in the possession of a man whose official business was dealing with North Americans seemed hardly surprising, let alone criminal.

When I first heard about the fate of the senior minder from my contacts at the Korean consulate in Toronto, I naturally disbelieved it. But when the same story was told to me by Mrs. Chun after she made yet another visit to Pyongyang, I knew it to be true. Strangely, she didn't appear too upset by Mr. Lee's arrest and admitted that her relationship with him had soured some time ago. She announced cheerfully that his replacement was much more lenient and flexible, and that if I were to return to North Korea for another visit, I'd have more freedom and access. Declaring that she never liked Mr. Lee in the first place, Mrs. Chun claimed to have reprimanded both him and his superiors for having treated me the way they had.

For their part, the men from the consulate, especially the one I liked to call Mr. Angibu, alleged that no one was more relieved to see my senior minder sent away than Mrs. Chun and speculated that she might have played a part in his arrest. This was quite an accusation, but I had to consider the source. Still, my curiosity was piqued, so I listened to the rest of the theory.

No one in North Korea had better insight into Mrs. Chun's business affairs than the senior minder, Mr. Angibu began. Mrs. Chun, who took over the *New Korea Times* and the family reunification organization after the death of her husband, didn't welcome the potential threat he posed. Mr. Lee knew the names of those who were trying to visit North Korea and how much some of them had paid Mrs. Chun for her services. Many expatriates paid generously, more often in cash than by check, for a chance to be reunited with their loved ones in North Korea. Some of the so-called service fee was supposedly "donated" to North Korea by Mrs. Chun on behalf of the family, but neither the donor nor the recipient ever knew how much the coordinator was keeping for herself—with the exception, perhaps, of the senior minder. "Now that he's gone, she is safe with her secrets," Mr. Angibu said. Furthermore, many expatriates were forced to continue sending "donations" to North Korea long after their visits were over, he claimed, because their families were harassed and pressured by the government, who urged them to write letters demanding more money from their rich relatives.

Mr. Angibu then announced that there was a North Korean man living in Toronto. A few years ago, so the story went, a young Korean-Canadian student was urged by her parents to enroll in Kim Il-Sung University in Pyongyang. When she graduated, she was held captive by the government until the parents agreed to let her marry a North Korean man, who then immigrated with his new bride to Canada. Apparently, his assignment was to recruit new North Korean sympa-

thizers and even lure some of them back to the country for spy training. If this was a true tale, this mysterious fellow would probably be the
only North Korean immigrant in Canada—if not in all of North
America. But I had to discount the story. The absence of any diplomatic
relationship between Canada and North Korea would make it impossible for the former country to legitimately accept immigrants from the
latter. And even were that not the case, the South Korean embassy would
immediately have alerted the media and tried to use the North Korean
as a propaganda tool, making it impossible for this man to live in peace.
Unless, of course, this phantom Communist was a double agent.

"What's his name and where do he and his wife live?" I asked.

"I don't know," Mr. Angibu said. "You're the reporter, so you find
out—and let me know when you do."

Telling me to be careful, he then explained that about 10 percent
of Metropolitan Toronto's fifty thousand Korean expatriates were
born in North Korea and moved to the South just before the outbreak
of the Korean War. Many of them, Mr. Angibu declared, were spies on
a recruiting mission. Toronto has the strongest pro–North Korea
movement in the West, and its leaders were making plans to form an
umbrella organization that would bring together all the like-minded
groups scattered throughout the United States—especially those in
New York and Los Angeles.

Pro–North Koreans spied on one another, the consulate spied on its
fellow South Koreans, and everyone, I was told, spied on me. Both Mrs.
Chun and the Angibu filed reports with their respective governments
after our meetings, and constantly tested my nonexistent allegiances.

While all this was going on, Yoon Kwang-Su, whom I had had the pleasure of meeting back in Seoul at my farewell dinner, was reassigned to
the Korean consulate about two months after my return from South
Korea. His sudden reappearance in Toronto surprised me, for it was
unusual, by Mr. Yoon's own admission, for a Korean diplomat to return
to a country he had already served in. I thought it was just a passing
coincidence, but then I reminded myself that this was the Korean intelligence service—and nothing it did was by coincidence.

Neither tactful nor subtle, Mr. Yoon invited me to dinner and asked me to hand over a copy of my manuscript for this book. When I refused, he first tried to woo me for several months, then followed that with attempts at bribery. He promised on behalf of the Korean government that the book would be translated and published in Korea, at no cost to me. But of course the government first had to read and approve the manuscript. When I didn't budge, he shook his head and asked if he could at least have a detailed outline. "Korean journalists do it all the time," he remarked disingenuously. "Doesn't it work like that in Canada?"

At our next meeting, he presented me with a carton of cigarettes as a peace offering and proceeded to assure me that the government was not in any way trying to interfere. The powers that be simply wanted to help me because I was young and unschooled in Korean history and politics. Wouldn't it be nice if the government corrected my mistakes before they came out in print? It was for my own good, he stressed.

"I refuse to even entertain your proposal. Besides, my publisher would never allow it," I said.

"You don't have to tell your publisher. It'll be just between us," Mr. Yoon said in a conspiratorial tone. "This is a Korean matter. Canada has nothing to do with it."

Having failed to convince me, Mr. Yoon then tried another tack and sent his colleague to meet with me instead. He was confident that the consulate's new press attaché would charm me with his impressive British education, his fluency in English, and his many exotic tales from Russia, his previous diplomatic posting. Intelligent and amusing, Lee Sok-Bae made a wonderful impression on me as he grumbled about the government, the consulate, and the Cold War games still being played on the Korean peninsula. "Do you know the saying, 'The dogs bark, but the caravan moves on'? Well, Korea is the dog." Just when I began to think I had found an ally, Mr. Lee asked for the manuscript. "But it's only for my own curiosity," he assured me. "I'm not going to give it to the government."

Taking note of the dramatic change in my attitude toward him, Mr. Lee tried to win back my affection by peppering his conversation with criticisms of Mr. Yoon and his archaic views, gently reminding me that he was on my side. Then, resignedly, he confessed that if he didn't get the manuscript, his career was on the line. He ran his index finger across his throat for effect, gently urging me to go easy on South Korea, especially the president. He looked skeptical when I told him President Kim Young-Sam wasn't even in the book.

Despite my repeated efforts to explain the nature of my book, neither Mr. Yoon nor Mr. Lee seemed to grasp the concept of a memoir. Of course, each time I refused their request to hand over my manuscript, they pursued me with a growing conviction that it contained military and political secrets from North Korea and criticisms of the South.

During one of my dinner meetings with Mr. Lee, I asked him if my book had anything to do with Mr. Yoon's reappearance in Toronto. "Don't you people have anything better to do than come after me?" I asked.

"What else are we to do?" he responded. "There's not much else going on in Canada. The trade relationship between Canada and South Korea is wonderful." Sadly, I was their chief concern of the day.

## II

It is one of the great ironies of Korean history that the artificial border which divides the two countries has created genuine hatreds. The propaganda emanating from both nations has been so effective that the people now believe they have nothing in common. Yet when South Koreans look at their neighbors in the North, they must feel as if they're looking into a funhouse mirror. They see their own image reflected, exaggerated, different but the same. How many times must they have wanted to break the mirror that symbolizes the barrier raised in their past and threatening their future?

Pyongyang is an artificial setting, a stage where the illusion of happiness is acted out against the backdrop of a beautiful landscape, monumental buildings, and the ubiquitous Kim Il-Sung statues. The Korean obsession with appearance is pushed beyond the limit in this socialist theme park, without the slightest hint of irony.

The absurdity of this grand scheme with its automaton participants menacingly reminds South Koreans of what they used to be, during a time not too long ago when they, too, went hungry and bowed down to a succession of bloodthirsty dictators.

Like a wealthy family ashamed of its poor relations, the South is embarrassed by the North. Rather than acknowledging their shared modest origins in front of their rich new Western friends, South Koreans shrug and claim they don't understand North Korea any better than the rest of the world does.

When Kim Il-Sung died, South Koreans swore they were just as shocked as North Americans by the frenzied display of mourning. Yet I remember that they, too, cried when their own dictator, Park Chung-Hee, was assassinated in the seventies. When they condemn the North for brainwashing their children into worshiping Kim Il-Sung, do they forget that once all little boys wanted to be just like one of the South's most authoritarian presidents, Rhee Syngman? As they criticize North Korea for violating their citizens' right to freedom of speech, do they not realize that South Korean political dissidents are still in jail today for exercising that right? Do they not remember that the people of Seoul were oblivious to the Kwangju Massacre until long after the soldiers stopped shooting because there was no freedom of the press? How quickly we forget.

Today, when North Korea is making world headlines with stories of catastrophic famine, cannibalism, and families selling their daughters for a handful of rice, South Koreans seem to have blotted out the memory of the global campaign in the 1960s to adopt their nation's orphans because the country was too poor to take care of its own children. They seem to have forgotten that there was a time, not too long ago, when they were the poor cousins and North Korea was prospering economically and technologically.

In the 1990s the world is dazzled by Hankuk's overnight economic success. Everybody applauds South Korea for a job well done, not always taking into account that very little has changed except the cash flow, and that any advances have been accompanied by bribery, scandals, and corruption. Beneath the ideal lies a morally crumbling, only quasi-democratic nation that has a long way to go before it can approach its goal of Western-style democracy.

## III

I spent most of my life running away from Korea, but I think I was running in the wrong direction: the farther I ran, the closer I seemed to be to my point of origin. I escaped from Regina because I didn't like the Korea I saw there, and reasoned that a handful of Koreans weren't representative enough of the country I left behind. In Toronto I found a Korea no different from the one before, and when I finally had the opportunity to revisit the real place, I came back disillusioned. I'm not sure which Korea I'd been searching for—perhaps the one that had filled my imagination in my childhood, when I remembered being happy and secure. That Korea seems to have perished, along with my prairie-princess fantasy. In a way, Korea will always remain an imaginary country for me, and the real Korea will no doubt remain divided, even when the border disappears.

# ACKNOWLEDGMENTS

I wish to thank the three people without whom this book would not have been possible.

My editor, Janice Weaver, taught me that writing can be neither rushed nor forced.

Max Allen, my producer and mentor, gave me the courage to tell the truth as I saw it. His dedication and commitment to storytelling taught me everything I know about good journalism. His friendship is a precious gift.

Most of all, I am grateful to John Haslett Cuff for his love and encouragement. He endured my hours of darkness and moments of rage with tenderness and patience. Our shared passion for literature and music and smoking kept me sane through months of rewrites.